PEACEMAKING
A Systems Approach to Conflict Management

Lynn Sandra Kahn, Ph.D.

with illustrations by Jennifer Hammond Landau

UNIVERSITY
PRESS OF
AMERICA

Lanham • New York • London

Copyright © 1988 by

University Press of America,® Inc.

4720 Boston Way
Lanham, MD 20706

3 Henrietta Street
London WC2E 8LU England

Printed in the United States of America

British Cataloging in Publication Information Available

Library of Congress Cataloging-in-Publication Data

Kahn, Lynn Sandra, 1946–
Peacemaking : a systems approach to conflict management / by Lynn Sandra Kahn :
with illustrations by Jennifer Hammond Landau.
p. cm.
Bibliography: p. Includes index.
1. Peace—Research. I. Title.
JX1904.5.K3   1988   327.1'72'072—dc19   87–31649 CIP
ISBN 0–8191–6782–7 (alk. paper)
ISBN 0–8191–6783–5 (pbk. : alk. paper)

All University Press of America books are produced on acid-free
paper which exceeds the minimum standards set by the National
Historical Publications and Records Commission.

to my mother and father, with love

TABLE OF CONTENTS

		Page
INTRODUCTION		vii
ACKNOWLEDGEMENTS		xv

Part I: TECHNOLOGY

Chapter 1:	PROBLEM SOLVING AND PEACEMAKING	3
Chapter 2:	TO THINE OWN SELF BE TRUE	31
Chapter 3:	GROUP ROLES	43

Part II: PSYCHOLOGY

PATTERNS OF CONFLICT

Chapter 4:	DEPENDENCY: Following the Leader	61
Chapter 5:	REBELLION: Fighting the Leader	79
Chapter 6:	SUB-GROUPING: Fighting Each Other	107
Chapter 7:	SCAPEGOATING: Blaming Each Other	117

PATTERNS OF HARMONY

Chapter 8:	PEACEMAKING: Bringing Together	127
Chapter 9:	SUPPORT: Holding Together	177
Chapter 10:	HEALING: Repair and Growth	195

Part III: THEORY

| Chapter 11: | A SCIENCE OF PEACEMAKING | 211 |

Part IV: APPLICATION

| Chapter 12: | DESIGNING PEACE CONFERENCES | 231 |

EPILOGUE		243
NOTES		247
INDEX		259

INTRODUCTION

Relax. Take a few deep breaths. Clear your mind of all that clutter. Breathe. Enjoy the rhythm of your breathing.

Imagine a scented breeze—the ocean, the pines, the cedars. Breathe in slowly. Let the scented air fill your lungs and cleanse your body.

Breathe out. Let the flow of air carry away tension. Let your feet feel firmly planted on the ground. Breathe. Again, breathe in and out slowly.

Now picture this world at peace. Go ahead. Picture an era of freedom, justice and well-being. Imagine families, neigborhoods, working organizations, nations, regions and the planet Earth as living systems of support and achievement. Imagine the planet at peace. Imagine technology in harmony with nature and aiding the pursuit of global peace. This is a time of transition, so imagine your role as change agent, facilitator or mediator.

Peace is a desired future state. Peacemaking is the activity which transforms the energy of conflict into the energy of creative cooperation. A peacemaker is a third party consultant who helps people in conflict discover shared solutions where all sides feel like a winner. This is more commonplace and more complex than you might imagine.

The science of peacemaking includes technology, psychology and theory. Technically, peacemaking means to identify, analyze and solve problems through face-to-face dialogue. Psychologically, peacemaking is a stunning, transformative journey requiring the courage of combat and honesty. Theoretically, peacemaking taps patterns of balance and rhythms of harmony across multiple fields of reality.

Peace-seeking dialogues may take place in a hospital, school, manufacturing plant, corporate Board room, City Council, state legislature, federal agency or international conference for representatives of nations and cultures at war. Whether the fight is about budgets, boundaries or bombs, the technologies and dynamics are the same when groups talk about peace. Peacemaking converts destructive conflict to cooperative achievement.

This book describes technologies to manage conflict and concepts to understand the dynamics of peacemaking. The foundation is the perspective of systems science. The intended audience is both the interested reader and the experienced practitioner. My wish is to add guidelines and hopefulness to the activities of peacemaking.

A LITTLE HISTORY

Peacemaking begins with the decision to talk about shared problems. Technically, peacemaking is the sum of all the tools and skills of creative problem solving. The technologies rely on genuine communication, effective listening, step-by-step problem solving and shared decisions about action.

When the focus is the analysis of conflict, confronting issues is not tearing into each other, but taking events apart and looking at causes, connections and solutions. The analysis of conflict brings balance to the dynamics of anger.

The conflict resolution technologies are in use all around us.[1] Participatory management in America, Industrial Democracy in Europe and Quality Circles in Japan are corporate philosophies which emphasize face-to-face discussion for solving problems. At least one million adults in the United States currently work in small teams skilled in the Quality Circle techniques of brainstorming, consensus, cause-effect analysis and roles of group facilitators, recorders and representatives.[2] With these tools, corporations have solved problems in production and quality, while introducing new ideas into the corporate culture.

Almost as a by-product of problem solving, large corporations have discovered that participation improves communication and repairs or prevents conflict. Oddly enough, large corporations are a major source of conflict resolution technologies, training manuals and toolkits.

Corporate and government leaders are more knowledgeable than ever about the value of human resources. In the 1980s, books such as *In Search of Excellence, Theory Z, The Art of Japanese Management* and *The Change Masters* reported the same basic finding:[3] profits and productivity depend upon a motivated, challenged and loyal workforce.

According to John Naisbitt, author of *Megatrends*, attention to human resources is now the competitive position.[4] Production, quality and satisfaction improve when organizations encourage employees to join together and solve problems. Paradoxically, systems that encourage participation require strong leadership.

In the Beginning. The university study of conflict resolution began in the 1940's when World War II pushed educators, psychologists, sociologists and political scientists out of ivory, academic towers and into the real world of war. Behavioral scientists designed, facilitated, mediated, analyzed and researched dialogues among racial and cultural groups in conflict.

Early pioneers made startling discoveries. In America, psychologist Kurt Lewin showed that group discussion could change attitudes toward eating liver and kidneys, thereby saving quality meat for wartime soldiers.[5] Change was more likely to occur when people met in small face-to-face groups to share and discuss information. Group discussion was more likely to change behavior and attitudes than lectures by experts or even individual instruction. Change occurred as people learned to **appreciate** and not simply attack differences in perception and values. Lewin brought these observations about group behavior to his consultations with racial and cultural groups in conflict, framed by his view of groups as fields of forces.

Also in the 1940s, at London's Tavistock Institute, Wilfred Bion began designing therapeutic communities where psychiatric patients were expected to make decisions about day-to-day activities and where staff groups met to talk about the "here-and-now" experience of such arrangements.[6] Bion concluded that groups exist on two levels: (1) the work group which aims to realistically carry out stated goals and (2) the "basic assumption" group which acts as if it were meeting for some purpose other than the stated goals. Bion went on to describe powerful, often unconscious basic assumptions of the group-as-a-whole, dynamics such as dependency, rebellion against authority and the patterns of pairing.

From the 1960s until the present, England's John Burton and Harvard's Herbert Kelman pioneered the study of the relationship between conflict and communication.[7] They and their colleagues designed and facilitated workshops for Turks and Greeks in Cyprus, Protestants and Catholics in Ireland, Palestinians and Israelis, representatives of the India/Pakistan/Bangladesh wars and a Somalia/Ethiopia/Kenya border dispute.[8]

Burton and Kelman emphasize the rational analysis of conflict issues and the exchange of perceptions through dialogue. In their workshop model, be-havioral scientists serve as session facilitators guiding discussion and giving feedback on progress. Burton and Kelman, both still practitioner-theorists, believe that focus on the analysis of conflict and the solving of shared problems is the best approach to managing social conflict. Analysis and problem solving counter the usual hostile, blaming, legalistic tones of diplomatic negotiation.

Strengthening Approaches. More recently, the conflict resolution technologies have been strengthened by a mediation approach called "single text negotiation" developed at the Harvard Negotiation Project and described by Roger Fisher and William Ury in *Getting to Yes*.[9] Here, a neutral facilitator helps opponents write a mutually agreeable treaty or contract.

From Camp David to Geneva, legal circles to corporate headquarters, the "single text" technique has influenced corporate, political and diplomatic use of negotiation technologies. At the same time, lawyers trained in mediation are shifting away from the adversarial approach of traditional law and towards the cooperative mediation of shared problems, especially in family law.

Peacemaking technologies have finally surfaced in international settings. In 1984, Chinese and Soviets, North Koreans and South Koreans, Romanians and West Germans as well as government and guerrilla leaders in El Salvador had face-to-face dialogues for the shared purpose of improving relations. In June 1985, a Syrian President helped negotiate release of thirty-nine Americans from TWA Flight 847 held hostage in Lebanon and Algeria by Shiite Moslems. In August 1985, India's Prime Minister mediated stalled peace talks in Sri Lanka between government and militant ethnic leaders, including minority Hindu Tamils and majority Buddhist Sinhalese. Also, in August, Lebanon's Christian and Moslem militias met with Syrian mediators in a mountain village to talk peace. However we judge the progress of peace in these and other battles, the technologies exist for the peaceful resolution of regional conflict.

The Fall and Winter of 1985 focused on Reagan and Gorbachev's impressive meeting in Geneva. Although Geneva's glow soon faded, the Challenger and Chernobyl explosions in 1986 drove more humble political leaders towards new negotiating proposals. Disappointment at the 1986 Iceland summit demonstrated the need for careful planning of diplomatic meetings.

Where We Are Now. As 1987 drew to a close, formal peace-seeking dialogue reached unprecedented proportions. There had been breakthroughs in arms control, super power summit meetings, Central American peace proposals and East-West German discussions, along with massive, democratic changes in eastern Asia, multiracial meetings in South Africa and continued, although quiet dialogue in the Mideast. There was a resurgence of "Citizen Diplomacy," the non-governmental, cross-national meetings such as conferences for scientists, physicians and athletes, the Fourth of July concert in Moscow and discussions between private citizens visiting foreign countries. Popular talk show hosts in the US and USSR had already hooked up their local audiences for simultaneous discussion, giving citizen diplomacy middle class acceptance. Modern electronics is now broadcasting the technologies and dynamics of peacemaking. More quietly, combined government and non-government interventions for peace are having a potent impact.

The U.S. Department of State, Center for the Study of Foreign Affairs (CSFA), uses the phrase "track two diplomacy" to refer to

> "... nongovernmental, informal and unofficial ... interaction between private citizens [who] have as their objective the reduction or resolution of conflict ... anger, tension or fear ... through improved communication and a better understanding of each other's point of view. (McDonald and Bendahmane, *Track Two Diplomacy*, p. 1)

Ambassador John W. McDonald, a forty-year State Department official, defines the context: "Track two diplomacy is not a substitute for track one, but rather is in support of or parallel to track one goals." (*Ibid.*, p. 12) Ambassador McDonald cites inspiring examples including journalist John Scali's role in the Cuban missile crisis and Bryant Wedge's contribution to conflict resolution in the Dominican Republic. Joseph Montville, Director of Research at CSFA, adds: "Track two diplomacy is a process designed to assist official leaders to resolve or . . . to manage conflicts by exploring possible solutions out of public view and without the requirements to formally negotiate or bargain for advantage." (*Ibid.*, p. 7)

Summary. There are a lot of names out there for all this technical activity—negotiation, mediation, conflict management, conflict resolution and creative problem solving. This book reserves the word "peacemaking" to include all the psychological dynamics underlying the words and techniques of problem solving. Peacemaking includes the psychological transformations which accompany the shift from YOU VERSUS ME conflict to YOU AND ME problem solving, where even enemies share systems of relationships.

Whatever the setting or issues, peacemaking requires communication, creativity and courage. Whatever the content, peacemaking taps internal mechanisms of balance and harmony.

THE DESIGN OF THIS BOOK

This book has four parts: **TECHNOLOGY, PSYCHOLOGY, THEORY** and **APPLICATION.** Each chapter begins with a one-page summary, goes next to behavioral description, then to psychological discussion and ends with "Working Guidelines" intended for the practitioner.

The case studies in this book are from newspapers and magazines, my work as a consulting psychologist from 1976 to 1987 and from colleagues, teachers, authors and researchers in the fields of conflict resolution and organization development. Woven throughout this book are conversations, statistics and conclusions from a 1975-76 research project at The American Unversity in Washington, D.C., here called the AU Research Groups and including a 1982 re-evaluation.[10] For this research project, 119 volunteers were randomly divided into nineteen male or female groups with a male or female consultant. The purpose of these self-study groups was to talk about and learn about their here-and-now group process. Each group met for eight 90-minute sessions, over a period of two days. All sessions had an observer who took notes and tape recorded everything that was said. Eight groups were chosen for analysis and a 238,404 word sample was fed into a computer program which tracked the rise and fall of word clusters such as Hostility, Analysis, Perceptions, Solutions, Action, Support, Pain and Belonging. Research results and edited conversations from these groups are scattered throughout this book, demonstrating quite clearly the wisdom of face-to-face discussion and how peacemaking taps internal wells of knowledge.

In both the AU Research Groups and the many case studies in this book, all research and client names have been changed and all organizational settings have been modified to ensure confidentiality.

Part I: TECHNOLOGY introduces the roles and procedures of conflict resolution, moving the reader from technical basics to the psychological arena.

Chapter 1: THE BASIC TOOLS   presents the **10∗STEP**SM **Problem Solving Model**∗ and its team of facilitator, recorder, timekeeper, representative and process consultants.[11] This model emphasizes creative problem solving, feedback about group dynamics and the careful design of conference meetings.

Chapter 2: TO THINE OWN SELF BE TRUE asks the reader to think about your personality. Are you extroverted or introverted? Pragmatic or intuitive? Logical or emotional? Spontaneous or scheduled?

Chapter 3: GROUP ROLES   connects technology and psychology. In face-to-face discussion we take on four roles: Functional, Meeting, Cultural and Process. Roles move the reader from technologies to psychological dynamics.

Part II: PSYCHOLOGY focuses on group behavior.[12] Four chapters describe patterns of conflict—dependency, rebellion, sub-grouping and scapegoating; three chapters describe patterns of harmony—peacemaking, support and healing.

Chapter 4: DEPENDENCY shows our magnetic attraction to authority figures and our conflicts about leadership and personal responsibility. Peacemaking reverses the dynamics of dependency—balancing the chain of command and group interaction.

Chapter 5: REBELLION   links Detroit automakers, California grape pickers, Polish dock workers, South African blacks and South Korean students. Rebellion is the push against authority to establish a balance of power. Living systems survive through the free flow of energy and information, so a balance of power is sought.

Chapter 6: SUB-GROUPING shifts analysis from the power struggles of dependency and rebellion to battles over values. Sub-grouping occurs when neighbors fight each other: Republicans versus Democrats, pro-life versus pro-choice, Moslem versus Christian or East versus West. On the surface, tension is channeled into sub-groups, underneath lies the struggle of Good versus Evil.

Chapter 7: SCAPEGOATING reveals how one or a few may be attacked for "causing" the problems of the system. Scapegoating includes the individual tendency to blame others for our difficulties and the group tendency to rid itself of discomfort.

∗ The **10∗STEP**SM Model is a service mark of LSK ASSOCIATES, San Francisco, California.

Chapter 8: PEACEMAKING details six case studies, then comments on dreams as tools of mediation. The chapter concludes with ten key guidelines for peacemaking: the focus on analysis of conflict, the use of third party facilitators, the reality of common ground, the influence of perception, the impact of individual style, our struggle with identity, the press of group dynamics, the value of feedback and the awareness of harmony.

Chapter 9: SUPPORT presents research showing that dialogue strengthens support and continued dialogue brings new learning and shared identity.

Chapter 10: HEALING tracks movements through pain to a third position of balance and harmony. Peacemaking and healing are inseparable.

Part III: THEORY asks: What principles of science describe how patterns relate to each other? What concepts guide the work of peacemaking?

Chapter 11: A SCIENCE OF PEACEMAKING answers: systems science is the framework, Jungian psychology is the heart, problem solving is the muscle, Tavistock group theory is the perspective and quantum physics is a metaphor to talk about peacemaking.[13]

As technologies turn problems to solutions, group life unfolds as patterns made of basic building blocks—hostility, analysis, pain, support, action, perception and belonging are a few. Patterns such as anger are voiced by individual role specialists such as Fight Leader and sometimes strike an archetypal chord. Research shows that group patterns take shape as pairs, Hostility attracts Analysis or Pain attracts Support. There are hundreds of these pairs, they are the internal balancing skills of group life.

At the same time, these patterns of balance are influenced by a background rhythm of harmony. Quantum physics describes the universe as an indivisible whole composed of interlocking fields of energy where opposites are unified through rhythm. In physics, the movements of space-time unify matter and energy. In psychology, the movements of belonging and separating unify individuals and groups.[14] The fundamental rhythm of the universe is the harmony of opposing forces.

Chapter 11 presents a theory of peacemaking: patterns of conflict contain patterns of balance and rhythms of harmony across multiple levels of reality. This means that all the ways in which we fight with each other are intimately connected to our ability to analyze anger, an internal sense of balance and a universal wish to create a healthy planet.

Part IV: APPLICATION grounds the reader in the pragmatics of conference design.

Chapter 12: DESIGNING PEACE CONFERENCES emphasizes clear boundaries, the analysis of conflict, true interaction, a press for solutions and conferences as systems with a logic of their own.

In summary, the technology, psychology, theory and application of peacemaking activities all revolve around internal mechanisms of balance. People joined together for peacemaking tap the inner wisdom of rhythms at the center of life. Here, duality is connected to unity and conflict leads to harmony.

ACKNOWLEDGEMENTS

I wish to thank these people for their assistance:

— Barbara Mullens, Margaret Rioch, Al Leventhal and Lanny Berman, professors of psychology at The American University, Washington, D.C.

— Donald Seelig, John F. Borriello and Elizabeth Cole Stirling, teachers of psychotherapy in the Clinical Psychology Training Section, St. Elizabeths Hospital, Washington, D.C.

— Georgia Strasburg, who co-authored the "rotating role model" for problem solving and process feedback and was my consulting partner for the U.S. Commission on Civil Rights, the White House Task Force on Women and the congressional staff groups writing the Domestic Violence legislation.

— Ronnie Koenig, Vivian Hopkins Jackson, Robert Shoffner and Susan Seliger for their friendship.

— Phyllis Palmer, Ronnie Feit, Norma Brooks, Barbara Knox, Sandra Tangri, Larry Porter, Herbert Kelman and John W. McDonald, for helpful conversations.

— Daniel Kegan, Kenneth Seelig, Stuart Baron and Blair Melvin for befriending a stranger in California.

— Fritjof Capra for conversations linking group dynamics and fields of energy, bringing metaphors of physics into the science of peacemaking.

— Dianne Reed, Donald T. Brown, Sharon Mulgrew, Nancy Ettrick, Bob Shellnut, Dani Perkins, Stuart Fliege, Dick Hendrickson, Dave Wigglesworth and Jean Gibbs for comments on the manuscript.

— Margaret Frings Keyes for understanding and encouraging my writing.

— Herman and Shirley Kahn and other family members for encouragement and support me even when they didn't understand my writing.

— The International Society for General Systems Research for opportunities to present and discuss my theoretical work.

— Lisa Hoogstra, Cythea Homitz, C. Michael Elling and Alma Taylor for typing assistance; Byron Brown for book design, computer typesetting and graphics; Ruth Ellen Miller and Alice Thomson for editing the final manuscript.

— The participants in the face-to-face meetings described in this book.

—L.S.K.

San Francisco, California, October 1987

Part I

TECHNOLOGY

Chapter 1:

PROBLEM SOLVING AND PEACEMAKING

Chapter 2:

TO THINE OWN SELF BE TRUE

Chapter 3:

GROUP ROLES

Chapter 1

PROBLEM SOLVING
AND PEACEMAKING

" Let us examine our attitude toward peace itself. Too many of us think it is impossible. Too many think it unreal. . . . We need not accept that view. Our problems are man-made, therefore they can be solved by man."

John F. Kennedy

The most potent tool for peacemaking is face-to-face group discussion. Group attention may be focused on individual, team, organizational, community or international problems and conflicts. In this model, conflict is redefined as A PROBLEM TO BE SOLVED.

Chapter 1 presents the **10∗STEP**^{SM} **Problem-Solving Model** with its team of facilitator, recorder, timekeeper, representative and process consultant. The model emphasizes creative solutions to shared problems, feedback about group dynamics and careful conference design. Many ideas are familiar to the general reader. The technology exists as part of our everyday life experience.

THE BASICS

Peacemaking begins as opponents decide to meet together, face-to-face, for the purpose of analyzing and solving shared problems. Peacemaking includes all the activities which shift anger to understanding and transform conflict to cooperation. In this approach, conflict is redefined as the target of problem-solving technologies.

Problem-solving sessions for groups of people who work together are generally enjoyable events. People learn more about themselves and each other, learn some techniques for finding creative solutions to shared difficulties, learn how to listen and communicate more effectively and, along the way, solve some troublesome problems. At the very least, people usually feel relieved that underlying tensions have surfaced and been addressed in a participatory manner, especially when there is an emphasis on action and results. Despite any initial reluctance to openly confront the issues at hand, people typically are satisfied with the group effort, delighted with their personal learning and individual contribution, and surprised that they enjoyed the whole thing. Furthermore, the group learns that even nasty conflict can be transformed through participation, communication and ground rules of analysis of problems and agreement on action solutions.

Many of the thirty-six case studies in this book use a specific technology to change conflict to achievement. The next six pages detail the basic components of that technology: the 10∗STEP$\underline{SM}$ Problem-Solving Model, five problem-solving roles and the systems view. In this approach, peacemaking occurs in a conference setting where participants use ten steps and five roles to solve problems while an outside consultant balances discussion and dynamics through systems thinking. First the technology, then two case studies, then more about conference design before the third, longer case study.

The three case studies in this chapter spotlight roles, procedures, dynamics and a conference design for problem solving and conflict management. These first three examples of peacemaking took place in a bank, a hospital and an accounting department in a large corporation. People had been brought together in special training or team-building sessions to pause in their day-to-day work and address communication and relationship issues. Each group had the services of an outside consultant who designed the structure of the sessions and helped keep the group on task.

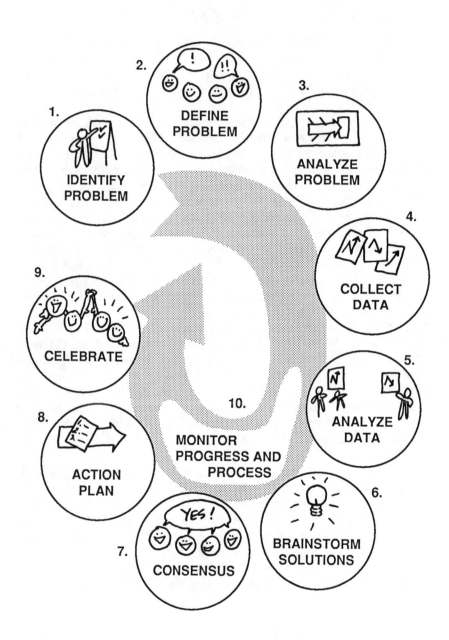

THE 10∗STEP^{SM} PROBLEM-SOLVING MODEL

Step 1: IDENTIFY THE PROBLEM. The group brainstorms and ranks a list of problems or focuses on one presented to the group. Brainstorming is the free-wheeling sharing of ideas.

Step 2: DEFINE THE PROBLEM CLEARLY. Describe the problem in concrete, observable terms. The facilitator helps the group restate the problem in one sentence.

Step 3: ANALYZE THE PROBLEM. Analyze problems by looking at causes, connections and contributing factors: How? Who? What? Where? When? Why? Look at all parts of a system: purpose, policies, people, technology, values, environment and culture. Draw charts and diagrams!!

Step 4: COLLECT DATA. Get facts by counting the problem: how much absenteeism, how often broken. Interview anyone who understands the problem.

Step 5: ANALYZE THE DATA. Bring data and information to the group for discussion. Answer the question: "What does the data tell you about the problem?"

Step 6: BRAINSTORM A LIST OF ALL POSSIBLE SOLUTIONS. Brainstorm ideas in a concentrated, time-limited fashion. One idea sparks another. CRITICISM IS OUT! Do not evaluate during brainstorming.

Step 7: SELECT THE BEST SOLUTION BY CONSENSUS. Consensus is group agreement; consensus is not a majority vote. Consensus is the decision everyone can live with. At the very least, consensus means everyone believes their viewpoint has been genuinely heard and understood by the group. Step 7 takes time.

Step 8: TAKE ACTION. Accept responsibility for action and follow-up. Action plans state who does what by when.

Step 9: CELEBRATE. Appreciate the courage of talking about conflict. Reaching any decision by consensus is an effort to be applauded.

Step 10: MONITOR PROGRESS AND PROCESS. Give feedback about progress toward goals and group dynamics. Groups become self-correcting systems when they discuss "How are we doing as a problem-solving team?"

PROBLEM-SOLVING ROLES

The **10∗STEP**SM **Model** uses five basic meeting roles: facilitator, recorder, timekeeper, representative and process consultant. The roles may be assigned to group members or taken on by a consulting team. Observation shows that the roles arise naturally in most group meetings. Experience suggests that consultants and group members can share the roles and that rotating the roles over time teaches everyone basic problem-solving skills.

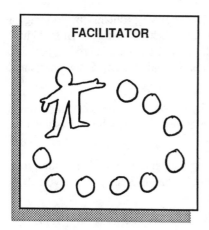

1. The Facilitator is both coach and active listener, setting up procedures for problem solving and moving the group through its agenda. Facilitators may ask the group to create an agenda, assign time limits to items on the agenda, call for clarification or brainstorming, poll the participants or check for consensus. The Facilitator does not express personal opinions about the problem issues, but rather reflects back to the group its progress through problem solving towards goals. The Facilitator focuses on problem solving until there is closure on a particular issue.

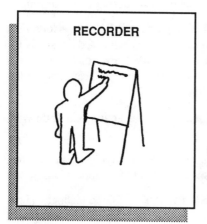

2. The Recorder writes out the group's ideas, solutions and decisions on flip charts or large sheets of paper taped to the wall. The visual record lets all group members see what is being recorded. During brainstorming, the visual record captures the group's creativity. During conflict, the visual record can bring order to the chaos of dialogue.

TIMEKEEPER

3. The Timekeeper helps the group keep track of time limits assigned to agenda items or individual speakers. Gentle reminders are most valuable: "You have five minutes left, Speaker," "We have ten more minutes for this topic" or "We have used up half of our time." Experience suggests that strong time boundaries, such as starting and ending meetings precisely as scheduled, help groups exchange a great deal of information and feel safe enough to explore the most explosive issues.

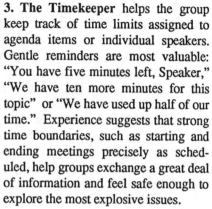

REPRESENTATIVE

4. The Representative goes outside the group to talk with other people or groups, often to collect or share information. Representatives have many forms. A neighborhood group may elect its most articulate member to represent them at city council meetings and voice the local position on the new prison site. If the Representative talks to the council and convinces them to move the prison away from the schoolyard, then the Representative would have been Messenger, Spokesperson and Negotiator.

PROCESS
CONSULTANT

5. Process Consultants give feedback to the group about internal, group-wide dynamics. Process Consultants may comment during meetings ("The group sits in a circle but only talks to the General"), ask questions ("How would you describe our group dynamics now?") or lead Process Review at the end of meetings ("How are we doing as a team?"). Especially when the primary consultant is working alone, it helps to have one or two group members also take on the role of Process Consultant.

THE SYSTEMS VIEW

Peacemaking brings together opposing forces for creative problem solving. A problem-solving team is a living system composed of interacting people who connect by talking, touching, coordinating activity and forming psychological relationships, all influenced by larger social-political-cultural events. The systems view puts all this in perspective.

A system is any whole with interacting parts. Systems science studies how parts of a whole relate to each other and uses principles (like feedback, interaction, boundaries and balance) common to many fields of study. The systems view reminds the problem solver that the behavior of individuals cannot be separated from larger networks of events and relationships. When in doubt, think in systems.

The Work System. The systems view gives the problem solver a framework for diagnosing conflict by identifying the parts of a whole. Organizations, their divisions and their working teams all have seven components: purpose, policies, people, technology, culture, values and a surrounding environment.

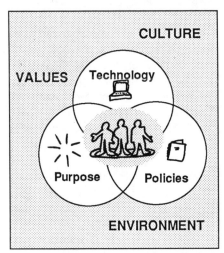

1. **Purpose** is the primary mission.

2. **Policies** are rules and regulations, formal or informal.

3. **People** are the human roles, relationships and dynamics.

4. **Technology** is knowledge, skills and machines.

5. **Environment** includes surrounding conditions.

6. **Values** are the core truths we believe.

7. **Culture** is "our way of doing things."

As shown on page 14, the seven components can be diagrammed to track sources of problems and conflict.

Group Life. The systems view is the most useful perspective for understanding group dynamics. A face-to-face group is a living system different from and more than the sum of individual members. Group life is a tapestry of multiple linked patterns of psychological relationships. The patterns include dependency, rebellion, sub-grouping, scapegoating, peacemaking, support and healing. The systems view reminds the problem solver that we are always embedded in family or group relationships.

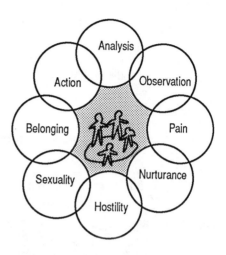

The Big Picture. The systems view reminds problem solvers to look at values, culture and environment. Peacemaking through dialogue places a conflict in a particular culture and environment. Forces outside the boundaries of a system in conflict can influence events. For example, the presence of the mass media effects decisions of Mideast terrorists, while American business decisions try to affect South Africa's apartheid policies. It helps to remember the potential impact of larger systems on relationships.

In summary, these are the basics—ten problem-solving steps, five meeting roles and a systems approach to problem analysis, group dynamics and conference design.

The **10∗STEP^{SM} Problem-Solving Model** is:

Step 1: Identify the problem.
Step 2: Define the problem clearly.
Step 3: Analyze the problem.
Step 4: Collect Data.
Step 5: Analyze Data.
Step 6: Brainstorm solutions.
Step 7: Select the best solution by consensus.
Step 8: Take action.
Step 9: Celebrate.
Step 10: Monitor Progress and Process.

The ten steps need five roles:

1. The Facilitator keeps the group on task.
2. The Recorder writes out group themes and ideas.
3. The Timekeeper keeps track of time limits.
4. The Representative speaks for the group.
5. The Process Consultant tracks group dynamics.

The systems view provides perspective:

1. A systems analysis tracks causes and contributing factors.
2. The systems model describes the patterns of group dynamics.
3. The systems view puts problems and conflicts inside the culture of the surrounding neighborhood.

Peacemaking and conflict management take place within a conference setting where participants use the procedures and roles to solve problems, while outside consultants balance activities through a systems perspective and clear conference design. If the primary consultant encourages genuine interaction, the potential for balance which exists in every living system will rise to the surface. Two case studies follow.

In Case Study #1, the twenty-six employees of a small town bank met for two 4-hour sessions on consecutive Saturdays in Spring 1982. The employees were paid overtime; they generally enjoyed these training events. After introductions, the two consultants (a lawyer and a psychologist) taught the **10∗STEP^{SM} Problem-Solving Model**. The employees were divided into their naturally occurring groups—Tellers (two groups), the Accounting Department, Computer Services and the Supervisors. The five groups were asked to brainstorm lists of Positives ("What do you like about working here?") and Problems ("What would you like to change?") and then pick one problem to send through the **10∗STEP^{SM} Model**.

Case Study #1: Tellers versus Computer Services

Step 1: Identify the Problem. Group #4, Computer Services, after choosing one person as facilitator and another to record what was said, picked "The conflict between the Department of Computer Services and the Tellers."

Step 2: Define The Problem Clearly. "Tellers get angry when Computer Services reports a mistake in numbers. Tellers take our questions personally."

Step 3: Analyze The Problem. The group brainstormed causes of the conflict: policy changes without notice, lack of professional attitude, unclear priorities, people don't understand each other's jobs, jealousy and pettiness, lack of trust, tellers read criticism into Computer Services' questions.

Step 4: Collect Data. The group decided what information would help their analysis and designed a simple survey. For one week they would rate as "positive" or "negative" every response to a Computer Services question.

Step 5: Analyze Data. The following Saturday at 8:00 AM, Group #4 reviewed the data collected. They found sixteen of twenty-three reactions to Computer Services questions were "negative," including nasty comments, nasty looks, sarcasm and refusal to investigate mistakes. The group decided their communication problem was not just with the Tellers and they redefined the problem: "People get defensive whenever we ask a question. They don't understood our job."

Step 6: Brainstorm Solutions. One person suggested "training" to help employees understand each others jobs; another said that even a five-minute description of what everyone does would help. A third person said Computer Services could give more information to other employees.

Step 7: Choose Solutions. At 9:30 AM, all groups reported back the problem chosen for analysis and recommended solutions. Group #4 reported a solution reached by consensus: "More cross-training—learning who does what here."

Step 8: Take Action. A request was made to use part of staff meetings to learn about people's jobs.

Step 9: Celebrate. The staff applauded its efforts and results.

Step 10: Monitor Progress and Process. A follow-up meeting was scheduled, the group reviewed its discussions and a closing ceremony asked each person to give a word describing his or her reactions to the two-day workshop.

•   •   •   •   •

This is the basic model. Participants use meeting roles to move through problem-solving procedures. The third party consultant designs overall events, trains and educates, gives feedback and manages progress towards closure. in the next case study, more details are provided about Step 3: Analyze The

Problem, as twenty-four nurses address the issue of perceived favoritism in promotions.

Case Study #2: Favoritism in Promotion

Step 1: Identify the problem. The nurses brainstormed a list of problems and then chose one for focus: "More than one qualified person applying for the same position."

Step 2: Define the problem clearly. Their one sentence: "Management is at risk and staff are under stress when unclear policies are used to promote or hire one person when several applicants have comparable abilities, qualities, credentials and qualifications."

Step 3: Analyze the problem. The consultant gave these directions: "Brainstorm a list of causes and contributing factors, then put the causes on the Analysis Map according to category—purpose, people, policy, technology, culture, environment and values." This diagram is a modification of a Quality Circle procedure called a cause-effect diagram or a fishbone analysis.[15]

THE ANALYSIS MAP^{SM}*

ENVIRONMENT

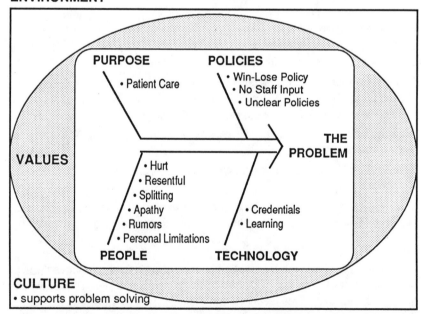

* The ANALYSIS MAP^{SM} is a service mark of LSK ASSOCIATES, San Francisco, California.

Step 4: Collect the data. Most unit promotions in the last few years had caused tension or conflict.

Step 5: Analyze the data. The nurses discussed their history and the data analysis and concluded (1) promotions were a serious problem and (2) "Almost all causes were listed under policies and people; we've lost sight of our shared purpose and skills." There was agreement to talk it all out.

Step 6: Brainstorm list of all possible solutions.
1. Management clarifies promotion policy, especially assistant head nurse slots. Who's decision is it?
2. Management actively seeks staff input regarding promotions.
3. Management considers survey on attitudes and promotions.
4. Staff discusses if fights about promotions represent other issues.
5. Manangement clarifies whether staff input is a vote.

Step 7: Select the best solution by consensus. All five solutions were chosen.

Step 8: Take action. Follow-up discussions at regular staff meetings were set.

Step 9: Celebrate. Applause for the game plan.

Step 10: Monitor progress and process. A follow-up survey was suggested for six months later and the group reviewed its solutions and process.

• • • • •

As the next section shows, when the roles, procedures and systems approach are put inside a conference setting, action becomes more complicated.

DESIGNING PEACE CONFERENCES

Some problem solving meetings are informal, spontaneous and on-site—the four-hour dinner conversation about the family summer vacation; the six-hour team meeting when the client rejects the new marketing plan; the Friday afternoon discussions when the senior partners decide which young lawyers will be advanced to junior partner status. Here, participants know each other and while there may be differences in opinion, even angry and bitter exchanges, the group has already established a base line of trust.

At other times, participants may not know each other, may have a history of hostility, may anticipate deceit and manipulation or may not be able to imagine an outcome generally acceptable to all. In these situations, a carefully designed series of meetings builds trust and meaningful communication.[16]

Case Study #3 shows a conference design that opens with a welcome and statement of ground rules, then gives people the opportunity to inertview each other, talk about common goals, the executive's management philosophy, personality styles and warm-up games before training begins in the 10*STEP[SM] Model. Only after all this "pre-work" do participants start the problem identification and problem-solving phase of the conference. The same design will reappear in Chapter 8: PEACEMAKING with more people and more anger. The basics first.

Case Study #3: Team Building During Reorganization

This two-day team-building workshop was for the Manager and five supervisors of an Accounting Department about to be de-centralized. Corporate headquarters had decided the department should cease to exist as a separate office. In ninety days, forty-two accounting employees would be divided up and reassigned to three operating departments (manufacturing, sales and distribution) rather than serve as a central processing branch for all corporate functions. In the team-building workshop, the Manager and five supervisors tried to deal with the re-organization.

Day 1

Opening. The Accounting Manager began the workshop with a welcome:

> I am happy to see you all here. I welcome you to our team building session and I'm looking forward to our discussions and to getting to know each other better.

The consultant also made an opening statement:

> I am a consulting psychologist with a specialty in group dynamics. This team-building workshop was designed to strengthen the sense of common goals on the management team and to set the stage for a smooth reorganization.
>
> From today until Thursday you will get to know yourselves and each other better and we will mostly spend our time analyzing and solving the issues at hand. I ask that you follow seven ground rules:
>
> 1. Listen to people when they speak.
> 2. Group decisions are by consensus.
> 3. We take breaks and meals at the same time.
> 4. There is no physical violence.

5. It's okay to have fun.
6. There are no side conversations—speak to the group.
7. Confidentiality means you can talk about the sequence of events and what you have personally learned and said to anyone, you may not quote or report what other people say.

My emphasis is on the procedures and dynamics of effective teams. The Agenda is as follows:

AGENDA

TUESDAY

1:00 – 1:15	Opening and Purpose Statement
1:15 – 1:45	Introductions
1:45 – 2:45	Management Philosophy
2:45 – 3:00	Break
3:00 – 4:30	Individual Differences

WEDNESDAY

8:00 – 9:30	Warm-up Games
9:30 –12:00	Problem Solving
12:00 – 1:30	Lunch
1:30 – 4:30	More Problem Solving

THURSDAY

8:00 –10:00	Finalize Problem Solving
10:00 –12:00	Application, Review and Closing

We have finished the Opening, are there any questions? Now, on to the Introductions.

Introduction. The group heard these directions from the consultant:

Look around the room and find the person you know the least well. Go interview that person for five minutes. Then, change roles and have your new partner interview you for five minutes. Ask the usual questions (where are you from, how long in this job, what are your major job responsibilities, what are your hopes and concerns about the job, career plans, favorite hobbies) and also ask 'What do you want to happen in our two-day meeting, what do you not want to happen?' In ten minutes, come back and each person will introduce their partner to the group.

The Accounting manager and her five supervisors were intrigued to learn they had been working for this organization a total of $64\frac{1}{2}$ years.

Management Philosophy—Vision and Values. Discussing vision, values and management philosophy gives participants the time to understand the style and values of their boss and discuss their common goals. Technically, the consultant introduces the boss who begins by describing work purpose and objectives, personal and organizational values and style.

Discussion helps group members better understand their common goals and the style of the organization and their boss. Sometimes, the consultant adds comments about personal vision—especially when a group is very angry and needs help with a vision of harmony. Vision helps groups move through time. (This section may be called management philosophy if the word "vision" makes people nervous.)

The Accounting Manager gave a brief and beautiful Philosophy Statement:

> I run the Department and I expect you as supervisors to manage and run your units. This is a chain of command organization where a great deal of authority is delegated and much decision making is decentralized. Make decisions. I expect you to do your work without interference from me. I expect you to do operational reviews, monitor production reports and meet with your employees without reminders from me.

> I want you to go through channels when you or your subordinates need to work something out with me. I will not sabotage your authority by negotiating with your subordinates without your knowledge.

> I believe in the open door policy, a casual atmosphere, with awareness of the rules of the company. Integrity and honesty are of primary importance. I want you as supervisors to work out differences at the section level. My one complaint is that I think you come to me with too many issues that could be worked out at a lower level.

When the Manager finished, the consultant asked for reactions. There were positive statements about the Manager's words, comments about the "open door" and questions about when supervisors need to see the Department Manager. Some supervisors thought the Manager's door was too open and she clearly got interrupted a lot. The Manager then revealed she often took work home on the weekends. "Door" here was a bit of a metaphor, as their "open space" offices had few walls, fewer doors and almost no privacy. Spontaneously, the group began brainstorming "When do we think we need to see the Manager?" The consultant chose not to interrupt the conversation, even though it was about 3:15 in the afternoon and problem solving was not scheduled until 10:00 the next morning.

The consultant acted as Recorder and took notes on newsprint taped to the walls:

**WHEN SUPERVISORS NEED TO SEE
DEPARTMENT MANAGER**

- For regulatory approvals
- For procedural differences which could not be resolved at the section level
- When the manager needed to talk to someone above the manager's level (i.e., the vice-president)
- When frustration was too high
- When a breath of fresh air or an outside view was needed
- When there are or might be labor grievances

Next, the group gave suggestions about how the Chief could slow the flow of interruptions when she was working on a project or important paperwork:

HOW THE MANAGER CAN STOP INTERRUPTIONS

- The Manager and her secretary could monitor interruptions better.
- The Manager could set aside quiet time for getting regular paperwork done.
- The Manager could use red and green flags near her desk to indicate when she is available and when she is not.
- The Manager could delegate more work, including regular production reports.
- Supervisors could learn to work out their differences, ask for help from one another, share more information, and seek guidance from each other on a more regular basis.
- Supervisors need to remind employees this is a chain of command organization and if employees have an issue with another section they are to go through their supervisor and not just go storming into the other unit.

Individual Differences. After a short break, the group took a personality profile (described in more detail in Chapter 2), called the Myers-Briggs Type Indicator.[17] The production-oriented team learned that as a group they had striking psychological similarities. The six supervisors were all SENSING (rather than INTUITIVE) types. SENSING types take in information about the world through their senses—what they could see, touch, hear, taste, feel. SENSING types are pragmatic, they like step-by-step procedures and want only the facts. They especially trust whatever they can count. SENSING types are thorough, conscientious and rely on facts to understand the world around them—good traits for handling clients' money. The consultant admitted she was the opposite—INTUITIVE, taking in information about the world through hunches, intuition and dreams.

The group of six were all also JUDGING (rather than PERCEIVING) types which means they liked closure, efficient decisions, numbers and organizations with "boxes and lines." They even like the regularity of production reports. The consultant, with a grin, admitted to being the opposite type—PERCEIV-ING. PERCEIVING types do not like closure or structure and collect a lot of information before making decisions which are typically done at the last possible moment.

Together, the Manager and her five supervisors were all SENSING-JUDGING types (the SJs). According to Myers-Briggs, SJs are quite at home in an organization which delegates through clear chains of command and a produc-tion atmosphere with clear goals and standards. SJs are reliable, loyal to the organization, and will follow through on the details while the INTUITIVE-PERCEIVERS (NPs), often the most creative group members, are exuberantly starting up new projects, solving new problems and otherwise moving on to the next adventure. The group of six realized they were quite suited to their work and understood why they seemed to communicate so well among themselves. They wondered if their sameness would lead to dull problem solving. As *Day 1* ended, they were asked to give one or a few words which described how they were feeling now. The consultant recorded the list:

PROCESS Out—Day 1

- I know people better.
- I know my own feelings better.
- I better understand everyone's perceptions, including the
  Manager.
- I know more about myself.
- Relaxed.
- I feel good.

Day 2

After a quick "Check-in," the morning started with a warm-up game.

Warm-Up Games. The Wilderness Game is a series of twelve questions about survival in the woods.[18] For example, one question is:

"You are hungry and lost in the forest. The best rule for determining which plants are safe to eat (those you do not recognize) is to:
(a) try anything you see the birds eat
(b) eat anything except plants with bright red berries or

(c) put a bit of the plant on your lower lip for five minutes; if it seems all right, try a little."

(The answer is in footnote #18.)

Participants answer the questions first as individuals and then answer the same questions by consensus in small groups. The "correct" answers are given out and then comparisons between the individual range of scores, the individual average and the group score are made. The important learning comes in the ensuing conversation about group dynamics, problem solving and decision making.

The group of six managers answered the twelve questions first as individuals then as a team. The individual scores were: 0, 4, 5, 1, 4, and 3 correct answers for an individual average of 2.8. The group score was seven correct answers.

With this game, the group score is typically higher than the individual average, so people learn about the benefits of teamwork. Often, slower groups score higher than groups working quickly, so teams learn about quality. When individuals score higher than the group, competition or fear may be keeping individual knowledge secret from the group. There are many such games around. *The Facilitator's Handbook*, published yearly by University Associates, is an excellent source.

Almost always, warm-up games are quick demonstrations that group creativity is more than the sum of individuals in the group. Results and dynamics also offer the opportunity for discussion about individual styles, group dynamics, the influence of the corporate culture and the nature of genuine communication.

Process Feedback. After the warm-up game and the discussion about group behavior, the consultant asked: "What are you learning about problem solving and your group dynamics?" The consultant wrote out the group's responses on paper taped to the wall, under the heading Process Review:

PROCESS REVIEW

- There are technical experts—some people have more facts than others.
- Expertise influences more than status and gender.
- The group is more than the sum of its members.
- Discussion has influence.
- Stating thoughts out loud makes them clearer.
- "Weird" answers are worth discussion.
- Confidence has influence.
- It helps to ask "Why do you think that?"
- Sometimes we all agree on the wrong answer.
- Dialogue brings out creative alternatives.

Problem Solving. After a short break, the consultant asked the group to brainstorm lists of "Positives" and "Problems or Issues." The issues list included:

ISSUES

1. Being asked to finish someone else's work.
2. Understanding the Manager's assignments.
3. Being a stronger team.
4. Coping with radical change.
5. Think things through with upcoming changes.
6. Being more cohesive.
7. Being able to admit mistakes.
8. Giving feedback to the Manager.
9. Maintain self-esteem and pride during changes.
10. Help with people's fears about changes.
11. Union activity.
12. Work problems as a team, don't dump them.
13. Passing the buck.
14. Retaining good employees.
15. Supporting each other.
16. Self-development.
17. Using planning and control reports better.
18. Are "The Girls from Chicago" a sub-group?

The consultant reviewed the list and identified two major clusters of issues—"doing it better now" and "dealing with the reorganization." The consultant recommended that the group deal with the two clusters in that order and handle any left over issues at the end of the day.

The consultant described the **10∗STEP**^{SM} **Model.** The group brainstormed factors which would help "doing it better now" and discussed factors which interrupted top quality work. They listed seven action solutions:

SOLUTIONS

1. Follow the chain of command.
2. Take suggestions as suggestions, not criticism.
3. Stop passing the buck, work issues to closure.
4. Remember, it's okay not to know.
5. Be more pro-active, more supportive.
6. Do more cross training.
7. Ask employee's ideas on making work better.

The Manager then said "I'd like to raise an issue for the supervisors—your written memos leave something to be desired." Discussion generated a two-part solution and the consultant recorded their plan:

BETTER WRITTEN WORK

When the Manager delegates assignments, especially written memos:

- the Manager will give more information about overview, politics of the situation, style of memo or report.
- the staff will write genuine statements or explanations, not one liners, restating the main issues, giving why's and wherefore's, not use jargon and target their response to the audience.

The second issue was saved for the next morning.

Day 3

After a short "Check-In," the consultant opened the problem-solving discussion: "Problem #2, the reorganization, means the death of the group as it is now constituted." The group responded "No, we're not dying, just moving around. The work we do will still be done, just in different divisions." The consultant asked, "Well, how do you all feel about the changes?" This is what they said:

FEELINGS ABOUT CHANGES

- I understand the rationale, to cut overhead.
- I'm anxious about not knowing what division or branch I'll be in.
- I'm curious about the Action Plan that's being developed.
- I'm surprised they're moving us, after the investment of time and resources.
- There's always change, being successful means rolling with the punches.
- I feel really sad, cut off at the roots.
- I think it's stupid and some staff are angry.
- That's the problem, how can we keep the good employees. satisfied until the changes, how do we prevent early panic?

The conversation continued for a while:

MORE FEELINGS ABOUT CHANGES

- For some people, they'll still work in the same group, they'll just report to someone else; and we'll all still be in the same building.
- Now that we're talking about it, I feel really sad. The consultant's right, it is the death of our team; the work will still be done but not by Our Team. I really liked working with all of you.
- The only thing that stays constant is change. I've been through this before. You build something up and then pass it along and you move on.

The consultant then asked "What is the legacy of your group for this organization? What is the gift you leave behind?" The consultant drew a large tombstone marked with the group's name and wrote comments as individuals spoke:

OUR LEGACY

R.I.P. 1986

- Success
- Faster, better, clearer
- More teamwork
- Good morale
- Low turnover
- We produced
- Left improvements
- We were appreciated
- Our system worked

Then the question: "How will you manage the change?" Their responses:

MANAGE CHANGE

- Keep up on the paperwork
- Give employees information about changes as we learn it
- Encourage employees to "do this process" of reporting their feelings and stating their accomplishments
- Be pro-active in the transition, negotiate new responsibilities and relationships

---

The consultant asked, "How will you say good-bye to each other?" Responses included lunches, wakes, symbolic gifts and a cruise down the river. Someone said, "Let's not burn our bridges behind us." Others said that although they would be in different divisions, they would still do related work, need to communicate with, would be physically close and could always have lunch.

The group then spontaneously asked for "feedback from each other—What do we think and feel about each other?" The consultant said, "Feedback with a focus on behavior is most helpful." Participants gave observations about the Manager and each supervisor as each person asked for a turn. Their focus was changes and growth they had seen and what they appreciated about each other.

Closing. After the feedback segment, the consultant said:

We have spent 2½ days together. We learned about each other, the Manager's style and her vision for this team and your department. We had warm-up games, talked about individual styles, group dynamics and corporate culture. We analyzed and made suggestions about team communication and the reorganization. I hope you will apply what you have learned to the people you supervise. To close our workshop, I would like a word from everyone about what you are thinking or feeling.

PROCESS REVIEW

- Comfortable
- Very comfortable
- Thankful
- Learned more than I thought I would
- Relaxed
- Grateful
- (from the consultant) Satisfied

• • • • •

Technically, the workshop was a conference with standard elements: opening ceremonies, introductions, warm-up events, education, training, problem analysis, negotiations, solutions, joint statements, action plans, follow-up plans, celebrations and closing ceremonies. In the next case study, similar events and dynamics occur in an international setting.

Case Study #4: The Geneva Summit

When Reagan and Gorbachev met in Geneva in November 1985, five of eight hours designated for formal summit meetings were face-to-face dialogues. This review of events is condensed from magazine accounts (*TIME* and *NEWSWEEK*, November 25 and December 2, 1985).

Tuesday Morning: On November 19, at 10:00 AM, Gorbachev came to the U.S. base at Chateau Fleur d'Eau and Reagan immediately proposed that they meet without advisers. For sixty-four minutes, they "educated each other on their divergent world view." Gorbachev commented on America's military-industrial complex, Reagan talked about government and economics. They then touched on regional issues including Soviet advisers in Nicaragua, American support of rebels in Afghanistan, Soviet influence in Ethiopia, and American influence in El Salvador. Gorbachev hinted at a political solution in Afghanistan.

Tuesday Afternoon: Problem solving became the focus on the key issue of arms control. In animated discussion, Reagan critiqued the U.S.-USSR history of mutual threats and described his dream of rendering nuclear weapons obsolete. Gorbachev replied, "You can have dreams of peace, we have to face reality." Gorbachev angrily demanded the ban of space weapons. Then a dramatic exchange:

Gorbachev: Why don't you believe us when we say we will not use weapons against you?

Reagan: I cannot say to the American people that I could take you at your word if you don't believe us.

Gorbachev: It looks as if we've reached an impasse.

Reagan: How about a change in atmosphere and a walk.

Gorbachev: Ah, fresh air may bring fresh ideas.

Settled in the pool house by the lake shore, conversation flowed from personal careers to arms control. Reagan presented six topic areas: the Soviet idea of a 50% reduction in nuclear arms, separate interim agreements, verification, chemical weapons ban, nuclear proliferation and risk reduction centers. Gorbachev rejected the package which allowed the U.S. to continue Star Wars research, yet declared "We must continue to talk." Still blocked by the Star Wars issue, the two superpower leaders climbed back up the hill. A few words seemed to shift gloom to hope:

Reagan: I think we agree that this meeting is useful.

Gorbachev: Yes.

Reagan: Then we must meet again. I invite you to the U.S.

Gorbachev: And I invite you to come to the Soviet Union.

Reagan: I accept.

Gorbachev: I accept.

Tuesday Night: At a dinner given by the Gorbachevs, conversation centered on career, marriage and grandchildren.

Wednesday Morning: Reagan again requested a private talk, to raise issues of human rights, individual freedom and imprisoned dissidents. Departing from the traditional response that human rights are an internal matter for the Soviet Union and not the business of the U.S., Gorbachev lectured on Soviet notions of individual freedom: freedom from hunger, freedom from unemployment, freedom to secure health care. Gorbachev also talked about America's abuse of its racial minorities.

Wednesday Afternoon and Evening: Rejoined by advisers, the impasse on Star Wars resurfaced. At 3:30, the two leaders sent their Foreign Ministers off to review issues preventing a joint statement. At 10:00 PM, leaders and advisers reconvened. With Reagan and Gorbachev sitting together in the American residence library, a turning point occurred. Shultz stated that negotiations at the staff level were going poorly and he criticized a Soviet official: "Mr. General Secretary, this man is not doing what you want, he is not working in your best interests." *TIME* magazine reported that Reagan played good cop to Schultz's bad and turned to Gorbachev: "This is a first for us. Our predecessors have not accomplished a helluva lot. Let's you and I work together. To hell with the rest of them." Gorbachev agreed and they shook on it. Many called this the most dramatic moment of the summit.

At 4:45 AM, American and Soviet aides found compromise language for the joint statement: the 50% reduction to nuclear arms would be "appropriately applied." For the first time, the Soviets agreed to substantial cuts in offensive weapons without simultaneously insisting on a Star Wars ban.

Thursday Morning: Reagan and Gorbachev appeared together to issue the joint statement. Although the talks had failed to solve the most pressing arms control problems, the leaders called it a "fresh start" and their allies called the summit a success. There were new affirmations to halt nuclear proliferation, reduce conventional forces in Europe, and outlaw chemical weapons; progress on discussion of human rights; agreements to improve air safety in the North Pacific, resume direct air service between New York and Moscow, set up new consulates, cooperate on environmental preservation and nuclear fusion research, and re-establish educational, scientific, cultural and athletic exchanges and hints about a political solution in Afghanistan. There were other more subtle changes: Gorbachev's unusual 90-minute press conference; Reagan's debut on Soviet television and the front page of *Pravda*; and uncensored Soviet coverage of the closing ceremonies and final press conference.

Throughout, televised images of political leaders and historical enemies articulating shared problems, shared needs, unique perceptions, dreams of peace, analysis of issues, proposed solutions and written statements were teaching the technologies of peacemaking to the global system.

• • • • •

Process Review. I was not at the Geneva summit and had nothing to do with the design of events. The summit is presented as a case study to show the basic conference elements in conflict management—elements which are both planned and emerge spontaneously.

From a technical standpoint, the Geneva summit meeting contained all the basic technologies: time for opening ceremonies, warm-up chatter and introduction of main issues; preparation and lists of issues and alternatives; flexibility so the main participants could meet on their own as needed; understanding of cultural differences and integrity.

From a psychological perspective, there were intriguing dynamics in Geneva. Along with the dance of diplomatic negotiation, there was the factor of quick rapport between the two leaders apparently based on their similar outgoing, intuitive styles and their similar comfort with both thoughts and feelings.

Both leaders appreciated the impact of cultural dynamics. Reagan, for example, was briefed on cultural differences regarding the word "compromise," which Americans generally see as positive behavior and Russians generally see as a sign of weakness. This understanding apparently led to their private discussions of human rights with little information released to the media.

Both leaders made many intuitive suggestions that brought harmony to tensions of the moment. Reagan often suggested actions that relieved tension and Gorbachev often made intellectual observations that relieved tension through words. For example, Reagan immediately proposed meeting without advisers and his comment, "How about a change in atmosphere and a walk?" also resolved tension and led to better communication.

Gorbachev made several statements that served as feedback about summit dynamics. His comment: "You can have dreams of peace, we have to face reality" is an observation about dynamics that contains opposing themes—DREAMS/REALITY. One of the principles in Chapter 11 is that opposing patterns—those which appear to be contradictions or paradoxes—contain the potential for balance. In problem solving and peacemaking, the pivotal learning is about perception: different people see the same event in different ways. Awareness of the tension of contradiction brings participants to the level of creative solutions. There was another paired opposite (REJECTION/ CONTINUING) when Gorbachev rejected the American plan yet declared "We must continue talking." At the Iceland summit, the final interchange was a paired opposite (NO/YES):

Gorbachev: I do not know what else I could have done.
Reagan: You could have said yes.

Spontaneous statements revealing underlying dynamics contribute to the progress of peacemaking.

Summary. So there it is. Roles, procedures, clear conference design and systems thinking will transform conflict to cooperative solutions most of the time. As Part II: Psychology will show, when rational analysis breaks down, feedback about group dynamics saves the day. Before jumping into group dynamics, however, Chapter 2 reminds you to check your SELF out first.

Chapter 2

TO THINE OWN SELF
BE TRUE

"Our future depends on the rate at which people can listen to their own story."

C. G. Jung

Peace-seeking dialogues mobilize a lot of psychological energy. Whether participant or facilitator, conflict resolution requires a strong awareness of our personal SELF: What sort of person are you? Extroverted or introverted? Pragmatic or visionary? Thinking or feeling? Spontaneous or scheduled?

Each of us is a unique person who arrives at this time and place with our unique history and unique way of perceiving the world. From awareness of this unique SELF flows the ability to observe differences among others. The pivotal learning in problem solving and peacemaking is: DIFFERENT PEOPLE SEE THE SAME EVENT IN DIFFERENT WAYS. Perception and culture influence our understanding of reality and the dynamics of conflict and peacemaking.

This chapter asks you to think about who you are as a person before stepping into the roles and patterns of conflict management. This chapter asks you to think about yourself and the topics of personality style, motivation and culture.

MY SELF

Our sense of self is that portion of our personality which consists of I or me. Ask yourself: What kind of person am I? Carl Jung said the SELF is an archetype which develops during middle age and includes the ability to be mindful, to be more aware.[19] According to Jung, life makes more sense after age forty, although our sense of personal identity is always unfolding.

As we mature, we become more aware. We learn who we are and how things work. We learn most of this through interaction with people and nature, often by seeing how we are similar and different.

Dialogue shows these differences in many ways. We have different personalities—styles of behaving, feeling and thinking. We have different motives, needs and values. We differ from each other according to our preferred sources of information—when learning something new, do you prefer to hear it, see it or read it? Which of the senses do you prefer?

Some of our differences are genetic. Most of our social differences were learned at family gatherings, where we first found out about relationships.

Our parents (whatever the image means) set the stage for our typical behaviors. Our families taught us ways of touching, communicating and understanding intimacy and anger. We learned about power and authority, forming friendships, rising above pain and opening up to happiness. We learned this and more, all in a style appropriate for male or female.

Our families were influenced by the norms of the prevailing culture. Culture is "our way of doing things" including shared behaviors, beliefs and assumptions. For example, the word "compromise" has negative connotations in the Russian culture, implying weakness or giving in on principles. In the West, "compromise" has positive connotations, suggesting ability to work with different groups.

This "compromise" example is what political scientist Linda Groff calls "cultural mindsets."[20] We take our cultural values for granted, they are like water surrounding a fish. To identify cultural mindsets, think about your first reactions to these words: masculine, feminine, work, authority, privacy, friendship, motherhood, the sacredness of land, success, money, power, death, birth, the planet and nature. Our cultural mindsets influence our sense of SELF and group dynamics.

There are hundreds of ways in which we differ from each other, including gender, race, age, ethnic origin, citizenship, education, employment, marital status, political power and energy level. The easiest way to understand these differences is to focus on the topics of personality styles, motivation and culture.

PERSONALITY STYLES

Taken altogether, our typical ways of behaving, believing, gathering information and making decisions define our personality. There is no right or wrong style, though differences clearly influence teamwork.

In corporate and government circles today, the most popular personality inventory is the Myers-Briggs Type Indicator (MBTI) designed by Isabel Meyers in the 1960's and based on Jung's psychology of individuals.[18] The MBTI defines personality along four dimensions:

1. **EXTROVERT/INTROVERT.** The **EXTROVERT** is sociable, action-oriented and focuses on external events. The **INTROVERT** needs privacy, focuses on internal responses and thinks before acting. The **E/I** scale tells us where we get our energy—externally or internally.

2. **SENSING/INTUITIVE.** The **SENSING** type is pragmatic, detail-minded and relies on facts. The **INTUITIVE** is visionary, thinks in patterns and relies on hunches. The **S/N** scale shows how we take in information— through details or hunches.

3. **THINKER/FEELER.** The **THINKER** relies on facts, logic, objectives and policies while the **FEELER** is concerned with values, intimacy and harmony. The **T/F** scale tells us how we decide about information—by logical analysis or impact on people's feelings.

4. **JUDGING/PERCEIVING.** The **JUDGING** type needs structure, closure, conclusions and outcomes, while the **PERCEIVING** type likes options, spontaneity and awareness of process. The **J/P** scale describes our general life style—structured or spontaneous.

So, sitting in a meeting, the extroverts start the discussion, the introverts wait and think, the sensing types list details, the intuitives have visions, the thinkers design the structure, the feelers seek harmony, the judging types ask for closure and the perceivers open more options. Often, the strongest disagreements are between sensing types who think in details and intuitives who decide through feelings. Bringing these differences together is part of the art of peacemaking. In *Please Understand Me*, David Keirsey and Marilyn Bates organize the types into four categories:

1. The **SPs** (Sensing Perceivers) hunger for action and freedom. They are detectives, mountain climbers, race car drivers, violinists and gunslingers— they live in the moment, show perfection in action, are good with tools and terrific in a crisis. They don't like a lot of structure.

2. The **SJs** (Sensing Judgers) hunger for membership. The SJs are usually nurses, teachers, accountants and personnel directors who focus on

tradition, duty, details and obligation. They are loyal to the institution, they have trouble turning down an extra request and they like structure.

3. The **NTs** (Intuitive Thinkers) are motivated by a hunger for competence and understanding. The NTs are the scientists and thinkers, they want to understand everything; they want to control, predict, describe and have power over nature; they are perfectionists for whom work is work and play is work. They often see the big picture.

4. The **NFs** (Intuitive Feelers) hunger for self-actualization. The NFs are the psychologists, who search for self, relationships, authentic dialogue and larger significance—the perpetual wanderers. In a meeting the NF will be most sensitive to group emotions, taking in the process as "gut reactions." Physical exercise helps NF's throw off group process. Swimming and jogging are great.

Understanding individual styles can ease difficult communications. The three following case studies show the importance of understanding individual differences.

Case Study #5: Thinkers versus Feelers

In August 1984, an NT (Intuitive Thinker) hospital executive shared her MBTI personality profile with a young department manager. Both were Chinese-American women. The NT executive thought she and the manager were rarely on the same wave length and she wanted to improve communication. The executive thought MBTI scores showed an analytic executive and a feeling manager. The NT executive said she would try new behavior to improve communication. The executive's strategy was to be less formal and more supportive. Over several months, the executive would "walk and talk" with the manager, give more support for work well done. She tried talking less about technicalities and quality measures, she thought the manager needed more personal comments. Within several months the relationship was smoother and the younger manager seemed more attentive to details.

$\bullet \quad \bullet \quad \bullet \quad \bullet \quad \bullet$

Case Study #6: Spontaneous versus Structured

In April 1985, at a two-day team-building retreat, five law enforcement managers, their division chief and staff assistant shared MBTI profiles. Managers and chief had been federal agents in the field. The four male managers were SJs, the female manager was an NT, the female staff aide was an SJ, and the male Division Chief was an NF. Discussion linked MBTI scores and their staff meetings:

Division Chief:	"Managers complain about meetings, now I see why. I'm informal, I go in the meeting and ask 'What's up?' The SJs want agendas."
Group Manager #1:	"You're great, we appreciate your support, but your meetings drive me nuts."
Group Manager #2:	"Yeah. I like to check things off an agenda, to make sure everything is covered."
Group Manager #3:	"It's the same with the Task Force on Continuing Education. You set it in place but we need more structure and guidelines. What objectives do you have?"
Division Chief:	"Okay, more structure from me."

•　•　•　•　•

Case Study #7: Begin-Sadat, Reagan-Gorbachev

In his journal about the Camp David peace talks, President Jimmy Carter frequently noted that Begin and Sadat had very different styles. Carter called Sadat "a shining light" and admired Sadat's insights spoken in broad terms with emphasis on strategic implications and concern for the views of all parties—Egyptian, Israeli, American and other Arab countries. Sadat made Egypt's decisions himself and spent little time with his staff.

On the other side, Begin was not as conceptual but rather more thorough, methodical and relied heavily on his staff. In Carter's words:

> His [Begin's] questions were not about substance. He was concerned about the daily schedule, the procedures to be followed, the time and place of meetings, how a record of the proceedings would be kept, how many aides would be permitted on each side and so forth. (Carter, *Keeping Faith*, p. 329)

After some bumpy starts, Carter worked out a strategy at Camp David to deal with the different styles. He talked with Sadat about the larger concepts and overall plan; he negotiated with Begin over details.

The Camp David events may be compared with the Geneva Summit. Reagan and Gorbachev's instant rapport appears to be the connection of two extroverts who enjoy story telling, two intuitives who prefer fundamentals to details and two mature men comfortable with themselves, their position, their families and their feelings.

•　•　•　•　•

In Case Study #5, peacemaking emerged from an executive's ability to observe, innovate and adapt her behavior to new understanding. In Case Study #6, peacemaking emerged from an executive's willingness to listen, look within and compromise. In Case Study #7, peacemaking emerged from presidential strategy and compatible, personal styles. Unless we understand that people have fundamental differences in the way they approach reality, our efforts to communicate will be filled with unnecessary stops and starts.

MOTIVATION

Aside from the enduring features of our personality style, we differ from each other according to the forces which motivate us at a particular moment. Motivation means "why" people behave as they do, what internal needs drive us. In the 1940s, Abraham Maslow wrote that human needs are arranged in a hierarchy so that physical needs (hunger, thirst) push our actions until these needs are met, then "higher order" needs (love, self-actualization) motivate us.[21]

The concept of a hierarchy of needs and motivation can help practitioners diagnose groups in conflict. Brainstorming a list of "positives" or "problems" is a diagnostic activity. If the list of problems contains comments like "fear of reprisals," "fear of being hurt" or "fear of being on the Hot Seat, " the group is in conflict at the level of lower motivational needs. Creative problem solving cannot occur until the group meets the more primitive requirements for survival and safety. If problems like "training," "payroll and personnel" or "not enough respect" are on the list, the group may need to satisfy concerns about psychological safety before solving technical problems such as cost savings.

More recently, psychologists such as David McClelland have described motivational drives such as power, achievement and affiliation.[22] Systems science now suggests that these needs as well as sexuality, identity, anger, analysis and others operate simultaneously.[23] A tapestry of motives and forces influences our behavioral choices.

Within the tapestry, the darker motives of greed, control, power and hurting others also have influence. Jung reminds us that these Shadow motives are always present. In *Getting To Yes*, Fisher and Ury remind us that sometimes you negotiate with people who are more powerful, refuse to play by the rules or resort to "dirty tricks." Peacemaking often gets "down and dirty."

Negotiating the agenda and ground rules, learning an arsenal of alternate tactics and speaking strongly and timely are part of the technology of conflict management.[24] Understanding the Shadow that lives in us all and working with the darker energy of dialogue are part of the psychology of peacemaking.

The mix of personality, motivation and situation generate different styles of responding to conflict. According to Kenneth Thomas and Ralph Kilmann, there are five typical ways of dealing with conflict:[25]

1. **Competition** is the power move: "DO IT MY WAY!"
2. **Avoiding** is side stepping: "It's not my problem."
3. **Accommodating** is self-sacrifice: "I'll do it your way, fighting isn't worth it."
4. **Compromising** is finding the middle ground: "Let's split the difference."
5. **Collaboration** is deeper exploration: "Let's dig in and explore all options, generate solutions through discussion and consensus."

According to the Thomas-Kilmann model, we may operate primarily with one style and a back-up, or move from style to style depending on the situation.

Whatever the content of the conversation, personality and motivation can be barriers or bridges to effective communication. Throughout, the pervasive influence of culture must be recognized.

GENDER AND CULTURE

The characteristics of our births influence social behavior. The culture we were born to, live and work in, influences our perceptions of reality. Culture is shared patterns of behavior, beliefs and assumptions affected by gender, race, ethnic heritage and the style of our families, neighborhood and workplace. The circumstance of being male or female seems to carry fundamental cultural influences.[26]

Girl or Boy. We all arrive at this level of existence as a member of a small group—the family system. In the first starring role, the infant's task is to be nurtured, loved and protected. To survive, infant and child are dependent on an effective and supportive connection with other members of the family system. As the child grows, cultural expectations about male and female roles are reinforced. Almost universally, the mother has had primary responsibility for feeding, nurturing and child raising. Wherever this condition exists, the developmental task of the first six months of life is to bond with the mother.

Fused with the nurturing female, the infant has no sense of separate self. About the end of the first year of life, the child begins to separate from the mother and learns about being not-mother. The child begins to develop a personal identity. By about age three, children have learned that boys and girls are different, and that the adult world expects different behaviors from males and females. As the child continues to grow, the cultural and social order have more and more influence on being male or female.

Wherever girls were trained for motherhood and reinforced for gentle or friendly behavior, they became nurturing, submissive and emotional. Wherever boys were trained for economic responsibilities and reinforced for exploratory or independent behavior, they became achievement oriented, assertive and analytic.

For some writers, the **Female** has a poorly defined, even negative sense of self. She lacked the power and status of the male child. She received less reinforcement and less opportunity to explore outside the home. As a young adult, she entered the social/economic/political world of work where women had less power, authority, status and prestige than men. Given this combination of culture and social conditioning, an inadequate sense of self is internalized.

For other writers, the **Male** has a poorly defined, even negative sense of self. His adult model is absent or distant. The male child establishes personal and sexual identity through statements telling him what not to do ("Big boys don't cry") and by learning not to be like girls. According to psychologist James O'Neil, the dangers of becoming male include difficulty expressing and acknowledging feelings in self or others; overemphasis on control, power, authority, dominance and influence; and a bias toward competing against rather than working with.[27]

In group dialogue, pure, stereotypical behavior is rare. It is impossible to predict how someone would behave only knowing that person's gender. Yet, gender has influence, especially in face-to-face dialogue.

In their comprehensive review of the research on sex differences, psychologists Maccoby and Jacklin found several, well-documented sex differences: males are physically and verbally more aggressive, have better visual-motor and mathematical abilities and have poorer verbal abilities than females.[28] They found no sex differences in activity level, competitiveness, emotionality (fear, timidity, anxiety, friendliness), self-confidence, achievement, motivation and analytic abilities.

About the same time, in the mid-1970s, psychologist Elizabeth Aries published her findings on sex differences and group dynamics.[29] In a New England university town, she studied communication patterns in same-sex and mixed-sex groups. The goal of the groups was getting to know each other better.

Aries found strong differences in male and female themes. Men in the all-male groups talked little of themselves, their feelings or their important social relationships; women in in the all-female groups talked at length about these topics. Male themes were competition, aggression and fears of intimacy; female themes were affiliation, personal relationships and conflicts about leadership. Competition was less frequent in female groups and the theme of aggression nearly absent. Aries concluded that mixed sex groups allow men more freedom in their interpersonal style, but are more restrictive for women.

The AU Research in the late 1970s showed themes of aggression and competition as frequent in female groups as in male groups.[30] In the AU Research Groups, men in all-male groups talked intensely about themselves, their feelings and important relationships including the growing bonds of the "here-and-now." The AU Research Groups found three important sex differences: (1) women use more words of SUPPORT; (2) groups voice more HOSTILE words with a woman in authority than with a man in the same position of leadership; (3) groups pressure the sexes to behave in the traditional fashion and tend to scapegoat men expressing softness and women expressing anger. Further research questions that may someday be explored include: in negotiation, are men reluctant to show vulnerability in all-male groups? Do men feel pressure to show aggression or at least bullying behavior? What is the impact on the dynamics of mediation and peacemaking if groups tend to scapegoat women who voice anger and men who voice softness? Can gender-related dynamics block peacemaking efforts in all-male groups? How do gender-related dynamics help peacemaking?

Recently, a comment by a political leader showed the interaction of culture, gender and sense of self surfacing in global politics. In August 1985, President Pieter Botha gave a hard line speech about South Africa's policies of strict racial separation. In a radio interview, one sentence stood out: "Negotiation is not a sign of weakness." Botha was defending dialogue and negotiation as "not weakness." The words showed concern about perceptions of softness and an awareness of tradition.

Gender has influence. Groups expect their men to be tough and achieving and their women to be supportive. In dialogue, this all interacts with ethnic and national traditions.

The Melting Pot. Just as the accident of being male or female influences group behavior, so do the traditions of national origin and citizenship. As the American workplace becomes multi-national, we are confronted with our stereotypes. The influx of new immigrants from Asia, South America, Central America and Eastern Europe pushes us to examine our assumptions about culture.

Cross-cultural communication can be brutalized by difficulties in translation, different attitudes toward physical contact or male-female relationships, different negotiation techniques and the value placed on individual versus group efforts. Even interpretation of nonverbal gestures can have a bearing on conflict and peacemaking.

At the same time, cultural and racial stereotypes interact with group dynamics. Psychologist Sara K. Winter researched interracial group discussions.[31] She described the role of Black Male Leader, an assertive and provocative figure who easily voiced sexual and aggressive feelings. Discussion showed that expectations about "appropriate" behavior for black men were related to stereotypes of the super-masculine black male and the impotent white male. Winter concluded that this role and the group's response were a function of cultural myths about race and the dynamics of a self-study group.

Multi-cultural groups need take special care to guarantee that communication is accurate. "Slowing the process down" to discuss cultural differences aids problem solving and peacemaking. If "blood vengeance" is part of your ethnic history, however, creative problem solving may be difficult at first. We return to the topic of culture and negotiation style in Chapter 12.

Organizational Culture. In a similar way, every group setting has its own culture, its standard way of doing things. These norms may include codes of dress and behavior, as well as shared beliefs and values. For example, "managers wear suits" and "staff freely question authority" may be norms in some cultures, but not in others. Cultural differences from one organization to another can be as dramatic as national styles. The intuitive-emotional strengths of animal keepers in a zoo can be contrasted with the pragmatic, analytic step-by-step culture of accounting firms.

Consultants Terrence Deal and Allan Kennedy remind us that the organizational culture is maintained by individuals who take on roles to pass along norms and rituals.[31] So "Storytellers" share company legends with new employees and the culture grows stronger.

Almost paradoxically, conflict resolution through dialogue strengthens our sense of unique identity by revealing the similarities and differences which both separate and join us. Feeling grounded in self identity and understanding personality, motivation and culture helps peacemaking efforts. As shown in the next chapters, differences are the source of both conflict and peacemaking.

The problem-solving conferences of Chapters 1, 8 and 11 generally begin with participants introducing themselves, sharing individual histories and stating personal expectations. This initial, even brief assertion of individual identity helps participants feel grounded in self before jumping into the universe of group process.

CHAPTER 3

GROUP ROLES

"All the world's a stage and all the men and women merely players."

William Shakespeare

Roles are our customary behaviors in social situations.[33] In face-to-face discussion, people take on four types of group roles:

- Functional
- Meeting
- Process
- Cultural

Roles exist in many forms, on multiple, interacting levels of awareness.

Roles are expressed through words and actions, linking individual needs, the group process, organizational requirements and cultural influences. Understanding roles will help the reader make the transition from the technology to the psychology of peacemaking.

This chapter looks for individual roles and finds the patterns of group life.

GROUP ROLES

Type	*Example*	*Activity*
FUNCTIONAL ROLES	• Head Nurse • Lt. Colonel • Vice-President Sales	Job Description
MEETING ROLES	• Chairperson • Facilitator • Timekeeper	Balance Task and Process
CULTURAL ROLES	• Male • Irish • Hindu	Social History
PROCESS ROLES	• The Analyst • The Fight Leader • The Peacemaker • The Good Mother	Express Psychological Needs

FUNCTIONAL ROLES

If an interviewer asked, "What is your role at work?" the answer would most likely be a job description: "I am a plant manager, personnel director, accounting supervisor, assistant floor manager or assembly line worker." Functional Roles carry information about the content of our jobs and our rank in the social hierarchy at work.

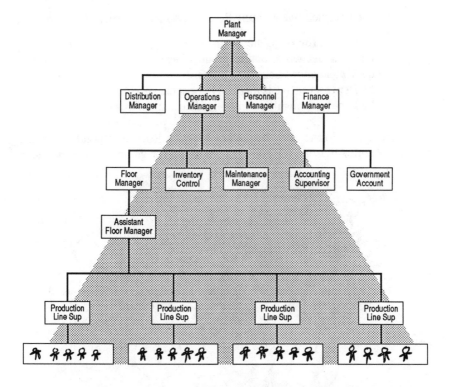

In most organizations, hierarchy is the main structure; information flows through the chain of command and the rumor mill; and objectives are accomplished through a division of responsibilities and the creation of functional departments. The organizational chart above shows a manufacturing plant with four departments: Distribution, Operations, Personnel and Finance. There is an overall triangular shape to these functional relationships.

Work systems survive through the effective flow of communication. Often, rank, authority and functional roles block the flow of information. If Operations is fighting with Finance, or if upper-level management does not listen to line supervisors, then Functional Roles interfere with effectiveness.

Chapters 4 and 5, Dependency and Rebellion, consider the influence of authority on group process. For now, this brief description of Functional Roles provides one lens to view the flow of interactions in group discussions. We move on to a second perspective which is less hierarchical and more interactive. Functional Roles may or may not correspond to Meeting Roles.

MEETING ROLES

Chapter 1 defined five Meeting Roles necessary for groups to do work:

> **The Facilitator** keeps the group on task.
> **The Recorder** writes out the group's ideas.
> **The Timekeeper** tracks time limits.
> **The Representative** is messenger or spokesperson.
> **The Process Consultant** gives feedback about dynamics.

Groups, of course, may define any Meeting Role to respond to current needs. Health Advisors, for example, are useful for groups who work under great stress.

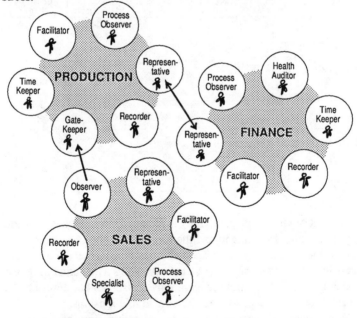

As shown above, Meeting Roles have a circular rather than hierarchical relationship and encourage a networking style of interaction. The model is a way-station as discussion moves towards more subtle group roles.

CULTURAL ROLES

Cultural Roles are the behaviors learned through gender, race, ethnic heritage and the style of our families, neighborhoods, workplace and nation. In group dialogue, gender and culture has influence. Groups still expect their men to be tough and their women to be supportive and may scapegoat those who do not meet these expectations. The impact of racial, ethnic and national heritage is less clear but still powerful. Chapter 12 will detail the influence of national style on negotiating strategies and dynamics. The interactive questions are just now being asked by social scientists: Are negotiating styles influenced by such cultural traits as aggression, passivity, kinship or competitiveness?

Assumptions and beliefs about gender and cultural mind-sets interact with the dynamics of face-to-face discussion. Cultural Roles help us understand the larger social context. Process Roles, the primary focus of this chapter, channel conscious and unconscious psychological patterns.

PROCESS ROLES

Writing in the 1920s, Sigmund Freud approached the topic of group roles by making a distinction between members and leaders.[34] He thought that a major condition for a collection of people to feel like a "group" is leadership—either an actual leader or a lasting idea. Group members identify with the leader, whom Freud called a "father surrogate," relate to each other and develop a sense of "group" through the common tie with the leader. The taking-in and sharing of the leader is a source of group identity.

In the 1940s, Fritz Redl greatly expanded Freud's view.[35] Redl introduced the concept of the "central person" who mobilized group activity around specific issues: "the Patriarch," "the Tyrant," "the Organizer," "the Bad

Influence" and "the Good Example." Redl tied group roles to the study of leadership, where leadership means mobilizing group activity around specific issues.

In the 1950s, when group roles were studied in the university, Robert Bales of Harvard's Department of Social Relations found that small problem-solving groups needed two types of leaders to be productive: the Task Leader moves the group through problem solving and the Support Leader facilitates tension release.[36] These roles are like the family system where the father provides for economic needs and the mother provides emotional support.

Since then, researchers have expanded the definition of psychological roles in face-to-face groups.[37] People voice internal needs through the words of role specialists: concepts from the Analyst, support from the Good Parent, anger from the Fight Leader, sexuality through the Lover and anxiety through the Distressed Participant. Process Roles are behavior clusters which channel the dual needs of individuals and the group system. People take on roles to meet both personal and group needs. There are hundreds of Process Roles, although social science research shows five are frequently on stage:

1. **The Analyst** uses words of perception, comparisons, concepts and categories, often providing a perspective for understanding:

   "It looks like what's happening is . . ."
   "It seems to me what's going on is . . ."
   "We're talking to each other, not listening or understanding."

   The Analyst observes what is happening at the moment, a natural talent that arises spontaneously in all face-to-face discussions. This finding encourages optimism about conflict resolution through dialogue.

2. **The Support Leader** uses positive words and gives emotional support:

"I appreciate that."
"I trust you in the Emergency Room."
"It would help if you moved your chair in closer."
"I feel good about that."

Support leaders are self-disclosing and expressive. They offer warmth and caring: "I am really glad we met." Research shows significant increases in support words in all groups—male and female—over time. Another nice finding.

3. **The Fight Leader** uses words of hostility, voicing frustration, tension, anger and rage as a personal statement and for the group system:

"That's a pathetic and ridiculous effort."
"I'm furious.
"I'd like to strangle that guy."
"I resent her orders and statements."

In groups where members do not express their feelings but make theories about them, the Fight Leader talks abstractly about control, power and influence: The Fight Leaders may be seen as "aggressive" by other group members.

4. **The Distressed Participant** is the role assigned to the member who uses words of stress, discomfort, pain, inadequacy or anxiety:

"I think our tension is underlying everything."
"I feel like my guts are still turning a bit."
"It's hard to stay with this, I'm embarrassed."
"My fears are more in the area of tenderness."

In some groups, the Distressed Participant becomes the Scapegoat, the object of group-wide attack. As seen in Chapter 5, scapegoating is a complex pattern.

5. **Nature's Child** is the role associated with words of sexuality, gender and touching:

"I can be physical with my friends. I can hug them."
"I was surprised when you touched my arm."
"Why is quiet conversation interpreted as seductive?"

Research suggests that Nature's Child is often the person who talks about nature, dreams, birth and death.

Patterns and Roles. Process roles are the behaviors which transmit psychological needs. Five such needs are achievement, nurturance, anger, sensuality and stress. These issues are addressed through the process roles of Analyst, Good Parent, Fight Leader, Nature's Child and Distressed Participant. These roles are, so to speak, the head, heart, defense, creative and stress-sensitive organs of the group system.

Any social-psychological theme may become associated with any group member. Any role may become center stage at any moment to allow the group system to resolve its internal tensions. Keep in mind that process roles voice both individual and group needs; all group behavior has this dual aspect. For example, in the second case study below, when Henry says "I'm angry," he is expressing both his own anger and the group tensions. You may "hear" the anger as only a personal statement or "hear" the individual/group connection and understand the group process. Experience shows that the most potent information for group problem solving is feedback about group dynamics. Listening to individuals and hearing the group process is a conflict resolution technology.

Case Study #8: The Play of the Roles

The transcript below is from the AU Research Groups. The case study shows how groups spontaneously put people in roles although no roles have been assigned. For example, Frank is not the consultant yet other group members perceive him as a leader, at least initially. Roles are given out intuitively, quickly and almost non-verbally.

Group 1 (Male Members, Male Consultant)

Session 1: Getting Started

Frank: How old are you? I'm 28.

Karl: 29.

Chris: 25.

Richie: 22

Tom: Just a virginal 19.

Neil: 29.

Frank: Has anyone been in something like this before?

Tom: No, I think you've assumed leadership of the group. You're asking the questions.

Richie: I've never participated in anything like this before.

Frank: Well, this is hideous. I was thinking, I'll get here and this fellow, the consultant, will be sitting here and say, "Why don't we start by asking why you're here?" I was going to say, "What a stupid question," and now I'm thinking that's what I ought to ask. That's what I'd be curious about. I don't see how we can do anything else, since I certainly don't know what Kahn's thesis is about. I don't see what else the group can do unless it finds out why people came.

Neil: I don't see what difference it makes.

Tom: I do. I think it makes a big difference, especially since this is an all-male group. I think everyone came to this workshop because they thought they would be personally enriched, and it was billed as an exercise in male-female relationships, and quite frankly I'm a little let down.

Neil: Yeah, I just read that over, and it's very trickily worded.

Chris: What does it say?

Neil: It says something about relationships among men and women instead of between men and women, and it says something about the sexual composition of the group.

Frank: I guess how things are affected by their composition.

Later: Assigning Roles

Tom: Well, we have you, Frank, as our leader, and he's, Neil, like playing the Bastard for us here.

Frank: I went into a therapy group when a girl friend left. It was a reaction to that specific trauma. I just stayed for a while, until the pain of that had subsided.

Karl: What was so painful?

Neil: I just wanted to say that now two of us and Frank are to some extent being used to work things through for the group. In other words, I was assigned the Bastard role and I was sorta floored a little bit. Why would I be that, and now Frank's switched from Leader to Sick Person, and now that's being looked at. How could this happen? There wasn't much said about your analytic stuff, Chris?

Frank: What do you suggest?

Neil: I'm not suggesting anything. I'm just saying that I think somehow boxes have been designed and assigned, and it's being used by the group.

Karl: I don't think you're such a bastard, just because Tom specified roles.

Frank: That really got under your skin; it didn't bother me that much.

Neil: It did something.

Chris: I think there's some purpose to the choice of roles you got now. I don't mean so much specifically that it's you, so much, but that role has been found. I think there's a search now for some level of intensity, something important enough to warrant our being here, and a Sick Member is a good purpose.

Session 3: Analyzing Roles

Neil: I have a very low voice, and I was thinking maybe I'm uncomfortable because I'm the opposite extreme in the way I was behaving. Not necessarily in terms of how either of us would be perceived outside the group in a social setting, but in here. I was being somewhat cold, not being real, gentle or facilitative towards people, and striking more of a caricature of masculinity as it is perceived not as it may be really. The voice thing being part of it. I was discomforted by the carving out, well, here's the feminine role, thinking maybe, well, I have a voice at the other end; maybe I should be the other, and not really liking either of them.

Chris: Your voice seems to be getting lower.

Frank: Deeper.

• • • • •

Process Review. The members of face-to-face groups spontaneously see each other in psychological roles and intuitively grasp this development. In fact, roles are attributed rather quickly based on very little information. In this group, in the first fifteen minutes of the first session, Tom has labeled Frank "The Leader" after Frank imposed the "structure" of asking two questions. He labelled Neil "The Bastard" after two sentences of disagreement. Immediate impressions can be powerful, long lasting and incorrect.

By Session 3, the strangers have known each other for four hours. On the level of content, they are discussing group roles, masculinity, vulnerability and authority. On the level of process, patterns of pain, support, protection, aggression and analysis are surfacing. The patterns are voiced by individuals.

The next case study sets the stage for a more detailed analysis of psychological roles. In 1982, in a large, community hospital, a conflict arose between five senior nurses and the head nurse on a psychiatric unit. The group of five were angry about favoritism, unclear decision making and an allegedly punitive management style. The head nurse, medical director and some nurses were angry that the group of five had gone outside the unit to complain to the hospital administrator who called in an outside consultant.

Case Study #9: Healing the Split

At Unit Meeting #1, twenty-two staff members identified 104 Problems and forty-eight Positives about the unit. At the end of this meeting, the staff decided that the most important agenda item for the next meeting was "to integrate the five" and heal the split between staff members. Unit Meeting #2 focused first on this split and open discussion surfaced the staff's anger. Some of this conversation is presented below to generate details about group roles. Kate and Jan are two of the five nurses who complained to the administrator.

Henry: I'm angry about your procedure. By going outside the unit you negated all of us.

Beth: Yeah, you could have used staff meetings.

Kate: I didn't think anyone would believe me. I brought the issues up in staff meetings. I didn't feel heard.

Susan: You labelled me a recipient of favoritism and I'm angry and hurt. You're denying my qualifications.

Kate: I'm angry you're angry. I'm angry no one's been listening to my anger.

Mary: Look, you people don't speak for me. I love working here.

Ethel: I don't know if we can solve this.

Jan: We were afraid of reprisals. I was afraid we'd be fired.

Sarah: I respect the five of you for raising all this. I respect the administration for supporting our need to work issues out.

Sue: I had no idea this was going on.

Gene: I didn't know either.

CONSULTANT: Communication is blocked within the team and between some staff and managers.

Anne: Some of it has to be let go. You can't resolve 100%.

Janet: Our anger won't go away until we work together.

About here, two hours into the discussion, the consultant asked the group to "work together in the here-and-now" by generating a philosophy statement which answered the question: "What is a healing community?" Soon, the staff had shifted from confrontation to team work.

• • • • •

Table 1 below shows the individual/group connection for each sentence in the hospital dialogue above. For example, Henry's words "I'm angry about your procedure" is the role of Aggressor voicing the group theme of hostility.

Table 1

WORDS, ROLES and PATTERNS

Staff	Words Used	Individual Role	Group Pattern
Henry	I'm angry	Aggressor	HOSTILITY
Beth	meetings	Solver	SOLUTIONS
Kate	not heard	Denier	NEGATION
Susan	angry/hurt	Distressed One	ANGER/PAIN
Kate	I'm angry	Aggressor	HOSTILITY
Mary	love	Supporter	SUPPORT
Ethel	don't know	Denier	NEGATION
Jan	afraid	Fearful One	FEAR
Sarah	respect	Supporter	SUPPORT
Sue	no idea	Denier	NEGATION
Gene	didn't know	Denier	NEGATION
CONSULTANT	communication	Analyst	CONCEPTS
Anne	let go	Solver	SOLUTIONS
Janet	work together	Solver	SOLUTIONS

The hospital dialogue had a fine troupe of players: two Aggressors, three Solvers, four Deniers, two Distressed Participants, two Supporters and one Analyst. In the end, a split staff became more united.

SHARING ROLES

Role types become less distinct over time.[38] Through dialogue, individuals model new behaviors for each other and adopt favorable aspects of other roles. Or, uncomfortable with old behavior, individuals search for new patterns and change roles. Over time, we become more flexible and learn a greater variety of behaviors. As conflicts represented by particular role specialists are worked through, or passed by for the moment, new players take center stage.

The natural group process operates to share role functions over time. In many ways, sharing roles is the mark of a mature group. Sharing roles is also visible as increased coordination and increased creativity. Evolution and learning occur as individuals explore more of the roles and characters that live within us, as shown in the next case study, from the AU Research Groups.

Case Study #10: Sharing Roles

Group 4 (Male Members, Female Consultant)

Session 3: Compartments

Kyle: My immediate thought was "there's your protector." That's what I've been thinking because I have openly admitted that I protected you.

Hal: Yeah.

Paul: That's your role.

Kyle: That's how I've been seeing myself.

Hal: That just changed. I saw that interaction as totally different. I didn't see you as an aggressor. And you came out and you were angry, very angry. I could see it in your eyes, spitting fire. I think I had you compartmentalized someplace else, not in the angry category.

Kyle: I did the same with you—focused on a frail person who really does have more to offer. I hope you continue to get in touch with the fact that you have something to say, and that you don't need as much help from us as you think.

Hal: I wonder if I haven't compartmentalized everybody into ascribed roles.

Session 4: Balance

Jake: The assumption is that the absolutely worst thing that one man could say to another is he's a little bit like a woman.

Zeke: This is what I'm trying to say. I'd like to say it in my own words. Every person has both feminine and masculine qualities, to varying degrees of balance. Because of social roles and society certain qualities have been typed as feminine, [others] as masculine qualities. Each of us have both masculine and feminine qualities in us.

Jake: There's two stereotypes—one of women, meek, mild, dependent, needing help, needing protection. And there's a stereotype of men as being aggressive, active, independent, giving help, giving protection. Something is happening in here. To whatever extent those qualities exist in me, the feminine stereotype, in here, in an all-male group, I know that the group is stopping me from exhibiting those at all. It's drawing out all the supposedly masculine things.

Zeke: I go along with that. Somehow I've come off a little different than
         I mean to. The qualities I abhor most are usually labelled mascu-
         line like aggressiveness. I like gentleness, peace. Almost all my
         friends are women. This is sort of a novel experience for me,
         sitting around with a group of men. And yet, today, I've found
         myself coming off more masculine. So maybe there's something
         about a male group that's making me and the rest of you come off
         more masculine.

Hal: Yeah, you can't be vulnerable.

Session 5: Variety

Tim: But if he puts it down, if he doesn't learn from his feelings, then he
         might as well not be here.

Paul: We all have a variety of feelings, and I think we should all get in
         touch with that variety. It's unfair to role-type a person, cast
         someone. It inhibits that person from experiencing other stuff
         because we don't allow them to step out of role.

Hal: Protecting me denies my ability to protect myself.

• • • • •

Process Review. Group 4 learned about role types when Kyle was
shifted from the "calm protector" to the "aggressor" category. Simultaneously,
Hal moved from the "naive, vulnerable male in need of protection" to an
articulate "observer" of group behavior. The disadvantages of typecasting
were beautifully summed up by Paul in Session 5: "Once Kyle gets identified
as the angry guy, we're not gonna let him be the nice tender guy that he might
want to be at times." The unasked question behind Jake's words is intriguing:
What group forces are "drawing out " particular patterns?

As the group matures, roles are shared. The natural unfolding of the
group process encourages the expression of all behaviors given cultural traditions. Sometimes the patterns have a surprising intensity.

THE ARCHETYPAL CHORD

Individual and group needs are channeled through Process Roles. Any
theme or behavior associated with a particular person may be a Process Role,
such as The Fight Leader, The Bastard, The Protector, Fragile One, Task
Master, Negotiator, Cheerleader or Scapegoat.

Group members may experience a particular role in a very compelling
manner. Neil was "kinda floored" when assigned "The Bastard" role. Process
Roles are influenced by deeper, archetypal patterns.

According to Jung, the archetypes are the compelling, wordless images of individual consciousness—images such as Good Mother, Devouring Mother, Wise Old Man, The Hero, Birth, Death, God, Evil, The Child, The Jokester, The Self, The Masculine, The Feminine and The Way. In Jungian psychology, the darker motives—greed, rage, revenge—are referred to as The Shadow.[39] Observation suggests Process Roles may shift to archetypal images when disagreement with The Boss makes you The Hero or The Fool, your co-worker's grey hair carries the image of Wise Old Man or a female staff member's kind words activate an image of Earth Mother. The whole range of archetypal images is active during conflict and peacemaking.

During dialogue, individual role specialists voice the needs of the larger group system. As participants raise and resolve group issues, as conflicts are worked through, the Process Roles become less distinct and archetypal energy less impactful. We tolerate and then learn from differences in style and perception. We find the analysis, support, anger and creativity within us all and no longer struggle with rigid role assignments. Process Roles are shared and the group matures.

WORKING GUIDELINES

Clearly, there are many ways of viewing group roles in face-to-face dialogue. While this discussion so far has separated out Functional, Meeting, Cultural and Process Roles, reality is overlapping and interacting.

For example, a manager is expected to mobilize people and resources to get things done. The Functional Role of the manager is to organize for production and achievement. Functional activities include running meetings, making decisions and signing paperwork. A manager may adopt any Meeting Role, from authoritarian commander to facilitative consultant, though success generally requires the ability to observe, listen and communicate accurately.

If the manager is a Cambodian refugee, cultural stereotypes may complicate dynamics.

The manager is also a Process Role, associated with the psychological images of Authority. As described in the next two chapters, the manager represents archetypal authority and touches feelings of dependency, power, control, obedience, autonomy, belonging, individuality and freedom, as well as fantasies of Heroes and Heroines who overcome Evil and liberate the people.

Now that the roles have been identified, it's time to get on with the action. The next seven chapters describe seven clusters of group dynamics—dependency, rebellion, sub-grouping, scapegoating, peacemaking, support and healing. Although it is the efforts of individual people that move peacemaking along, it is the perspective of group process that allows facilitators to tap the balance and harmony of human systems.

Part II

PSYCHOLOGY

— *PATTERNS OF CONFLICT* —

Chapter 4:   DEPENDENCY

Chapter 5:   REBELLION

Chapter 6:   SUB-GROUPING

Chapter 7:   SCAPEGOATING

— *PATTERNS OF HARMONY* —

Chapter 8:   PEACEMAKING

Chapter 9:   SUPPORT

Chapter 10:   HEALING

CHAPTER 4

DEPENDENCY:
Following the Leader

"My office thinks of me as the Mother Hen."

anonymous engineer

Dependency is the search for protection, direction and answers when the situation calls for self-starting action. A dependent group wants directives and carries out orders without asking questions. They are good soldiers.

Dependency is built on a magnetic attraction to authority figures. Authority is the power associated with rank—The President, The Boss, The Head Nurse. Our fascination with authority is more than the formal and informal rules at work. We see authority as "larger than life." We follow the leader, even when obedience is disruptive or destructive, abandoning our capacity for wisdom and creativity.

Peacemaking changes the dynamics of dependency—shifting the communication emphasis from top-down pronouncements to genuine interaction among all participants.

This chapter explores the dynamics of dependency and the power of authority.

DEPENDENCY

THE BEHAVIORS OF DEPENDENCY

The search for direction has many forms. The forty-year old founder of
an East Coast engineering firm specializing in high-tech water purification
reported:

> My office thinks of me as the Mother Hen. I am constantly interrupted.
> People float in and out of my office all day long. Asking for approval.
> Asking for direction. Asking for suggestions. All of them—the office
> manager, the draftsmen, the engineers. They want my opinion and okay
> before they do anything on their own. It's not necessary. They are
> technically competent people.

These are the behaviors of dependency. The staff continually asked for
approval when management expected more self-starting action. To counter
this dependency, the Boss began explicitly asking for staff opinions while
stating clearly what he expected them to accomplish on their own. To improve
effectiveness, he changed the dynamics of dependency and encouraged everyone to speak up and make decisions.

Elsewhere, management may operate differently. Where values include
"Do what the Boss says" and "Don't question Authority," dependency reigns.
For example, a mid-level manager described arrangements in a firm with a
Defense Department contract:

> Walk with me through the Personnel Department. Interior design has
> taken its cue from the army barracks. You see row upon row of work
> tables, each desk situated with just enough space for sliding into a chair.
>
> All employees wear security badges, color-coded by rank: green for
> hourly employees, yellow for professionals, red for management. The
> constant reminder of "pecking order" reinforces the belief that
> employees are expected to take direction, not offer opinions or ideas.
> The "captains" have no interest in the prattle of "privates."
>
> The salute and crisp "Yes, sir" are missing, but the influence of rank and
> tradition are heard whenever staff bring up new ideas: "That's the way
> we've done it for years, don't make waves." We always seem to get the
> job done, but our turnover is tremendous and constant.

The security-minded culture reinforced dependent behavior. Physical design
and management values rewarded people who "do what the Boss says."

In many work, military and educational settings, conformity is reinforced
and dialogue or disagreement is punished. When workers, soldiers or students
spend their days sitting or standing in rows following directions from authority
figures, dependency builds. The culture of these settings teaches young and old

to take direction not initiative. As the next case study shows, too much dependency can be harmful.

Case Study #11: Another Mother Hen

With details changed to protect the storyteller, this is the story of a first line supervisor. In her section of the factory, eighty people sit in eight rows of ten, putting together by hand a little piece of what becomes a central part of the wheel assembly on airplanes. The wheel assembly itself is put together in another Midwest state.

The line supervisor walks up and down the rows answering questions, especially from new employees, and correcting mistakes. This line supervisor was employed by the factory for nineteen years and was a parent figure to the mostly female teenagers who worked there. She states:

> Well, we knew this was an important meeting because we didn't have to give up our lunch hour for it. And the Union Representative was there, all the way from Chicago. Nice-looking young fellow, too.

> The meeting began when the Plant Manager got up and said that all factory jobs were to be re-evaluated, including our section. An outside expert would come in and up-grade some jobs, down-grade others and most would stay the same. Since we would benefit from the changes, we were being asked to help pay for the study—$1.58 per paycheck for a year. Then the Union Representative stood up and said that the Union had negotiated with management in our interests, and this arrangement would save jobs, raise pay levels and was the best deal that we could get.

> Not one of my kids asked a single question. They just sat there, smiling and nodding. They were quite impressed with the Union Representative from Chicago. Most of these kids had never been to college. Most of them hadn't finished high school. Anyway, I watched every one of us vote for the re-evaluation study and one year's worth of payroll deductions. Me, too. I'm six months to retirement, and I'm not rocking the boat. If I got fired now, I'd lose all my benefits.

> When the report came out everyone in our section got a forty-two cent-per-hour pay cut. I got a thirty-eight cent-per-hour pay cut and they transferred the other supervisor. I now get paid less to supervise twice as many workers. And we all just let it happen to us, paying out money every pay period for someone else's study.

• • • • •

Dependency and power go hand in hand. According to sociologist Rosabeth Moss Kanter, an excessive division of responsibilities generates a pervasive concern for power and political alliances.[40] In larger organizations, such as factories or multi-national corporations, dependency is built into relationships because "the work" is divided into small parts of complicated procedures. In a dependency organization, adults soon start learning to maneuver and manipulate.

According to Kanter, organizational power is the ability to influence others for production and accomplishment. The organizational source of this power is access to resources—money, supplies, support and information. Access to resources depends on connections to all parts of the work system, especially outside the group and up the hierarchy.

The darker side of organizational life is that control over resources may be used to keep workers in line by rewarding compliance and punishing disagreement. Then, dependency turns into obedience, creativity disappears, individual responsibility is replaced by loyalty to impersonal authority, rebellion simmers and the Shadow reigns.

OBEDIENCE TO AUTHORITY

Obedience to authority means simple assertions are accepted. Generally, people in positions of social control need only issue directives to obtain obedience. Our families, school, church, military and local government have taught us since childhood how to respond to rank, uniform, title and symbol. The traffic cop holds up one outstretched hand and lines of automobiles come to a halt.

In a famous series of experiments in the early 1960s, social psychologist Stanley Milgram studied obedience to authority.[41] He advertised in the New Haven, Connecticut newspapers to recruit volunteers for an experiment about learning. He was actually concerned with determining how far a person would proceed when ordered to inflict increasing pain on a protesting victim. At what point would the subject refuse to obey the experimenter, a white-coated scientist in the Yale University laboratory?

The volunteers were paired off as "teacher" and "learner." The "learner" had to memorize a series of word pairs read over a loudspeaker by the "teacher" who was in another room. Every time the "learner" made a mistake the "teacher" administered what was at first a mild shock. As mistakes increased so did the shock value. At 285 volts, the "learner's" responses were screams of pain. In truth, the "learner," an actor, received no shock, but the "teacher" did not know this until after the end of the experiment.

In the pilot project, no one refused to administer the first shocks. In several variations of the same experimental design, nearly fifty percent of the "teachers" continued until the last shock on the generator panel, despite the obvious stress of the "learner" and even the verbal protests of the "teachers" themselves. Subjects obeyed authority to a greater extent than predicted. Milgram called these results surprising and dismaying.

The subjects in the experiments were average citizens, not overly aggressive individuals. The ordinary person who shocked a victim did so out of obligation and commitment to the role of subject in a scientific experiment. Politeness, initial promise and the awkwardness of refusal were cited as factors which bound the subjects to the experimental conditions. Most importantly, Milgram concluded that obedience to authority is a mode of thinking.

When we enter a social hierarchy, first we sort out the power arrangements. We think less about the consequences of our behavior and more about the performance of duty. Acting under command, soldiers are less concerned with guilt about destruction, more focused on pride in performance: "I'm just doing what I'm told and trying to do it well."

The cementing mechanism which glues people to the words of authority is social etiquette. According to Milgram, the topic of conversation is less important than maintaining the appropriate orientation—equality or hierarchy. When the social occasion is defined as hierarchy, to disobey authority may be experienced as a moral transgression, accompanied by anxiety, shame and embarrassment.

Fortunately, a demand for total submission generally brings great turmoil. Many of those who played "teacher" showed doubt or dissent, and others eventually disobeyed instructions. To confront authority in this way requires tremendous effort. In Milgram's words, "the price of disobedience is a gnawing sense that one has been faithless." (p. 164)

Still, we look to authority for direction, pledging loyalty and faithfulness in return. Our search for leadership and attraction to authority sometimes distracts us from individual creativity and personal responsibility, impeding the work of problem solving and peacemaking.

THE POWER OF AUTHORITY

We are all exquisitely attentive to the behavior of powerful figures. From the moment life begins, we rely on the power of adults to take care of us as infants, then as children. An infant shows absolute dependence on its parents for life-sustaining nurturance. The child's sense that survival equals dependency on some powerful other is carried around through adulthood.

Dependent feelings surface in two ways when individuals join together in small groups. We depend upon each other for psychological survival and mutual support. The need to belong, to feel connected, to receive affirmation and to avoid becoming the odd one out are met by finding a secure place in a social network and a supportive group.

We also seek security by searching for powerful leadership. We want leaders to control the chaos that is human affairs, so we view authority, at least initially, as "larger than life."

Self-Study Groups. A self-study group is a collection of individuals meeting together for the explicit purpose of discussing the immediate, here-and-now experience of group membership. Thoughts, feelings and behaviors are the topics of conversation.

The AU Research Project described earlier was a series of self-study groups with consultants trained in the model of England's Tavistock Institute. Tavistock is a particularly useful tool for analyzing the dynamics of authority because the Tavistock consultant does not talk directly to any individual group member. The role of the Tavistock consultant is to give feedback about group process. The Tavistock consultant reflects back to the group its behavior as a system: "The group can't decide if it wants to break bread or break heads." The Tavistock consultant does not give or suggest direction, but simply reports observations of group process. This observer role of an authority figure contradicts the general expectation about how consultants "ought to" lead groups and stimulates great discussion about the nature of authority.

In the first short segment, Group 2, an all-male group of six with a male consultant, shows how attentive to authority the members have become. The consultant represents authority figures in general. The group's fascination with the consultant reflects a dependent attraction to authority.

Group 2 (Male Members, Male Consultant)

Session 2: Fascination

> Donald: The consultant gets more attentive at times. Sometimes he does peer forward and look at us.
>
> David: He gives us all sorts of verbal and non-verbal signs.
>
> Chuck: The foot movements. I've been trying to figure out what the foot movements mean.
>
> David: I don't think a folded-arms posture is natural. Personally, I think that is a role that he has been asked to adopt.
>
> Chuck: I think he's been in it too long for it to be natural.
>
> Donald: I see him as a statue, as marble.
>
> David: From what I know about group relations things, I'm sure that it is intended that he be as neutral as he can possibly be.

Chuck: I don't think he's neutral.

David: I don't think so either. I don't think it's possible to sit in the room and be totally neutral. His eye movements, the way he's reacting right now as I talk about him, although he just looked away, gives me information about what he's feeling, affects the way I interact with him.

Chuck: I don't think he's been neutral. I find him to be more authoritative, sort of pontifical. The statements that he makes seem to be measured and controlled in tone and that tone is directed in a certain way. I would not expect him to be that way normally. I find myself wanting to evaluate his comments in the same way he evaluates ours. I'm reading into that a little, maybe more evaluation than there is there, but that's the way I see it.

Process Review. For Group 2, the attraction to authority began with concentrated attention to the details of his physical presence. The authority's eye, hand, head and foot movements, as well as his tone of voice undergo the group's analysis. No wonder managers are taught to "dress for success;" the group does notice the shine on their shoes.

People are fascinated with authority, they are mesmerized. They see authority as endowed with special powers, "above and beyond" or "sort of pontifical" or "larger than life." People want authority to lead, or at least to help when they are stuck or blocked. The next transcript helps explain this magnified attitude towards authority. This conversation is from Group 4, six men and a female consultant. The transcripts begin early in Session 1, members are asking "Why are you here?"

Group 4 (Male Members, Female Consultant)

Session 1: Above and Beyond

Jake: I wanted to study group process. How I act in groups, for instance, our all-male group.

Kyle: It's interesting that you excluded the consultant. I see her as a member of the group. I didn't hear you say that.

Jake: She is a member, but she's a special member. I hate to say above and beyond us, but that is the way I look at consultants; someone who's employed with expertise and all.

Zeke: I think she is the one structural rigidity in the group that we can't control, except we could throw her out if we want. But there's no way we can force her to come in as a full participating member of the group.

Jake: Yeah. We're making an effort to point out how different she is
        from the rest of us. She's female, she's a consultant, she hasn't
        talked except to make observations, she hasn't talked to any
        specific person, et cetera. We're acting as if she's not here in a lot
        of ways. In fact, I'm not even looking at her, except occasionally
        when I get self-conscious about it.

Zeke: One question I have is whether she's going to lead us through our
        "blocks." I'm not sure she can lead us anywhere.

Paul: But there is a tendency to want the consultant to lead, to direct. I
        think that's what Kyle was saying.

Session 2: Control

Tim: Well, that's the function of the leader. She's the leader.

Paul: As long as you see her as the leader, that puts us in the position of
        being the followers or trying to figure out what it is that we're
        being led into or led to.

Tim: Not necessarily. We're given a consultant who could or could not
        be a leader, depending upon what we do.

Zeke: Where is the control over where this group goes as a group? Does
        she have it or do we?

Jake: It's split.

Zeke: Either way, you think she has really a lot of control over us. You
        set her up on a pedestal, for guidance, for leadership.

Jake: It is ridiculous to assert she doesn't have a lot of influence. As an
        indication, we interrupt one another, not her. While we might ig-
        nore what she says, we seem to think that whatever it is she says is
        either so valuable it has to be listened to or she has some sort of au-
        thority because she's part of the larger organization that set this up.

Zeke: There's a little bit of both, but it is hard to interrupt a ten-word
        sentence.

Jake: Because they are ten-word sentences, it's a little bit as if what she
        says are commandments from the mountain top, they're short and
        given by someone who's the representative of the organization that
        set this up and gave us whatever structure we have. She has a lot
        more authority than us.

Paul: I have trouble with that. True, the room, the times have all been
        designated, but it is like her comments are descriptive, an

observation of what we've been doing or what we've been getting into or what we've been avoiding. We can reject them or we can accept them or whatever, but the point is that it's what we're doing. The focus of the group is what we are into.

Process Review. Group 4 began its analysis of power, authority and leadership trying to determine if the consultant is "in" or "above" the group. Is authority a "special member?" What is leadership? Who has the power of influence?

A leader is not a leader without followers. Most people look to authority for direction and some look for guidance more than others. Leadership rests in this mutual relationship between authority and group members. The balance of control between the membership and the leader is "split," but authority has "special" influence. This influence has two parts. First, authority connects the group to the greater power of the larger organization; second, authority connects the group to the concept of power beyond the organization. Many theories about group behavior conclude that we give added powers to authority figures; in fantasy, we see them as god-like, capable of moral judgment. The dilemma is resolved through the recognition of personal responsibility.

Group 4 talks quite directly about the interaction of gender and authority. For some in this all-male group, "a woman consultant makes it harder to talk about myself;" others disagree: "There's a lot of things inhibiting my talking." The transcript continues with Group 4.

Session 2: Our Sunday Best

Paul: I keep struggling with it. What is her role? What are we doing here?

Tim: We seem to have a certain image in making sure she doesn't get her stereotypic image of an all-male group. We want to make sure we give her our Sunday best. And also, if you show me a bad point about myself in private, well, I'll analyze it and I'll think about it whether you're right or wrong. But if you show my bad points in front of a lot of people, then I'm gonna get pissed off. Especially in front of a woman.

Hal: Is it threatening to allow a woman to know too much about a man?

Chuck: Well, if you're vying for her favors you wouldn't want her to think badly.

Zeke: She has power over us. One-way knowledge: one person knows you and you don't know that person is a very powerful weapon. It's our custom to expose ourselves to a woman when the woman is also disclosing herself. The witness is reciprocal. Both have to maintain an equilibrium. I don't see that that is applicable here. There's certainly no possibility of mutual vulnerability—us and the consultant. If we view the consultant as a woman we're establishing a relationship with, then any exposure becomes even more impossible than if simply between men.

Day 2—Session 7: Authority in the Group

Zeke: I feel that authority rests in the group, not with her. At times, when I feel insecure or anxious, it's because I feel somehow apart from the group or attacked by the group, or in danger of ostracism by the group. I don't relate any of my feelings to her as an authority figure. I don't think it's because I feel threatened by her. I just don't relate to her that way. And I don't think my reactions would be any different if she were a male.

Tim: Mine would be. I don't think I would have exposed myself as much as I did during this group with a male consultant.

Paul: She takes on different roles for different people at different times. I generally see her as someone who is making observations about what is going on, who is looking at some of the same things I am looking at. I see the consultant as having certain responsibilities, a role and a function.

Zeke: How about what I said, my statement that there's authority that resides in the group?

Paul: Yeah, there is responsibility that resides within each of us.

Kyle: I can respect the fact that she's a consultant, a learned person, and is making observations, some controversial, some off the mark, some not. And that's how I prefer to see her, not as mother, not as mistress, not as nursemaid.

Zeke: The three of you have admitted to some kind of fantasy relationship with the consultant. The two of us can't conceive of a relationship with the consultant, or don't have any fantasies, or at least are not now aware of them. I don't know where that gets us except it shows a variety of approaches.

Tim: I'm blocking out the powerful aspects of her authority. I kind of put on a shield on that half. The only half I see is the gentle half of the authority, an authority that does not feel threatening.

Hal: The gentle part is in your head. I don't feel any gentleness. She hasn't shown herself to be a woman. She's an authority. She's just somebody who sits there and puts words out. Obviously, she's a woman, but she is not giving. It takes more than a body to make a woman.

Paul: Now it seems that we go back to yesterday's conversation about masculine and feminine.

Jake: That's what I'd say.

Zeke: For me, a female makes authority more threatening.

Process Review. For Group 4, discussion revealed different images of authority: mother, mistress, nursemaid, learned person, gentle, threatening. Talking about a "variety of approaches," they gradually understand that an observation from the consultant is neither judgment nor command. The words of authority are filtered through personalities. Authority is not magical and leadership is shared with the group: "There's responsibility that resides within each of us."

The dilemma of authority is resolved through recognition of personal responsibility and group leadership. Dialogue shows interacting issues of power, authority, leadership, dependency, individual responsibility and group maturity.

POWER, SEX, DEATH AND NATURE

Groups easily discover the nature of individual differences by describing their images of authority. These images often strike an intense chord: gentle, vengeful, nourishing, threatening, controlling, demanding, judgmental. The same behavior in authority may stir up different images for different members.

When groups give authority added powers and special influence, the attraction to powerful figures may seem sexual or erotic. Indeed, authorities have been known to exploit their positions of power through sexual harassment, and groups may negotiate with authority figures through flirtatious and provocative behavior (see Chapter 5).

In *The Denial of Death*, Ernest Becker concluded that our fascination with authority is a consequence of the immortality motive and not the sexual one.[42] Becker said our fascination with authority is a multi-dimensional "dialogue with nature," rich with the dynamics of power, dependency, loyalty and freedom. Our attraction to authority figures is a psychological mechanism which wards off the anxiety associated with the human condition, its temporary nature and unknowable origins. We hook onto powerful others to distract us from our fears of life. Our fascination with authority is fueled by anxiety not sexuality.

This fascination has lasted thousands of years. Our ancestors believed their chiefs and leaders could influence the storms and seasons of nature and the whims of wicked spirits.[43] In ancient Egypt, India, China, the South Pacific, Africa and elsewhere, community leaders performed magical ceremonies to bring sunshine, rain, food and other blessings of nature. As magic gave way to religion, ancient kings took on priestly duties and offered prayers, thanksgiving and sacrifices.

Our ancestors also sought the power of authority through the worship of the Mother Goddesses, such as Diana, goddess of fruitfulness. Diana was Earth Mother and Earth as Mother: warming, birthing and nourishing.

In the 1980s, conversations with authority figures are influenced by unconscious images of political and spiritual power. The modern search for leadership is connected to archetypal images of Sacred King and Earth Mother, activated whenever we deal with "The Boss" or any authority figure. Dependency, power, authority, obedience, loyalty, belonging, freedom and self-identity are some of the patterns which influence interactions between group members and authorities. These are the major patterns involved whenever conflict about power and authority is negotiated and discussed.

The next case study occurred in Spring 1985, when a consultant was called in by the Director of Nursing at a City Hospital for team building with all the Head Nurses.[44] The Director was clear thinking, straight talking, patient-centered, technically expert, loyal to her hospital and her nurses. She was a respected thirty-year veteran of a one hundred-year old facility with a national reputation for quality care. She thought the Head Nurses had a slight case of dependency. They behaved appropriately on their wards but when they came into the Head Nurse Meeting they were too quiet and too reluctant to speak up and solve problems. The Director requested a Head Nurse workshop on Communication, Team Building and Leadership which would meet requirements for Continuing Education credits, could be scheduled for several Monday afternoons and would take place without the Director's presence. The consultant was referred to the Chair, Head Nurse Meetings, for further negotiations.

Case Study #12: Dependency and the Head Nurses

In a brief meeting with the Head Nurses, the consultant described an all-purpose, team-building 10*STEP^SM Problem-Solving Model and then asked the Head Nurses what they would like to gain from such a participatory workshop. Responses, recorded with markers on a large flip chart, included: more participation, more communication, build morale, get to know each other, become a more effective group, for everyone to say what they feel, working together, feedback, learn management skills, improve corrective criticism, learn about motivation, more cooperation, clarify criteria for evaluation and solve chronic unsolved problems. The consultant responded: "Satisfaction guaranteed." The workshop was divided into four half-day meetings.

Meeting #1—Late October

1:00 - 1:15 Opening. The consultant reviewed the agenda: Introductions would help people learn about each other; a Lost in the Wilderness game would teach the basics of communication, consensus, individual differences and group dynamics; and Problem-Solving Training would settle shared concerns.

1:15 - 2:00 Introductions. Participants paired off, interviewed each other, and asked "(1) What do you want to happen in this workshop and (2) what do you not want to happen?" Partners then introduced each other to the whole group.

2:00 - 3:30 Lost in The Wilderness. The twenty-eight nurses were divided into four groups and given twelve questions about wilderness survival (see page 20) to answer first as individuals and then as a small group by consensus—i.e., when lost in the wilderness, do you freeze, run or climb a tree when a bear approaches you?[45] Participants compared correct answers, individual and group scores.

Here, group scores were better than individual averages so the first point was "group knowledge is more than the sum of individuals." When asked to "Process Review—describe what you've learned and observed about group dynamics?" the Head Nurses responded:

PROCESS REVIEW

- Everyone has a point of view
- Consensus takes time and means lots of listening
- Consensus helps motivate people because they feel like part of the team
- Sometimes 2 plus 2 is more than 4
- Saying things out loud makes them clearer
- It helps to ask questions like "what was your reasoning?"
- The group developed a rhythm of hearing each person's point of view and then moving in general directions together

---

The consultant gave a "five-minute lecture" on process feedback: discussing internal group dynamics completes a feedback loop, so information about system functioning is available for self-correction and perhaps self-transcendance. Process review reinforces new learning and allows participants to discover that each person has different insights and different viewpoints. In the physical universe, this is Relativity Theory—different individuals see the same event in different ways.

In this Head Nurse Workshop, the fastest group got the worst score and the two slower groups got the best scores. So the group also learned about quality and attention to detail. The Head Nurses fully enjoyed this activity and spontaneously raised the issue of the influence of their multi-cultural make-up. The twenty-eight participating Head Nurses (twenty-seven female, one male), were approximately twelve white, nine Hispanic, four Chinese American, one black, one Lebanese and one who sounded very British.

3:30 - 3:55 Review and Application. Discussion centered on personal learning, group dynamics and effective problem solving.

3:55 - 4:00 Closing. Asked to "Give one word to describe your feelings about our workshop so far," responses included: teamwork, communication and hopeful anticipation. This exercise is called "Process Out."

Meeting #2—Early November

1:00 - 1:15 Opening. After a five-minute relaxation exercise, the Head Nurses "Checked In by giving one word to describe events since we were last together." This helped participants "let go" of outside stresses and start interacting as a team. A few minutes for Checking In at the beginning and Process-Out at the conclusion of meetings set clear time boundaries and helped members begin and bring closure to their talks.

1:15 - 4:00 Problem Solving Training. The **10∗STEP**$\underline{^{SM}}$ **Model** with roles of facilitator, recorder, timekeeper, representative and process consultant was introduced. The Head Nurses were asked to solve the problem: What can be done to improve communication in Head Nurse meetings? The group brainstormed a list of concerns which clustered in three areas: the structure of Head Nurse meetings, the lack of mutual support and dealing with the Director of Nursing. By the end of this three-hour meeting, they had reached Step 4 Collect Data. They decided to analyze their Head Nurse meetings during the two weeks before the next workshop session. They would measure numbers of items on the agenda, how often people spoke up, how many spoke and the number of interruptions and verbal put downs.

Meeting #3—Late November

1:00 - 4:00 Analyze Data and Choose Solutions. After a relaxation exercise and a brief "Check In," the data collectors reported: "In the last Head Nurse meeting, more people spoke up than usual, but still not everyone participated; about eight times as many agenda items were submitted by Head Nurses in the past two weeks as in the previous six months; and there were more interruptions and put downs than they wanted to see." They moved to Step 6 Brainstorm Solutions and requested the fourth session to refine their action plans. During Process Review, they discussed dependency in Head Nurse Meetings and leadership on the wards.

Meeting #4—Early December

1:00 - 3:00 Small Groups Report Back. Representatives from each working team reported back to the workshop as a whole:

Small Group #1:
THE STRUCTURE OF THE HEAD NURSE MEETING

- The purpose of meetings is to share information and support, advise each other, and solve problems.
- Meetings are essential to Head Nurse teamwork and need to be regularly scheduled.
- Minutes are to be distributed within two weeks of meetings; agenda items are to be submitted to the chairperson one week before the meeting and distributed a few days before the meeting.
- When The Director joins the Head Nurse Meeting [about one hour into the meeting], the spokesperson will report issues, options considered and consensus recommendations.
- We need to revise the structure to emphasize problem solving using recorders, facilitators and spokespersons as needed.
- All hands will be recognized until there are no more hands and we will often poll the group.
- There will be a formal close of the meeting and possibly a new place and new time.

Small Group #2:
MUTUAL SUPPORT

- We will respect and recognize each other.
- There will be no more put downs, we will elbow the dominant ones so they learn to share time, we will help people trying to speak up, we will respond to sarcasm with silence and we will support anyone made the target of inappropriate criticism.
- We will monitor our efforts to improve mutual support.
- We will work together and go for consensus.

Small Group #3:
DEALING WITH THE DIRECTOR OF NURSING

- We recognize that the Director of Nursing likes strength, confidence, wants nurses to solve problems, has open door access, is dedicated and strongly patient-centered.
- We recognize that the Director wants excellence, expects Head Nurses to be informed, thinks fast and remembers everything.
- We believe the relationship with the Director will improve if we stay informed, be prepared, give solutions along with problems, use our new structure, maintain a united front and keep a positive attitude.

3:00 - 4:00 Review, Application and Closure. After a discussion about leadership, the nurses considered ways to integrate the six absent nurses into their new way of participating in meetings. After brainstorming "all the positives" about working at this hospital, the conference ended. The evaluations were unanimously positive.

• • • • •

WORKING GUIDELINES

The inclination of groups to follow leaders is a consequence of many events: the biological reliance of child on parent, the psychological need to bond with others, a wish for guidance and relief from anxiety, working organizations that reward compliance and unconscious images of powerful beings. The inclination to hook onto powerful authorities has a history which crosses centuries and continents.

Problem solving and peacemaking mean everyone learns responsibility for change and improved relationships. Putting the power of authority in its proper perspective requires individuals and groups to see the person behind the authority role and then express the knowledge within the membership itself.

When people join together for problem solving, participants naturally look for leadership. This search for direction is influenced by our complicated attraction to authority figures and patterns of dependency, power, obedience, loyalty and freedom.

Problem solving and peacemaking mean participants learn to counter their natural inclination to rely on authority for answers and direction. At the same time, authorities and local leaders must consciously encourage participation and discourage the dependent search for magical guidance. Consultants can counter dependent behavior by asking, "What does the group think?" or saying, "I want to know the group's opinion." Responsibility is strengthened when facilitators encourage interaction and remind participants to talk to each other and not direct their comments to the authority figure running or attending the meeting. Reporting observations of dependent behavior can also help problem solving. For example, "The group is sitting in a circle, but only talking to the General" is feedback which can help a group shift to a more interactive approach.

Of course, if leadership does not genuinely support group participation, people will resolutely (and appropriately) maintain a magnetic attraction to authority that interferes with creative problem solving. Yes, sir.

Chapter 5

REBELLION:
Fighting the Leader

"The harsh cry of Liberty or Death echoes down the ages."
                                                  Winston Churchill

Attitudes toward the people we call leaders includes both following and fighting. Dependency is the wish to follow a leader. Rebellion is the push to neutralize authority. In a single dialogue, dependency and rebellion may occur simultaneously.

Rebellion is the push against authority to establish a balance of power. South African blacks, Native American Indians, labor unions, most ethnic minorities, most third world countries, many women and children feel internal drives to balance power and influence in their surrounding social systems. Whatever the content, rebellion represents the group effort to balance power and vulnerability. The strategies of rebellion include challenge, sabotage, denial, seduction and hostile attack.

In work organizations, there is always some tension between employees and their supervisors or managers who represent authority. This is a natural outcome of the human need to resolve issues of identity, power, freedom and loyalty. Hostility toward women and minorities in authority is a more complex event. Hostility toward women in authority includes fears about emotional support, while hostility toward minorities with organizational power includes fears about cultural differences.

This chapter examines hostility toward authority, the balance of power and the patterns of rebellion.

79

REBELLION

THE BEHAVIORS OF REBELLION

Rebellion is the push against authority to establish a balance of power and influence. Rebellion is a remarkably frequent group dynamic appearing in many forms. On the homefront, teenagers growing their hair long or shaving it off or coloring it green are rebelling against parental authority. Here, confrontation with authority is an effort to establish identity.

In the American workplace, confrontation with authority revolves around an expectation of fairness and participation in decision making. People expect to participate; people feel free, more or less, to question authority. In high-technology research centers such as Hewlett Packard or Intel, to "question authority" in the pursuit of creative problem solving is applauded and rewarded by the system. In other settings, such as schools and hospitals, to question authority may bring disciplinary action.

On a global level, the most visible examples of rebellion are hostility toward repressive governments (South Africa, South Korea or Poland) and labor's hostility toward management (Minnesota meat packers or Bolivian mine workers). Whatever the setting, rebellion aims for a balance of power. This interpretation of rebellion links our understanding of family, office, cultural, political and global dynamics. Hostility toward authority is a group dynamic which connects Detroit autoworkers, Chicago school teachers, New York firefighters, California fruit-pickers, Polish dock workers, South African blacks, Palestinian refugees and Native American Indians. When authority controls through ruthless repression, the response can be violent revolution. Obviously, balancing power is easier in some places than others.

In its mildest form, group revolt means to question authority in the course of creative problem solving. In a stronger form, the relationship between authority and group members may be continually hostile. Work may be overdue, misplaced, sabotaged or shabbily done. Direct requests may be ignored, information distorted or meetings held in secret.

Case Study #13: Sabotaging Authority

Dr. R was a middle-aged, white female psychologist who replaced an older male, Latin psychiatrist as Division Director at a state mental health center. One of her first official actions was a request to the medical staff, composed of twelve physicians: eight Latin men, three white men and one Hispanic psychiatrist.

Dr. R's request was straightforward: "Please choose one of your staff to act as medical director." As a psychologist rather than a physician, Dr. R legally needed a cooperative relationship with a senior physician to co-sign certain patient papers. For six months, the medical staff simply ignored her request to choose a medical director. This rebellion was a challenge to Dr. R's role and responsibilities. Eventually, she made the choice herself.

• • • • •

Vandalism is a form of hostility toward authority, where the ripples of rebellion damage the community and our shared institutions. Hostility toward authority can be taken out on the physical symbols of an organization, as shown in this quote from *The Wall Street Journal:*[46]

> The General Accounting Office is investigating reports of forty-five acts of "apparent vandalism" by employees at the Social Security Administration computer complex. The reports tell of memory disks being intentionally scratched, tapes containing beneficiary information being thrown in the trash and damage to computer machinery, including one large computer disk-drive unit someone urinated on.

HEROES AND FIGHT LEADERS

Rebellion is a favorite topic of research in the field of group psychology for both Freudians and Jungians. In both camps, discussion connects the pattern of rebellion with the behaviors of a Hero.

In 1913, Sigmund Freud published *Totem and Taboo*, his analysis of revolt against authority.[47] Freud studied the tribal myths handed down through generations by village story-tellers from Australia, Africa and various South Pacific Islands. He concluded that people naturally form social groups, or tribes. Each tribe has its own way of dressing, talking, eating, reproducing, organizing and showing respect to nature or God. Religious beliefs are represented by totems, symbols of identity with the tribal unit. Totems can include shields, flags or insignias. Freud observed that different clans choose different religious symbols (totems), but all tribes had similar rules (taboos) about who could have sexual relations with whom.

Freud juggled his observations and with a conceptual leap devised the Theory of the Primal Horde: according to Freud, small groups unconsciously wish to attack father/leaders for the prizes of available women. This myth of the Primal Horde parallels some animal behavior in the wild. Among walruses, wolves, lions, and other mammals, the strongest male "owns" or has easy access to a harem of females. When the strongest male becomes too old to maintain his hold over the female harem and the male pecking order, the next strongest takes over. The Fight Leader is The Hero who rises up manfully against dictatorial authority, controlling his peers and winning the females for himself.

These ideas led to the theory that group dynamics and the human balance of power is influenced by sexual rivalries.[48] However, although the tensions between men or women and an attractive boss can be erotic, rebellion is more complex than sexual politics.

Another View. The Freudian view is that revolt against authority is aimed at winning forbidden fruit. Carl Gustav Jung suggests that revolt against authority is aimed at winning freedom.[49] According to Jung, the Hero is a timeless and universal archetype, usually a powerful man or god-man who overcomes Evil in the form of monsters and liberates his people. The Hero myth may include a miraculous but humble birth, early proof of superhuman strength, a triumphant struggle over Evil, saving beautiful women in distress, pride and overconfidence, fall through betrayal and heroic sacrificial death. The death and re-birth of the God-King is also a universal pattern.

According to Jung, Hero symbols have psychological presence whenever assistance is needed. The Hero myth represents our inner strength, their words inspire us through the ages, as shown in the next case study.

Case Study #14: Ancient Rebellion

The British rebellion against Roman authority in 60 A.D. was led by Boudicca, Queen of Iceni, from Southeast Britain.[50] According to Tacitus, the Roman historian living at the time, the enslaved British tribes took up arms under Boudicca's leadership and stormed Colchester, London and St. Albans, killing 70,000 Roman citizens and allies. When the Roman armies met Boudicca's tribes, the ancient Fight Leader addressed her troops before the final battle. Boudicca drove round in her chariot, her daughters with her. As they reached each tribal contingent she proclaimed:

We Britons are well-used to the leadership of women in battle. But I do not come among you now as a descendant of mighty ancestors, eager to avenge lost wealth and kingdom. Rather, I am an ordinary woman, fighting for my lost freedom, my bruised body, and the outraged virginity of my daughters. Roman greed no longer spares our bodies, old people are killed, virgins raped.

But the gods will grant a just vengeance: the legion which had dared to fight has perished. The others are skulking in their camps and looking for means of escape. They will never face the roar and din of the British thousands, much less our charges and our grappling hand-to-hand. Let us consider how many we have under arms and why. . . . On this day it is Victory or Death. (p. 141)

According to the Roman Tacitus:

> It was a glorious victory, equal to those of the good old days: some estimate as many as 80,000 British dead. There were only 400 Romans killed, and scarcely more wounded. [Near capture] Boudicca ended her life with poison. (p. 142)

• • • • •

For the observer of group dynamics, Boudicca's speech is a classic statement describing the archetypal drive of ordinary people for freedom from repressive authority. Boudicca also teaches us that our capacity for heroism contains the potential for cruelty.

History supports Jung's observation that Heroes emerge when assistance is needed. When any group experiences authority as repressive and controlling, the system response is rebellion. The pattern of rebellion may be voiced by the words of a single Fight Leader (i.e., Boudicca, Lech Walesa or Bishop Tutu) who represents the tensions of the whole system. The dynamics of rebellion in history share the characteristics of rebellion in the workplace and the dilemmas of authority in all social settings.

STRATEGIES OF REBELLION

History and Jungian psychology suggest that revolt against authority is aimed at freedom. In social hierarchies, the psychological press is towards a free flow of energy and a balance of power and influence.

Effective leadership balances a group's need for guidance, their dependent wish for direction and adult need to assert independence and make decisions. Over time, to meet the needs of the organization, group members always work out a power relationship with authority figures. If the relationship is not genuinely fair and just, an unresolved tension will always exist, rooted in a psychological need for the balance of power.

To unravel the patterns of authority and rebellion, the next section returns to the AU Research Groups. Transcripts from six different self-study groups show six different strategies to neutralize authority. The strategies include competition, challenge, seduction, resistance, attack and rape. Here, the consultant represents authority figures in general. As the self-study groups analyze their anger toward the consultant, they learn about the power and illusions of authority. Throughout, the potency and frequency of hostility toward authority point to rebellion as a major dynamic found in all group settings.

GROUP 2: CHALLENGING AUTHORITY

In the first transcript, rebellion begins when Chuck and David start ranking the consultant's comments: "That was an A, that was a D." The group responds that Chuck and David are challenging authority.

Group 2 (Male Members, Male Consultant)

Session 3: The Challenge

Donald: I think rating his [the consultant's] responses is in effect demeaning his responses, saying they're not important to us. In an attempt to get leadership, you two rate every response. I don't understand why.

Sam: They're acting as if they're teachers, giving grades to a student.

Donald: Like when you two do it, I think you're saying, "Well, that was an A, that was a very important comment to me." But when you said, "It was a D-," I think, "Well, consultant, you're an asshole, and don't make those kind of comments."

Sam: Yeah, like "that really missed the mark."

Donald: That's what I hear when you say that. Because to me, they're all equal. I think they're interesting.

Chuck: Well, there's no other way to answer him. There's no other way to interact.

Donald: You're trying for leadership when you say that.

Sam: You're influencing his decision on what he says, too.

Donald: You are. That's very interesting.

David: Competing with him, there's no question about it; he is in a complete role of authority.

Chuck: I acknowledged that right in the beginning.

David: Unapproachable.

Sam: But when you say that out loud the rest of us are influenced by what you think.

Chuck: It's a challenge; it's competition.

CONSULTANT: The members might ask themselves how they would feel if they could win the competition with the consultant.

Chuck: I can't imagine what winning would be.

David: Winning would be to end the consultant relationship.

Donald: Winning would be hearing emotion from the leader.

Session 6: The Analysis

David: A shorter, quicker statement, like "A-" or "D-" would allow you to direct the flow of the conversation.

CONSULTANT: The assumption is that an assertion of power left unchallenged becomes fact. Rather than allow an assertion of power to become fact it must be immediately challenged.

Chuck: Yeah, I agree with that.

Donald: In a larger group it becomes fact faster, and more and more solidly entrenched.

CONSULTANT: The more people who accept an assertion of power, the stronger the power becomes.

Donald: Right. The more difficult it becomes to overcome it.

David: That viewpoint is a viewpoint of protecting the group from unstated power—acting to protect the group.

Donald: I see it as you were acting to enhance your own power.

David: But I saw it as protecting myself.

Chuck: Maybe protecting my position in the group is a better way to say it.

Donald: Protecting your ability to influence the group.

Chuck: Protecting my ability to participate in the group. Yeah, in a way that I want to, or whatever.

Donald: Which is perfectly okay. It's very good.

Chuck: There's one other element, protecting the right of everyone else; in this sense, protecting the group, protecting the right of everyone else to do the same, to object to the consultant.

David: I think you very much set that tone yesterday. I think you succeeded in doing that. And persons who might not have felt comfortable challenging authority felt freer as the day went on to do so.

Chuck: Yeah, I felt the need to neutralize the threatening aspects of his power. One of the threatening aspects is that, left unchallenged, it would get to be too absolute, and therefore limit the way in which I would participate in the group and the way in which I would interact with others. I guess I felt that very strongly. Yeah, that the way he was interpreting and structuring interaction, if it got turned in that direction and accepted by the group, would be threatening to me.

David: I come back to that ultimately. I feel that a lot of the things I did yesterday I can speak of in terms of protecting the group, but ultimately they're protecting me.

Process Review. On the level of content, the group discusses reactions to the consultant as the representative of University authority. At the same time, on the level of process, the members are asserting their own power. Content mirrors process. Chuck and David have played out the roles of Fight Leader or Hero rising to "protect my ability to participate" and "protect the group from unstated power." In turn, their protection was seen as a power play: "You're trying for leadership."

For Group 2, rebellion includes an assertion of individual freedom, defense of the group system and a reflection of leadership seeded in the group itself.

GROUP 4: REJECTING FEMALE AUTHORITY

In this transcript, Group 4's initial response to the female consultant is confusion: "It's very ambivalent with a female leader." At first, this all-male group sees the female consultant as fragile, in need of protection. As the men become more self-disclosing, female authority seems more aloof, better defended and protection shifts to attack.

Group 4 (Male Members, Female Consultant)

Session 3: Protection

Jake: You can't help but wonder about these coincidences. The group is all men, and the group is competitive.

Zeke: Well, you have a single-sex male group. It's almost a cliche that men are going to be competitive with each other.

Jake: Something occurs to me. While perhaps it's even obvious that this is going to be a competitive situation, there's an attitude that she is not one of the competitive members of the group. Like Tim was saying, if we had a male consultant he would have more difficulty competing with him. With a female consultant, it seems to be assumed that it isn't necessarily competition, as if women don't compete.

Zeke: With a male consultant it would be very straightforward. It's very ambivalent with a female leader.

Tim: With a female consultant we can hit her much harder in a lot of ways than we could with a male consultant. Like, I don't know what went through her mind but she must have felt pretty bad when we grouped her together with the microphone and the chair as part of the environment. My impression of women is that it's usually pretty important to them that people notice their physical attractiveness.

Zeke: Some people here seem to think that we're competing with the consultant for leadership of the group. I wonder if that makes her a woman who needs protection.

Day 2—Session 6: Rejection

Jake: It bothers me that there's only one member of the group in particular who's only talking about what other people are doing or thinking, and never devoting any attention to herself. That really bothers the hell out of me. I dislike having someone in such an elitist position with judgment over us all. We can't throw any judgment back; she certainly won't throw judgment on herself.

Tim: I don't understand how she's avoiding judgment by us.

Jake: I'm more bothered by her role.

Paul: What strikes me most is that you're really pissed off about that. My feeling is okay, this is the role. I keep going back to the model and who's doing what, who's the group, who's the consultant, what does the consultant do, what does the consultant not do. The anger and the pissed off that I think we are feeling is we want her to tell us exactly where to go, what to do, what we're feeling, what we're thinking, 'cause then we don't have to do it.

Hal: Is it because she's a woman and she's manipulative?

Paul: And then we think that she is doing that when she makes suggestions. But it isn't clear. Then we think, yeah, she really does know it, but she's not giving it to us.

Tim: I think she's trying to give us things and we've been saying "shut up."

Paul: I don't know if she's trying to give us things.

Tim: We said all that yesterday. We were just pushing a rock, rejecting her statements, several times. Rejecting. If you really believe that she doesn't know what's going on, then you should believe that she is giving us her opinion. So she is giving us a part of herself.

Process Review. For Group 4, authority carries many images and hostility has many meanings. Jake is angered by the "elitist position" of the consultant and feels vulnerable before the well-shielded authority figure. Hal struggles with images of "manipulative women." Paul describes the resentments of dependency: "The anger and pissed off we are feeling is we want her to tell us exactly where to go, what to do, and what we're feeling, what we're thinking, 'cause then we don't have to do it."

Tim and Paul help the group see beyond the illusions of authority. Tim keeps repeating that the consultant is not so elitist, she is "giving part of herself," her role is filtered through a life history, her comments are observations, not judgments. Paul's questions also push the group toward a realistic view of authority: "What's the model, who's doing what?"

Anger toward authority arises for different reasons, influenced by different images and realities of power. Group revolt includes rage about the "lack of mutual vulnerability" and resentment about authority's failure to perfectly provide. Anger is channelled into insight as people learn that different individuals define and experience authority and power in different ways. In the next segment, these themes appear in different forms.

GROUP 1: CONFRONTING AUTHORITY

In this transcript, Group 1's confrontation with authority is a simple gesture. One member unties the consultant's shoelace.

Group 1 (Male Members, Male Consultant)

Session 3: Torture

Frank: Well, we have to give it up. I think we're not going to torture any wisdom out of the consultant, anything significant, except for those comments. We really have to stop and get back to ourselves.

Neil: Well, I just had an interesting fantasy of torturing something out of him. It's as if I have in my mind I'd like to see him act different than he's acting now. I would agree to that, torture, it's a good point.

[Ritchie gets up and unties the consultant's shoelace.]

Chris: How far would you go to get him to act differently?

Karl: We had talked about this earlier. Richie had said: "You're infatuated with the silence. Why don't you go and give him a yank on the beard and see what happens?" I could see this simple act evolving under, say less civilized conditions; actually pounding him on the head or beating him into the ground, trying to get something out of him. But in talking, we just entertain: "Well, go over and give him a tug on the beard and see what happens."

Neil: That would be starting at the top. Instead we started at the bottom, untying his shoelace.

Chris: There seems to be something more basic about whatever he represents to us. It's our lack of faith in ourselves as a group.

Neil: Our talk is to avoid dealing with your untying the shoelace. We're in a verbal frenzy to keep talking so he won't say anything about it, so he won't have a chance. If we keep talking, he'll have to interrupt.

Frank: I think his training equips him to deal with these situations in which his role is defined this way, but not to deal with situations in which there is actual action, physical confrontation.

Neil: Maybe he knows karate.

Richie: Why focus on the consultant?

Chris: Well, I think he represents—his stony and hard silence—represents the myth we all have, which is that is the way to woo women. We're castrated by our own nervous chatter and the contrast exposes us as nervous chatterers. And how attractive is that as a conventional male feature?

Neil: Yeah, it's pathetic that we can't get a response from him. We even untied his shoelace and that didn't get any response. It's really ridiculous.

Chris: I'm feeling like I did when I was a kid and I'd throw a snowball at a car. We have no potency to affect him.

Neil: So the central thing is that we're embarrassing ourselves in front of the consultant.

Chris: I think our more interpretive stance, Neil's and mine, is an attempt to be more adult, to show that we are worthy of colleagueship. Even as I'm saying that, I'm wondering, what do males have to offer each other? Perhaps you were looking for something when you mentioned skydiving—a good, healthy, robust male pursuit, to be discussed in the war room.

Karl: I thought you were trying to dissociate yourself from Richie's act. I thought you were trying to impress upon the consultant that you would never do anything like that, as childish as untying a shoe.

Later: Peer Pressure

Karl: Why do you attribute this act to all of us, when Richie was the only one? He was the perpetrator of the act.

Chris: Because there were smiles all around the room.

Neil: It evolved slowly out of him [Frank] mentioning the word "torture," me picking up on it, then Richie acting. It was a group thing; he did it but it evolved from those things.

Chris: Richie was acting out what was at least latent as a group norm, attacking the consultant in an active way.

Process Review. Here, rebellion is attempted, but the effort seems pathetic: "We have no potency to affect him." The irony is that of all eight research groups this is the only one which actually touched a consultant. Although other groups, as will be seen, became angrier, none physically touched a consultant. It was not a "pathetic" response, it was rather a direct, behavioral means of testing the relationship with authority. For this group, confronting authority was a test of power, adulthood and manhood.

Chris helped the group resolve the authority dilemma with an astute comment: "infatuation" with the consultant represents "our lack of faith in our-selves as a group." Attraction to authority is strongest when self-confidence is weakest. The psychological balance of power is only achieved when groups recognize their internal knowledge and responsibility.

Group 1 also clarifies a concept which surfaces throughout this book: individuals voice both personal and group needs. Although Richie was the one who literally untied the shoelace, he was carried along by the words, smiles and intentions of all group members. The same insight is achieved in Group 6 as they explore seduction and authority.

GROUP 6: SEDUCING AUTHORITY

Flirtation and seduction can be effective strategies to counter the powers of authority. In the next transcript, the women of Group 6 had been discussing sexuality in the office when Anna gives Fran a backrub after Fran had complained of feeling chilled and achy. The conversation shifted from "touching as communication" to "seduction in dealing with authority figures." The first two segments are from Day 1, the last segment from Day 2.

Group 6 (Female Members, Male Consultant)

Session 3: Power

Anna: When I first came in here today, I thought verbally we weren't going to bring him [the consultant] into being part of the group.

Arlene: Are you avoiding discussing whether or not you also use sexuality and seduction in dealing with authority figures? Or power figures? Do you think you use sex?

Anna: No, I'm not avoiding discussing that. I think I've already said that I do use it. But I felt uncomfortable initially even thinking in terms of using other than verbal means to deal with the consultant; to physically entice him into the group. I even find it difficult to sit here and look him in the eye saying that. I felt that I'd be dealing in terms of censure not only from the group but from my own feelings and from the feelings of the rest of the group.

Fran: What are you saying? That you want to bring him into the group?

Arlene: Or seduce him into the group?

Anna: I'd prefer to have him in the group.

Session 4: Seduction

Arlene: I was the first person, when I started discussing authority, saying openly that I used sex as a means of controlling authority figures.

Anna: And you brought it out in your discussion.

Arlene: But, Anna was the one that it all got focused on. I felt as though I had shirked responsibility for also being seductive.

Anna: And I thought I had gotten out of it. I have made, I feel, a great effort in trying to avoid being seductive with men?

Enid: Why?

Arlene: Well, I mean seductive for the purposes of manipulation. Or being seductive when I didn't mean it. It was pointed out to me within the last year that I was being very seductive with people in order to get things. Now I am trying to be very straight, I have been trying so hard to be non-manipulative with people, particularly with men.

Enid: Why particularly with men? Another one that wants to protect them!

Arlene: I want to fight them fair. I don't want to use sex.

Fran: One thing this talking has done for me is that I get really upset with the image I come across. I look younger than my age 25.

Enid: Yeah, you do look younger.

Fran: You're saying you seduce in order to get your way. I feel that sometimes I act like the little girl to get my way.

Arlene: That's another form of seduction.

Fran: I'm trying to put this all together while you're talking. I didn't make that connection until you said, "Well, that's being seductive, too, being a little girl." I kind of felt that it's more being dependent and being taken care of and not seeing the form of seduction.

Anna: My dog seduces me all the time.

Day 2—Session 8: Balance

Anna: Something I felt all today was less free than yesterday. It's bothering me this afternoon, this last session. Somewhere yesterday I made a judgment on my seductive behavior as being bad, wrong or negative.

Enid: Yes you did. I did too.

Anna: And I'm not using it today. I've felt very unfree today, all day. I think somewhere, probably not here and not now, but somewhere, I have a need to lay that out and take some of it back. I feel some loss of pleasure in myself and I don't want to lose any of that. Somewhere there's a balance.

Process Review. Group 6's conversation is remarkably candid, suggesting there are no easy answers to the dilemmas of power and sexuality. Some words and behaviors were intended "to physically entice" the consultant-as-authority out of role and "into the group." These efforts to "get things" without being "very straight" about what is wanted or needed led to discussion of different forms of seductive manipulation: flattery, flirtation, touching, to "act like the Little Girl."

The important point was that sexualizing the relationship with "The Boss" is a strategy to diffuse the power of authority by directly engaging the person behind the role. This gives the group some sense of power, even if the seductive pattern is acted out through one specific group member.

GROUP 8: RESISTANCE TO AUTHORITY

One strategy to diffuse the power of authority only seemed to occur in groups with female consultants: a wish to protect the female authority. The following transcript is from an all female group with a female consultant.

Group 8 (Female Members, Female Consultant)

Session 5: Confusion

Carla: I feel that I want to continue to protect the consultant. I feel willing to say anything that's necessary to keep the members of this group from feeling hostile towards her.

Gwen: Because you identify with the consultant?

Terrie: Why?

Carla: Because she has a special position. Maybe in some ways I feel competitive with her.

Gwen: I don't understand the suggestion that we think of her as a child. I think it's much more likely we think of her as a parent. Somebody who knows more than we do and tries to get us to behave in certain ways.

Carla: Yet all the things that we talked about—how some of the members of the group withdrew and observed as a way of being hostile as children—it just makes sense.

Gwen: So that her behavior seems more like a child's.

Carla: Sort of. And also my feelings of wanting to protect her are as if she's defenseless.

Gwen: Maybe. I think of parents as withholding people, because mine were.

Process Review. This segment demonstrates again that authority figures generate a variety of images—good leader, bad leader, Zeus-like oracle, fellow competitor, hostile child, withholding parent. The image of the authority as child-like, defenseless and in need of protection only occurred in groups with female consultants. The revolt against authority in this group carries little of the anger shown in the following transcript.

GROUP 3: THE RAPE OF AUTHORITY

Group 3 was composed of six men who made a conscious effort on *Day 1* to "work on exposing a much softer side of myself." They worked intensely and more of their conversations appear in Chapter 8: Support. After very personal self-disclosures, the group became distracted by the "removed presence" of authority and sexualized hostility erupted. The transcription begins on *Day 1*.

Group 3 (Male Members, Female Consultant)

Day 1—Session 2: The Non-Entity

Steve: But everything the consultant says, I treat her like a non-entity.

Hank: I don't think she necessarily says the most pertinent things. (To the consultant) Sorry, you can hit me when this thing's over.

Jerry: We tend to discount everything, act as if she's not there, as if she's sexless.

Steve: Well, I think what she does is bring us back to the here-and-now, the group interaction.

Hank: But as we start to get into things, she talks and that makes us very self-conscious of her removed presence, making it hard to talk.

Alex: How would you like her to be?

Jerry: Project anything you want on her.

Hank: I would want her to be supportive, emotionally and physically, so that I could work on exposing a much softer side of my self and not feel emasculated by it. I need it from her. That gives me a greater sense of what I can't get from you guys.

Day 2—Session 6: Vulnerability

Hank: Everything's surfacing. I mean, everybody is naked in a sense. You guys probably see through me in a way. I see through you. You all look ridiculous. You all look like a bunch of blubbering fools. I think I do also. We're running around like wild turkeys without our heads on.

Jerry: Blubbering fools. That implies some sort of standard. I don't see how there is any real standard against which you can apply this and say that we're blubbering fools.

Hank: I don't know. Before, I didn't feel that. Before, I had this thing of breaking down as a positive thing, coming to the real human self. But now I have this thing, the further we break down the more ridiculous we look to each other. It doesn't even matter what we say.

Jerry: You don't look ridiculous to me.

Alex: I'm getting angry because the group isn't going again. I feel like I really want to be vulnerable. I want to sit here and be open and be me. I've gotten a little closer to that.

Session 7: The Pseudo-Rape

Hank: Do you think Kahn could hear her screams down here?

Jerry: I don't think Keith [the observer] would do anything. [Pretending to hold a microphone] Ten-four, this is Hank, we're reporting a rape. We got intention to rape in Room 6, Building 1. Don't send help for sixty minutes.

Hank: [To the consultant] This is important, because if you want to be a psychologist you're going to be working with a lot of rape cases, and to be truly able to empathize you should have the experience yourself.

CONSULTANT: The group may want to look at why it feels it needs to threaten the consultant with rape.

Jerry: Why would we want to threaten the consultant with rape? To show off our male egos, our aggressive tendencies, or maybe it's a pseudo-rape of a surrogate mother, of the authority figure.

CONSULTANT: The group apparently feels the consultant's role is unacceptable.

Jerry: She's getting upset. Hear the quiver in her voice?

Hank: She's getting upset. It will be fun. I hope she really resists. The fight should be great.

Jerry: Alex is getting red in the face.

Alex: No I'm not.

Hank: I hope she uses dirty words.

Steve: I don't want her to get sick.

Jerry: You don't want her to get sick? That's very considerate.

Hank: What if she's on the rag.

Jerry: Gosh, no.

Hank: You pull it out of her. I can't do it.

Steve: Put her in stirrups.

Jerry: Anybody got any petroleum jelly?

Hank: No. You're gonna pull a Last Tango in Paris move. Marlon Brando gives it to Maria Schneider from the rear.

Jerry: I haven't had time to see movies in a long time.

Hank: She's starting to relax a little. Start teasing. She started to get hot. She wants it bad.

Jerry: Must be terrible being a consultant, especially if you can't even consult.

CONSULTANT: The group wishes to exclude the consultant or prevent the consultant from performing her role.

Hank: She's starting to stutter. And you thought this would be easy.
         You'd be the liberal psychologist. You never thought it would end
         like this. She could sue Lynn Kahn and the University. She could
         sue us.

Jerry: Could try to throw us in jail.

Hank: And it's all on tape. We can whisper so it's not even on the tape.
         Got her all wigged out.

Alex: There's a part of me that could get into this thing.

Jerry: You look up tight.

Hank: You got laid last night, didn't you?

Jerry: How long is this thing going to go on?

Hank: Let's see, it started at 1:30. She's got an hour. At the latest I want
         to get going by 2:15. That would be forty-five minutes. That
         would be fifteen minutes a piece. This will be a very peculiar study,
         a very interesting Ph.D. We should stop immediately. Maybe
         we'll get into a Nazi mentality, and I'm a Jew.

Alex: Did your parents ever go to church?

Jerry: No, they didn't. They had no religion.

Hank: Psychologists, they're amazing.

Jerry: You never know what they've been trained to do. Maybe she's a
         sex therapist on the side.

[At this point the consultant gets up, walks out of the room, takes a few deep
         breaths and returns.]

Jerry: What keeps us angry towards her?

Alex: She's really hard.

Hank: No she isn't.

Jerry: We broke her. We got her out of her role. She isn't that hard.

Alex: She's not hard in that respect.

CONSULTANT: What does the group have to gain by taking the consultant
         out of her role?

Jerry: It's insight. Insight into the limits to which we can break social
         laws. That's what we were doing.

Hank: Are you serious?

Alex: I'm serious. What you all did was good. I mean, I'm not saying I approve. It was blowing my mind.

Jerry: What do you think, Steve?

Steve: I don't know.

Alex: If we were all men in the world how would we live? How would we survive?

Jerry: There would be no particular point for aggression.

Alex: I don't know. We've tried to come up with a viable survival tactic, being all male here, and we haven't.

Jerry: Well, there's been nothing to do, no task to perform, no goals to set.

Alex: If there were tasks, it'd be easier.

Jerry: Yes, you take seven men, put them in a squad in the army, and march them together, and they think alike, and they act alike, and do their function, and they don't ask questions like what we've been asking. There is no need to. But if you put them in a box like this with four blank walls and two people who don't make comments, of course they're going to start.

Hank: You know what scared me about this? I didn't realize I had it in me to go that far. I don't know what I have in me and how far I could go.

Jerry: That's one of the things about the military. You noticed that I got in a kind of supportive role. I tried to draw them in.

Hank: You came in and he was in it. When you [Alex] came in I was getting a little scared.

Alex: As long as I stayed out it was safe.

Hank: Yeah, it was definitely safe. But I mean you get a group of five, six people together, you get that mob psychology.

Jerry: Yeah, sure. That's the basis of the seven- man squad. You take an average individual, a good American boy, he isn't gonna go out and shoot somebody.

Hank: So how is guerilla warfare so effective?

Jerry: Guerilla warfare is a group of seven men. That's the whole thing. It's not an individual man. It's seven men. They move fast. It's like My Lai. And everyone was saying, "shoot, shoot, shoot, shoot." You're telling your buddy, like I told you, "shoot, shoot,

shoot." And I get out my gun and start shooting. Get the group psychology going and you lose all your morality. You lose everything.

Hank: And it's much stronger than what we've been through because you're getting shot at.

Jerry: Even if you're not being shot at, even if nobody's threatening you. See, we've only been together for two days, and this is already what we're doing.

Process Review. As the six men of Group 3 "work on exposing a much softer side of myself," they become more aware of the "removed presence" of the female consultant. This experience of vulnerability gradually becomes the breeding ground of rebellion. Hostility towards authority erupts in Session 7.

When the tension cannot be contained, Group 3 turns on the consultant with a surprising intensity: "You know what scared me about this? I didn't realize I had it in me to go that far." Jerry's observations about "mob psychology" describe the fusion which bonds individuals together in small groups, particularly when those groups turn violent: "Get the group psychology going and you lose all your morality. You lose everything."

In general, groups revolt from an imbalance of power and a sense of vulnerability. When groups turn on female authority, however, the attack carries with it a quality of rage that deserves more attention.

WOMEN IN AUTHORITY

Social science research suggests that groups typically respond to female authority with negative feelings. Psychologist Fred Wright of the City College of New York studied co-ed groups and found that female consultants were rated less warm and less friendly than male counterparts.[51] Psychologist Carol Beauvais, also of the City College of New York, investigated all-male and all-female groups and found that female consultants were rated more negatively and perceived as more distant and more contemptuous than their male counterparts. Females were more negative than males toward female authority. Beauvais concluded that group concerns for nurturance in female authority overshadow the concern with her knowledge and competence.[52] Female power is equated with nurturance, not analytic competence. Women in authority, however, are perceived, experienced and evaluated differently than men in authority.[53]

In the eight self-study groups described throughout this book, more HOSTILE words were spoken in groups with a female consultant than in groups with a male consultant.[54] In other words, groups with women in authority became angrier than groups with men in authority. The anger was not necessarily directed against the female authority figure, sometimes groups just "got angrier." In either case, such turmoil reflects confusion about the images of female power.

Our psychological images of female power are inherently contradictory, both positive and negative. The positive Feminine gives life, warmth, shelter, nourishment and protection. All existence is dependent upon her nurturance. The negative Feminine steals life and warmth. Existence is dependent upon defense.

The shift from the positive to the negative Feminine is the shift from sheltered to captured, from life-giving to death-dealing. In the chilling words of Erich Neumann, "Among all peoples, the goddesses of war and the hunt express man's experience of life as a female exacting blood."[55]

The negative Feminine is also associated with the myth of Evil Seductress. That is, women stand for purity and nourishment or for darkness and sin. This split view of women influences group dynamics. Sexualized hostility (seduction or sexual harassment) towards female authority may be a group's unconscious attempt to control "feminine evil," the unstated power.[56]

The Double Image. The transformation of the Feminine image from positive to negative may occur slowly or instantaneously. This transformation is perfectly mirrored in folk tales about the Greek goddess, Pandora. In farming communities of ancient Greece, women's capacity to birth and nurse offspring was held in awe. This perception combined with the life cycles of Mother Earth created a tradition of goddess worship. Pandora was the Giver of All Gifts: plants for food, herbs for healing, flowers and trees, wonder and justice. Researcher Charlene Spretnak has concluded that the religion based on a judgmental, thundering Zeus and his Olympian gods was imposed upon the Greek mainland by Northern invaders about 3,000 years ago.[57] By the seventh century B.C., when Hesiod and Homer were recording the "classical" myths, the original nature of the Earth goddesses was altered: Hera became vindictive, Athena became cold and masculine, Aphrodite became frivolous.

In the "classical" version, Pandora was tempted out of wickedness or curiosity to open the gift box of the gods. She released sorrow and misfortune for all humankind. In the original version, Pandora, the Giver of All Gifts, released the seeds of peace. In the 1980s, women are struggling to balance stereotype with reality.

Not all groups have trouble working with a "woman boss," but many do. Women in authority are the targets for group projections. They may absorb group confusion and feel strangely incompetent, isolated or ignored.[58] Women managers, authorities or technical experts may feel valued only for nurturing qualities rather than analytic competence or system leadership. The double Good/Evil image of female power may influence organizational dynamics. A women in authority may stir up primitive fears about the availability of life-sustaining nurturance, triggering anger, sabotage and avoidance of the work at hand. These psychological results suggests that **mutual support** is a valid objective for all work teams. Anxiety about a woman manager is less likely when the culture emphasizes mutual support.

THE BALANCE OF RACIAL POWER

Some problem-solving situations require negotiating groups to discuss both power and cultural differences. The problems of South African blacks, Native American Indians and Palestinian Arabs are conflicts of both power and cultural differences. Dialogue between people of different color or religion inherently stirs up concerns about identity and survival. In the United States in the 1980s, as new waves of immigrants changed the flavor of America, whites, blacks, Asians, East Europeans, Hispanics and Native American Indians began to work side by side and eventually looked within to explore assumptions, values and stereotypes. Corporate America has discovered the benefits of training to manage a multi-cultural work force. For cultures historically at war, this self-study is both painful and healing.

Organizational theorist Vivian Hopkins Jackson has concluded that minority managers and technical experts must deal with some special group dynamics.[59] The sense of belonging may be confused, raising membership questions of "Do I really belong?" or "Will they let me in?" and "How important is this to me?" Power dynamics may be distorted, since the minority manager may need super-credentials. Malice, indifference and non-cooperation may prevent the development of trust. The militancy which results when there is power but no trust may also confront minorities with organizational authority.

In the American workplace, the interlocking issues of power, authority, and cultural differences are embedded in a heritage of black slavery. According to historian Phyllis Palmer, slavery in America allowed white men primarily, and white women incidentally, to "deal with" their insecurities by controlling strength, reproduction and rebellion in black slaves.[60] Psychologists attribute the power of these efforts of control to both greed and our fear of death. At the same time, for the black woman, American culture gave her two stereotypic images of power: Sapphire is dominant sexuality and Mammie is abundant mothering. According to Palmer, black women are celebrated as symbols of heroic womanhood rather than accepted as political partners.

We are quick to deny the realities of racism in America. Yet minorities know when they are acknowledged for their power rather than accepted as authorities or allies. For example, a black psychologist who joined a management training team in a large organization, but never felt welcome, said:

Within just a few months I found myself becoming quieter and quieter, volunteering less, risking less, keeping my ideas and observations to myself. I seemed to just act out the prevailing expectation, the lowered expectation, that I couldn't possibly know much about management training. In fact, I had more managerial experience than some of my supervisors. It wasn't until I had made plans to take another job that I felt acknowledged. Other staff said they were "amazed" that I was so knowledgeable about organizational issues.

Facing cultural or racial or religious differences and learning to work in partnership may mean giving up old meanings and categories. The minority manager may absorb the group's concern about the balance of power and its fear of internal diversity.

THE REBELLIOUS PHASE

As stated earlier, rebellion is a popular topic of research for group psychologists. Many believe that rebellion is a necessary phase of development in the life-cycle of any group system. In the 1950s, Warren Bennis and Herbert Shepard concluded that small groups must resolve problems of power, generally through some rebellion against the group leader, before understanding intimacy and affection.[61] Rebellion is the pivotal phase.

Sequence. The first major review of group development theories emphasized this sequence of authority, rebellion and nurturance. In 1965, B.W. Tuckman summarized the sequence theories in four steps:[62]

1. Forming is testing and dependence.
2. Storming is conflict with members or authority.
3. Norming is group cohesiveness and self-disclosure.
4. Performing is the productive work.

The sequence theories say that individuals and groups move through stages. The sequence is from dependency through conflict to affiliation towards maturity and achievement.

Later in the 1960s, psychologist Philip Slater concluded that rebellion allows groups to shift attachments from authority to each other.[63] For many members, group rebellion is their first true cooperative effort. Groups celebrate the events of rebellion, such as the totem feast or the Fourth of July. The public re-enactment of the revolt strengthens tradition and unity, often when renewal seems needed. At the same time, maturity and identity bring an awareness of death. According to Slater, groups which do not revolt show little sexuality, remain overly dependent, and avoid such issues as growing older and separation.

Cycles. Other group theorists have concluded that psychological activity in groups occurs in cycles, not sequence. Wilfred Bion, who introduced the technique of the self-study group, suggested that groups move towards or away from the patterns of dependency, fight, flight and pairing.[64] As the group develops, members participate in different ways. Patterns and roles become center stage in recurring cycles.

The work of William Shutz is also a cyclical view.[65] Shutz defined three interpersonal needs: inclusion (belonging), control (power) and affection (emotional closeness). These three group needs occur in cycles. From the beginning until the last phase of the group, the sequence is: inclusion, control and affection. As the group experience ends, the sequence is a reversal: affection (affectionate bonds are broken), control (control is stopped) and inclusion (members withdraw from the group).

Multiple Events. Recently, attempts have been made to integrate the two views. Group theorists Graham Gibbard and John Hartman describe authority and nurturance as the two central themes in group activity.[66] Gibbard and Hartman add Freud's notion that sexual rivalries influence rebellion, and Slater's view that rebellion allows members to become more independent of the "leader" and more involved with each other. At the same time, the "we-ness" or nurturing capacity of the group becomes more influential over time. According to Gibbard and Hartman, group members are constantly struggling with submersion and separation, or "we-ness" versus individual freedom. When emotionality runs high and the boundary between individual and group feeling is blurred, members may demonstrate their separateness through distance (flight) or conflict (fight).

According to Gibbard and Hartman, revolt against authority is a struggle with the balance of power influenced by sexual rivalries and a simultaneous struggle with the nurturing capacity of the group system. These themes coincide with a fundamental group rhythm—the balance of individual and group needs. When power is out of balance, The Hero is born "to protect myself" and "to protect the group."

In considering how groups "mature" over time, it is useful to remember the multiple, simultaneous quality of group life. Multiple roles and patterns become center stage, according to the logic of internal needs. Negativity towards authority, the balance of power, the search for nurturance, the exploration of intimacy, the development of self-awareness and "pride in our group" are overlapping interactions. As group theorist Donald T. Brown concludes, groups are inevitably drawn towards maturity and towards some productive balance in the relationship with authority, or the group does not survive.[67] A final statement of group development is made in Chapter 8: Support.

The behaviors of rebellion occur in sequence, in cycles and simultaneously with other patterns in all group settings. Group systems continually work towards a balance of power, and rebellion is a natural component of this growth towards maturity. Authority may respond to challenge with defense and counter-attack; or authority may channel rebellion into creative problem solving. The following example studies rebellion as a healthy sign of group creativity restricted by the narrow interpretation of the local hierarchy.

Case Study #15: Heal Thy Revolt

This story occurred in a public mental hospital. One day, the Evening Shift sent the Day Shift a note: "It's winter again. There's so little recreation for our locked ward patients. Would you please see what can be done to hurry up the Repair Shop and get the TV set fixed. It's been three months."

The Day Shift replied into the Communication Book, "We know. We've sent four memos. Volunteer Services got th Ladies Auxiliary to give us one more night of Bingo in November. Why aren't we more grateful?"

The very next day a fire drill coincided with a rainstorm. The drill began and everyone was shuttled off to B Cottage, which was abandoned and cold but out of the rain. Inside B Cottage, Nurse Johnson and Nurse Aide Michaels, after taking the third count and finally agreeing everyone was there, looked around the empty ward. Yes, they saw a television set which they turned on, and it functioned perfectly. Joined by Nurse Aide Jackson, who loved getting in on stuff, the three hoisted the TV onto the bus, while the driver looked the other way. When the fire drill was over, patients, staff and TV headed back for the locked wards. For four cold, winter nights there was TV, quiet conversation and somehow a lot of cookies for patients and staff.

On the fifth day the Supervisor found out. Somebody had reported a theft. Two reprimands and four memos later there was no TV and more than a few grumpy staff and patients on the locked ward. Three months passed before the ward's only TV was fixed.

• • • • •

Process Review. What did the rebellion represent for the larger system? In part, this was a creative response to an organizational impasse. Fighting authority represented a heartfelt response to the inefficiency of the larger system. It was a spontaneous effort by a beleaguered group to respond to the task at hand—patient care. It was also an important sign that this particular staff had shaken off its burn-out and had developed a secure sense of group identity. Indeed, a new Head Nurse had clearly communicated her faith in the abilities of this staff. Her faith sparked renewed energy and led to the courage of rebellion.

WORKING GUIDELINES

Authority confronted with rebellion must separate out individual, group and organizational contributions to the conflict and hostility. This means looking at individual leadership style, group reactions to authority and cultural values. It is useful to remember the question: What does the conflict represent for the larger system?

Personal Style. When hostility greets authority, analysis begins with self-study. Does the leader encourage open communication, value participation in problem solving and listen to opposing points of view without panic? Does the leader provide a vision for the future and clear expectations of group goals? Do group members feel free to speak up and risk creative solutions to shared problems?

The most useful strategy for authority confronted with rebellion is to maintain clear expectations about system goals, hold regular discussion meetings and strongly encourage open communication and shared problem solving. This will help the group system balance power and influence appropriately. This move from confrontation through dialogue to cooperation and shared achievement is the appropriate strategy for organizational and political systems torn by the anger of rebellion.

Group Patterns. Hostility toward authority, even anger voiced by a single Fight Leader, represents a systems issue. Lech Walesa may symbolize the power conflicts in Poland, his words and actions speak the tensions of a great many people. The behaviors of the individual represent group-wide patterns. This occurs in both political systems and face-to-face groups. The individual speaks for the group.

What does rebellion represent for the larger system? At least seven psychological choices:

1. To a great degree, hostility toward authority is an effort to balance power and influence. Rebellion is often the system response to the threatening aspects of an imbalance of power and influence. Here, rebellion is a symptom of serious problems and the best response is dialogue.

2. At the same time, for some group members, rebellion represents the shift from dependency to self-assertion and bonding with peers. Here, rebellion is a natural phase of group development.

3. At other times, the meaning of group revolt is entirely different. Groups may rebel to test the limits of a new leader. In this case, authority learns when to hold the line, when to compromise or yield and when to listen.

4. An overly dependent group may expect authority to perfectly guide and provide. Here, the group projects superhuman abilities onto authority and then reacts in rage when they feel more vulnerable.

5. Hostility towards authority sometimes represents "our lack of faith in our-selves." Here, the leader encourages group initiative.

6. When the organizational authority is a woman, hostility may rest on psychological images which show women as life-giving, death-dealing or seductive. A women in authority may find her unpopular decisions greeted with more anger than anticipated. She may be evaluated more negatively than necessary. She may be confronted with anger or sexualized hostility more intensely than expected. In these cases, she must consider the primitive nature of group responses to female power while taking a careful look at her individual style, including the chips on her shoulder.

7. Similarly, minority managers may find themselves supervising a workgroup which is more hostile than anticipated. Minority managers, by their physical presence, force groups to face cultural differences. Survival means learning that diversity provides the foundation for creative problem solving.

Rebellion is a complicated event. Although the form and meaning may vary, the core issue is a balance of power, influence and vulnerability. In any setting, the most effective response to rebellion is to listen, analyze the conflict on its merits and collaboratively solve the problem.

Cultural Values. Rebellion is a dynamic embedded in a larger con-text—the structure and culture of a family, workplace or political system. Where authority behaves or is perceived to behave as controlling or judging, where rewards favor compliance and punish disagreement, the group response is dependency, impotence or anger. Organizations and cultures built on forums for participation in problem solving prevent most forms of rebellion.

The psychological dynamics of rebellion link families, work settings and political systems in turmoil. Indeed, the examples of reconciliation between management and labor are healthy models for parents or political leaders struggling to design democratic systems.

CHAPTER 6

SUB-GROUPING:
Fighting Each Other

". . . the most enduring form of human hatred: ethnic and religious rivalry."

Don Podesta

Sub-grouping occurs when neighbors fight each other: blacks versus whites, East versus West, doctors versus nurses. People generally fight about power or values or both. Dependency and Rebellion are conflicts about authority, Sub-Grouping shifts analysis to conflicts between neighbors and fears about differences in values.

Humanity seems terrified of diversity. We often act as if war is the only response to the irritation of differences in opinion. Dialogue is an alternative to war. When we confront diversity and stop to talk, we enter a new frontier. In dialogue about peace, individuals analyze and solve problems, struggle with questions of identity, become a living system of interacting patterns and continually confront archetypal images of Good and Evil. Fortunately, opposing forces are fertile soil for both conflict and peacemaking.

This chapter looks at sub-groups in conflict, the identity dynamics, the splitting of Good and Evil and the concept of duality.

SUBGROUPING

THE BEHAVIORS OF SUB-GROUPING

Sub-grouping occurs when neighbors fight each other. Everywhere you look, tension in living systems is channeled into opposing camps, The Sub-Groups: sales versus production, doctors versus nurses, liberal versus conservative, Protestant versus Catholic, Tamils versus Buddhists, Sunni Moslem versus Shiite Moslem, blacks versus whites, pro-life versus pro-choice, preservationist versus land developer, hawk versus dove, old guard versus new wave and East versus West.

Sub-groups in conflict are parts of the same larger system (people are all partners on this planet), but act as if one were more important than the other. The dynamics of sub-grouping represent difficulty dealing with internal differences and trouble seeing parts of the whole.

Conflict is not solved. The energy of conflict can be transformed into creative problem solving. This systems approach looks past personality differences and asks: What does this conflict represent for the larger system? Peacemaking begins by identifying sub-groups, a task more complicated than first meets the eye.

OVERLAPPING SUB-GROUPS

Frustration turns to aggression at some triggering point of intolerance.[68] When conflict erupts, people engage the opposition and move to destroy the source of irritation. They look to friends for support.

Conflict generally improves teamwork as individual wagons draw themselves into a cohesive circle. When tension turns to conflict, the flag is raised, swords are drawn and loyalty is sworn. A common enemy strengthens shared identity. Knowing who to hate bonds groups together.

Rensis Likert, founder of the Institute for the Social Research at University of Michigan, considered the behavioral and perceptual changes that occur when groups are in conflict.[69] When the battle begins, actions and reactions escalate hostility in a spiraling manner. Control is assumed by the most verbal or the most aggressive, setting the stage for later power struggles. Attacks, counterattacks and the expectation of continued threat block the shift to cooperative problem solving.

Likert and many social psychologists believe perceptual and intellectual distortions interfere with communication between groups in conflict. When groups are at war, demands are overstated, similarities are ignored, information is misinterpreted and memory is selective. The views of the other side are misunderstood, the needs of the larger system are poorly served. There are no forums to exchange accurate information and develop shared solutions.

In complex, social conflict, numerous and overlapping sub-groups further block communication and effective problem solving. As the next case study shows, sometimes the genuine analysis of underlying problems never occurs.

Case Study #16: Republicans versus Democrats

Marie Helen McGlone and Melody Brooks Balick analyzed the conflicts surrounding the Equal Rights Amendment (ERA) at the 1980 Republican and Democratic National Conventions.[70, 71] At both conventions, the conflict focused on content—the **wording** of the amendment to be adopted. At the level of process, overlapping sub-groups aligned and collided, ultimately to be mediated by politicians or the media.

The Republicans. The Republican Party had supported ERA since 1940, but a large anti-ERA group now wanted to reverse tradition. At the convention, the Platform Committee delegated authority to the Sub-Committee on Human Resources to decide "support or non-support" of the ERA. McClone described the Republican Convention as a DAD and MOM system because all Committee and Sub-Committee groups had a male Chair and a female Vice-Chair. McGlone found seven important sub-group conflicts influencing the Sub-Committee:

1. **Supporters versus On-The-Fencers versus Non-Supporters.** At first, there were three sub-groups—pro-ERA, Undecideds and anti-ERA—called The Saints, The Save-ables and The Sinners by the anti-ERA forces.

2. **Pro-ERA versus Anti-ERA.** Lobbying helped the Un-decideds decide and there were then two major sub-groups: pro-ERA and anti-ERA. There was little open conflict and no outward anger on the Sub-Committee, but later in the Convention, 4500 people marched through Detroit in favor of ERA.

3. **Liberal versus Conservative.** The anti-ERA people saw the ERA as liberal support for woman's issues, not a male-versus-female split. The primary sub-groups were pro- and anti-ERA, often described as liberal and conservative.

4. **Politicians versus Vote Your Conscience.** Some Undecideds counted up the votes and did not want to be on the losing side. According to one delegate, "One politician was sympathetic, but knew the ERA would lose."

5. **Chauvinist versus Non-Chauvinist.** The chosen Chairman of the Sub-Committee withdrew because of illness. Instead of the female Vice-Chair taking his place, the Republican leadership sent in a man who was not a member of the Sub-Committee to act as chair.

6. **Well-Informed versus Non-Informed.** Some members chose the Sub-Committee on Human Resources because ERA, abortion and the "family"

were strong personal concerns. Others seemed less involved and less knowledgeable. Some asked: "How am I supposed to vote on this?"

7. Islanders versus Mainlanders. The two pro-ERA males were from Hawaii and the Virgin Islands. Said one, "Perhaps the islands are more liberated than the mainland."

McGlone concluded that the politicians played a mediating role when it came time to write the anti-ERA plank. The politicians, more practiced in the art of compromise, did not want "strict" language in the plank. They softened the "lopsided" anti-ERA enthusiasm and negotiated compromises in service of party unity. Later, the full Platform Committee added a sentence acknowledging the "legitimate efforts of those who support or oppose ERA." On the national level, however, the female Vice-Chair of the Republican National Committee supported ERA and was fired from her position.

The Democrats. Balick's analysis of the Democratic Convention shows similar dynamics. Conflict also focused at the level of content, the wording of Minority Report #10 (MR #10): the Democratic Party would "withhold financial support and technical assistance" from candidates who do not support ERA. Women's groups saw MR #10 as a strong commitment to women's issues. Politicians and party loyalists were concerned about the wording: "You reward people for doing right, you don't punish them for doing wrong." At least five sub-group conflicts influenced the debate:

1. Pro-ERA versus anti-ERA. For the first time in American history, women were almost 50% of the delegates at a presidential nominating convention. The pro-ERA forces clearly outnumbered the anti-ERA forces. The debate was about the wording of the plank. Is "withholding support" a good tactic?

2. Kennedy Women versus Carter Women. According to Balick's analysis, MR #10 was not a Carter-versus-Kennedy issue. Carter opposed the punishment intended in MR #10 and Kennedy was neutral. For both Carter and Kennedy forces, the wording was a problem: "If you don't help a Democrat, you help a Republican."

3. Feminist First Women versus Party Loyalty Women. The ERA debate soon became a conflict between Feminists pushing for strong commitment to women's issues and the Loyalists' concern for candidates, the election and the party's image: "If you're a delegate to a national convention, you're a politician first and a feminist or something else second. You have to think about your candidate, the party, your image and consistency."

4. The Coalition versus Anti-ERA. During the convention, some of the leaders and members of various women's organizations formed an ad hoc committee called the National Coalition for Women's Rights. This coalition of Carter and Kennedy women tried to put aside political differences to broaden support for MR #10. Although most Coalition members supported ERA, many were divided about abortion and most were split about an "open" convention.

5. Open Convention versus Binding Rule. To "open" the convention would break the "binding rule" and allow delegates to vote for the candidate of their choice rather than the candidate they had favored in the primaries. Advocating an open convention produced controversy within the Coalition, since an open convention was thought to favor Kennedy. The Kennedy Women's Caucus waited until they lost the vote on opening the convention, then worked at the last minute to support MR #10. Balick concluded that the Open Convention versus Binding Rule conflict split the Women's Coalition.

Balick identified these sub-group conflicts and then described how the National Education Association (NEA) played a mediating role in the sub-group conflict. The NEA had the largest bloc of delegates: 302 delegates, 70% women. NEA was in the middle of the argument backing both Carter and ERA but not agreeing to the language of MR #10. When the White House requested that MR #10 be withdrawn or rewritten, the Feminists refused, and the NEA was caught in the middle. According to Balick's analysis, the media had subtle and pervasive influence. A common fear among convention delegates was that the defeat of an ERA tactic (such as MR #10) would be seen as an anti-ERA position. Many felt that media coverage needed to show support of ERA resolutions, even if the wording was troublesome. NEA decided to support MR #10 about $1\frac{1}{2}$ hours before the plank was due for a vote on the floor of the conference. Carter delegates were told to vote as they wished, and MR #10 passed on an "overwhelming voice vote."

Some delegates and observers thought the controversy brought party unity: "Everybody felt terrific. It was a big victory. The place went euphoric when it passed." Participants learned they could "hold ground and compromise." Politicians in conflict unified around a special interest.

• • • • •

Summary. Many conflicts at the 1980 political conventions surfaced around the ERA planks. At both conventions, the debates were focused at the level of content—about the wording of a policy decision. At the same time, multiple, overlapping sub-groups were forming and reforming both inside and outside the convention centers influencing the dynamics of the conference as a whole system. The analyses of McGlone and Balick show how tension in a living system is channeled into opposing forces and that a psychological potential for balance encourages the rise of neutral, mediating sub-groups.

The analysis of the 1980 political conventions also demonstrates how structure and culture influence conflict and peacemaking. Although the conventions allowed time for debate, there was little space for dialogue and few formats for collaborative problem solving. The win-lose philosophy of the political culture kept the conflict focused on content and prevented the shift to problem solving. For example, a shift from win-lose to win-win would have delegates solving the problems of unwanted pregnancies, rather than debating the ethics of abortion. To resolve internal conflict, the conventions need language and authority to address internal dynamics, such as the forming and re-forming of sub-groups. As seen below, the language of internal dynamics includes awareness of the human tendency to "split" Good and Evil.

SPLITTING GOOD AND EVIL

During conflict, we generally know what the fight is about, though we may lose track of some of the multiple, overlapping issues. As leaders debate content and sub-groups organize, individuals choose sides. If the fight is about values, choosing sides stirs up conscious and unconscious images of Good and Evil. The sub-groups labelled The Saints, The Sinners and the Save-ables show how easily conflict is connected to our notions of right and wrong.

In the 1940s, psychoanalyst Melanie Klein wrote that children tend to separate forces in conflict into the elements of Good and Evil.[72] Today, many psychologists believe that "splitting" Good and Evil is a fundamental psychological mechanism in children, adults, small groups and large political systems. Usually, human nature takes the Good inside "My Self" or "My Team" and projects the Evil onto the Enemy. In this way, splitting Good and Evil controls the anxiety of contradiction by momentarily "getting rid of" confusion about right and wrong.

Psychoanalyst Elliot Jacques has described this splitting when nations go to war:

> The members of each community put their bad objects and sadistic impulses onto the commonly shared and accepted external enemy. . . . The bad, sadistic enemy is fought against, not in the solitary isolation of the unconscious world, but in cooperation with comrades-in-arms in real life.[73] (Gibbard et al, *Analysis of Groups*, p. 283)

People justify warfare by seeing Evil in the Enemy, ignoring the existence and consequences of destructive impulses.

Political leaders are just beginning to learn the folly of attempting to solve conflict by assigning blame to the evil enemy. According to writer Georgeanne Geyer, when differences in opinion become arguments about spiritual superiority, warfare is more likely than dialogue. Most recently, an

American President has shifted from repeated accusations of "The Russians are Evil" to recognition of the value of face-to-face dialogue. Peacemaking means individuals learn to see the enemy as human, not Evil. From this perspective, evil is unconscious fear or anger which erupts destructively.

At the same time, peacemaking requires participants to "own" the darker motives, the Shadow which exist in all people—rage, vengeance, deceit, lust for power and the capacity to hurt (see page 57). Peacemaking means all parties claim their contribution to an interconnected network of events and own their piece of the Shadow.

Accepting the Shadow is easier said than done. As the Shadow leaks into awareness, people become anxious and try to avoid it. Organizational consultant Peter Vaill helps people "own" the contradiction by describing the Shadow as our "weak suit."[74] For example, for the corporate executive, the weak suit is the opposite of traditional managerial characteristics:

- hierarchical position versus network member
- decision maker versus floating with ambiguity
- program performer versus "I'm winging it"

Accepting the Shadow means accepting the dual nature of human behavior. By acknowledging the human capacity for destructiveness, balance emerges more easily. The reconciliation of Good and Evil leads to maturity and underscores peacemaking.

THE IDENTITY STRUGGLES

Conflict often improves teamwork, team spirit, personal and group identity. A common enemy pushes individuals to bond together quickly and strongly. As team members pull together, a boundary clearly separates the groups in opposition. Within this boundary, emotions run strong and identity issues become intensified. While groups debate content, individuals balance the issues of My Side versus The Enemy, Self versus Others and Self versus Group.[75]

My Side versus The Enemy. The boundary which separates groups in conflict defines a territory for belonging. Generally, hostility demands that we take sides. Conflict heightens our awareness about the choice—my team, my department, my town, my country.

Bonding together to outsmart the enemy carries along the patterns of fear, courage, loyalty, shared identity and the understanding of Good and Evil. As these dynamics are played out and as team spirit rises and falls, individual participants are also learning about identity of Self.

Self versus Others. Our sense of Self, that portion of personality known as I or me, is always unfolding. My sense of Self as Lynn Sandra Kahn has some old and familiar elements, some new and changing ones. In part, I learn who I am by looking around and seeing who I am not. I interact with people and nature, then assert my vision and values and my sense of Self becomes stronger.

The separation of You from Me intensifies during conflict and becomes crucial during peacemaking when people learn to speak up, take risks, show differences and give support. Problem solving and peacemaking strengthen the sense of unique identity by revealing the differences which separate my Self from Others.

Self versus Group. Personal identity interacts with group identity. People balance their sense of Self with their feelings of team spirit. The fundamental rhythm of all human systems is this separating out as a unique individual and fusing with the energy and process of the group system. This shared individual and group identity is experienced as the rhythm of separating and belonging.

When emotions run strong, the fundamental rhythm of separating and belonging is intensified. Fusing with the energy of the group can feel comfortable or confusing. Group action may turn to mob riot, and belonging may become terrifying. At the same time, the rhythms of belonging and separating move systems towards balance and new learning. Individuals learn to stand apart and join forces. This book returns to the topic of rhythm and balance in Chapter 11.

Summary. When tensions bursts into conflict, individual Fight Leaders and opposing sub-groups turn on each other. At the level of content, conflict may take the form of debate, confrontation or attack. At the level of process, conflict includes hostility, power, analysis, support and shared identity.

During conflict and peacemaking, individuals struggle with personal questions: What is this fight about? Which side are my friends on? How do I fit in? How do I show my separateness? Who's right and who's wrong? The unfolding of individual and group identity, the understanding of right and wrong, the analysis of shared problems and rhythms of separating and belonging all underscore conflict and peacemaking.

WORKING GUIDELINES

Conflict is rooted in structure, content and process. Structure is the organization's policies and procedures. Content is the topic of conversation. Process is how people relate. Structure, content and process overlap and interact, influenced by the dynamics of the larger social system.

Structure. The structure of an organization is its policies and procedures. Absent, inefficient or confused policies contribute to conflict, often in very subtle ways. Unclear goals and vague roles are common, structural sources of conflict and problems. Case Study #16 shows how a structure which relies on majority vote and win-lose debate makes problem solving and peace-making more difficult. The distinctions between majority vote and consensus decisions are just now emerging in federal agencies. Democracy is shifting from majority vote to consensus, from manipulation to participation.

Content. For the most part, conflict is fought and managed at the level of content. Analysis of the situation generally begins by identifying the "oppos-ing parties" and their perceptions about the issues at hand. Conflict can sometimes be discussed, analyzed and resolved at the level of content.

If important issues are ignored, however, resolution is incomplete. The systems approach to peacemaking looks closely at all components and aspects of the conflict under study. Analysis can shift conflict to cooperation only if all issues, players and teams have been identified. For example, the ERA debates represented multiple, connected problems, including the role of women at American political conventions, the role of special interest groups in American politics and the influence of the media on political decision making.

Process. Conflict is the opposition of forces. Looking in on a system in conflict, opposing forces are seen on the level of content ("Support or Non-Support" of a policy decision), individual process ("Am I pro-ERA or anti-ERA?"), group dynamics (the interplay of hostility and analysis) and larger organizational dynamics (the win-lose philosophy of political cultures). Throughout, interactions are continually influenced by our conscious and unconscious understanding of Good and Evil. Duality, which means separation into two parts, is the concept describing opposing tensions. It is useful to remember that Jung believed all psychological patterns come alive along with their opposites. Duality is always connected to unity. Duality is the foundation of quantum theory in the physical sciences. In the behavioral and psychological sciences, duality is the source of both conflict and peacemaking, for creative solutions emerge from the interplay of opposing ideas.

A systems approach to conflict resolution considers structure, content and process. Searching the structure for sources of conflict may be quite complicated. The search must be careful and patient. The key to resolution is balancing and listening to all the sub-groups.

CHAPTER 7

SCAPEGOATING:
Blaming Each Other

"The fault, dear Brutus, is not in our stars, but in ourselves that we are underlings."

William Shakespeare

Sub-grouping conflict may turn to scapegoating when the group blames one or a few for the tensions of the whole. Scapegoating occurs when a group ignores, criticizes or drives away the people who represent unpopular, unfamiliar or frightening group behaviors and beliefs.

Scapegoating includes the individual tendency to blame others for personal difficulties and the group tendency to rid itself of discomfort. Under stress, people point fingers and push someone away. When stress is most extreme, the group turns on members or neighbors with a vengeance that often hides great fear. When the group is most aroused, it acts as if its survival depended upon some point of view being suppressed: "You are destructive to us."

At its core, scapegoating represents the tensions associated with the unknown, human limitations and mortality. Whatever the content, a successful, non-violent response requires the shift from confrontation to self-exploration. Groups at war must learn to talk about inner tensions to deal with internal diversity. Only by allowing the expression of all points of view can a group discover the creativity necessary to solve problems and heal itself.

This chapter describes the patterns of scapegoating, the human fear of diversity and the consequences of ignorance.

SCAPEGOATING

THE HISTORY OF SCAPEGOATING

For thousands of years, our ancestors believed that Evil caused all pain.[76] Physical, psychological and community suffering were attributed to the magic of enemies and the evil of wicked spirits. Misery was relieved through ceremonies which transferred pain to objects, animals or other people who would bear the suffering of another.

In *The Golden Bough*, published in 1922, Sir James George Frazer described the ceremonies intended to drive away suffering.[77] There were two styles. Pain could be expelled directly by choosing the appropriate ritual—banging tin pans to create an uproar which drives away cholera demons. Or pain could be expelled indirectly through the transfer of evil to a material vehicle or scapegoat—a goat is let loose in the wilderness after the high priest has symbolically laid the sins of the people on its head. Driven off, the goat carried along the pain and sins of the community.

Historically, scapegoating is the process by which malignant forces are loaded on some vehicle (object, animal or person) which is then beat, burnt, buried or otherwise driven off, carrying away the pain, evil and sins of the community. When faced with problems or conflicts, people have a long history of finding fault, blaming someone and deluding themselves into believing they have "solved" the problem.

Modern science has not freed humanity from a murky belief in evil forces. When faced with trouble, people still act as though difficulties are the fault of someone else and by simply getting rid of that individual, miseries will be relieved. We are still quick to blame—the boss, the wife, Democrats, Communists, Blacks, Jews or Palestinians—whoever happens to be handy. Someone is attacked to drive away Evil, as if dialogue were sinful.

Because the ones chosen to bear the blame for community suffering have often been ethnic, religious or racial minorities, psychology has traditionally studied scapegoating under the topic of prejudice.[78] At first, scapegoating was seen as a community response to fear or deprivation, deflected from the true source of the difficulty and directed at some ethnic group.

More recently, scapegoating has been studied in other arenas, such as the family, the workplace and global politics. In each of these systems, the descriptions of scapegoating coincide with Frazer's cross-cultural observations that the scapegoat role is often laid on a social outcast, someone who does not quite fit into the group.

Scapegoating occurs when a group ignores, attacks or drives away the member who represents the group's internal struggles. Under stress, group members try to separate themselves from thoughts, feelings or behaviors which are frightening. They blame one or a few for the tensions of the system, momentarily easing the anxiety of difference. At its core, scapegoating is the illusion that we can conquer death by avoiding the unknown and driving away Evil.

THE BEHAVIORS OF SCAPEGOATING

Scapegoating means to blame one or a few for the tensions of all. Scapegoating occurs when a system tries to solve its problems by destroying a few people seen as "the cause of the problem." The behaviors of scapegoating include avoidance, criticism, attack and genocide. Although scapegoating is an ancient pattern, modern versions are potent and ever-present.

In the workplace, scapegoating is a remarkably frequent group event. Daily, management blames labor, the boss blames the secretary, division directors blame their assistants, sales blames production and doctors blame nurses.

Outside of work, teenagers blame parents, parents blame teachers, teachers blame state governments, governors blame Washington, D.C., and the White House blames the last administration. Blaming is often mistaken for problem solving and conflict resolution. Blaming and scapegoating do not solve problems. Dialogue about differences does. Scapegoating shifts to genuine conflict resolution as opponents move from confrontation to exploration and analysis of shared problems.

Nine examples of scapegoating follow: seven from the workplace and two from the AU Research Groups. In each case, it is useful to ask the question: "What does the conflict represent for the larger system?"

Case Study #17: The Odd Dresser

In the Sales Department in a large electronics firm, scapegoating pushed the odd one out:

> I remember how the group used to tease Jerry. We mostly dressed southern California—carefree polyester suits. Jerry dressed like a university type—jeans and jacket, boots and vests. We used to laugh and call him the Ivy League Cowboy. I remember the day he quit. The funny thing is, he was the best salesman we had. He made the highest commissions.

The salesman who dresses differently gets teased. No doubt his top commissions contributed to his isolation. Still, the group shoves out rather than holding together and learning. What does the conflict represent for the larger system? Here, the group drives away stylistic differences and scapegoats technical competence.

•　•　•　•　•

Case Study #18: The Quiet Ones

These are the words of a graduate student in a Business course which emphasized participation and where students rotated the role of facilitator.

> Several members of the class constantly remind the group that CERTAIN MEMBERS do not talk as much as others. Some are reluctant to say anything. Others speak only infrequently. Those who do a lot of talking keep bringing up the matter that there are those who do not talk. The atmosphere of "Talk or Die" is always present. I think those who are comfortable talking in large groups feel let down by those who are less participative.
>
> Something else is going on, too. Criticism occurs when the discussions run out of steam. Whenever things get dull one of the talkative members speaks out. This person either continues the boredom or announces "There are CERTAIN MEMBERS who are not being helpful."
>
> As Facilitator, I intend to have more meaningful and productive discussions. I will ask the group to give more time and thought to the Agenda and to how discussions should continue. I will get group commitment not by acquiescence or silence, but by eliciting responses from everyone in the group. My goal is group commitment, not group endurance.

What does the conflict represent for the larger system? In a classroom with a participatory structure, scapegoating quiet members distracts the group from responsibility for its boredom. They have freedom to create the class agenda.

· · · · ·

Case Study #19: The Company Scapegoat

In the same class, a Japanese American engineer from a high technology business in California's Silicon Valley gave another example of workplace scapegoating:

> Quality Control is the company scapegoat. The president just cut us back from a staff of seven to two, the manager and assistant manager. There was no reason given or discussion allowed by the president.
>
> Quality Control is usually caught up in the conflicts between Sales and Production. The two most powerful departments are Sales and Production. Production wants quantity and Sales wants quality. It is almost guaranteed that if one is happy the other is not.
>
> This illustrates the basic difference in American and Japanese attitudes towards quality. In America, quality and quantity are opposites. The

attitude is that one must be given up for the other. In Japan, quality is the means towards the end of quantity. If you get the first one, the other is automatic.

Here Quality Control is unjustly blamed by Sales and Production, making us the company scapegoat. Recent cutbacks fall unfairly on Quality Control. Quality Control is being "driven away."

What does the conflict represent for the system? Quality Control represents the conflict between Sales and Production. Quality Control is also the place where there can be a happy medium. Too bad the company doesn't see this.

• • • • •

Case Study #20: The Dumb Computer

From the same class, a computer analyst described the dynamics when people blame the computer for business errors:

Computers process data at astonishing speeds precisely as instructed. Computers do not make errors of interpretation. The computer will process data only according to the well-defined statements of the computer program. The computer program says this or that. The computer itself is always right.

A computer program of any use requires hundreds of well-defined statements, all demanding precision. Writing complete programs requires strong doses of humility and honesty. I personally always blame the computer.

What does the conflict represent for the larger system? Blaming the computer distracts us from personal responsibility for precision and quality in the workplace.

• • • • •

Case Study #21: The Angry Woman

A pattern visible in all eight AU Research Groups was the criticism and sometimes vicious attack directed at members behaving counter to sex role expectations. The criticism was strongest when women expressed anger and men expressed distress.

In each of the four female groups, the women seen as expressing the most anger toward either the consultant or other group members was at some point called "masculine," "sexless," or "destructive," labels which had strong emotional impact. The "angry" women found that their hostility led to (at least initially) a negative reaction: "You are helping us pit ourselves against each other."

When groups are pressed to analyze anger, even vicious fault-finding can turn to powerful insight. In each of the four female research groups, the woman who voiced the strongest anger also clearly expressed her ambivalence:

> I thought I was being brave because I knew there had been no feeling like that [anger] expressed in the group and I thought it was important to express it. But there's a conflict in me because I still have a protective feeling inside of me. I don't want to be responsible for someone else feeling bad. (Group 8, female members, female consultant)

In describing their mixed feelings, these members made it easier for others to respond to their dilemma more sympathetically. In fact, all four female groups considered and discussed the difficulties inherent in expressing anger and still being considered a "good" group member and a "feminine" woman.

The "angry" women responded to group criticism and turned the scapegoating process around: by describing their awareness of the group's disapproval ("I feel like I'm being kick out"); by describing their sense of expressing something for the group-as-a-whole ("I've been feeling pressure from everybody to express anger"); and by asking if they were the "only one" who felt any anger. For all four groups, these comments contributed to the shift in group behavior from criticism of the "angry" member to self-exploration of unspoken resentments. Every time, attack led to analysis and balance.

At first glance, driving off discomfort seems easier than listening to anger. What does the conflict represent for the larger system? Looking more closely, attacking angry women is the group effort to expel the intolerable—feminine rage.

• • • • •

Case Study #22: The Gentle Men

Similar dynamics were operating in all four male groups. Men who reported anxiety or vulnerability were labeled "sick," "naive" and "feminine." Group responses to these "softer" men implied weakness: "You carved out the role of a fragile person who might be hurt by our rough-house activities."

Again, as in the female groups, discussion turned the group around. Men responded more sympathetically to the role of the vulnerable male. Several groups agreed that gentleness in a man was important, even though the burden was still that "gentle men are called homosexual . . . and ostracized." Other groups came to understand that the group can exert a kind of pressure on individual behavior: "Protecting me denies my ability to protect myself." Exploration of these issues allowed some male members to identify with the conflicts of male vulnerability: "I feel like yesterday I came across as pretty insightful ... I want to be able to appear extremely stupid, weak and all that and be supported by all of you."

Not all male groups, however, were open to this sort of discussion at all times. Group 3 (male members, female consultant) was a highly disclosing group on Day 1; but on Day 2, the man who expressed discomfort with the intensity of the verbal attack on the female consultant ("the pseudo-rape of our surrogate mother") was ignored and he dropped out minutes before that session ended. Overall, two of the "distressed" males dropped out but none of the "aggressive" women did. One possible interpretation is that male vulnerability was less acceptable in male groups than female aggression was in female groups.

What does the conflict represent for the larger system? Attacking vulnerable men distracts the group from the conflicts of male nurturance. By scapegoating gentle men, the group drives away those who represent softness and perhaps peacemaking.

• • • • •

Case Study #23: The Older Woman

When President Carter banned the shipment of agricultural produce to Latin American countries violating human rights guidelines, social service agencies in several Washington, D.C. communities benefited. Springtide Nursing Home (not the real name) was contacted by a chicken-processing company and asked how many chickens the Home could use that week. Somehow, Mrs. Smith, Assistant Administrator, returned the call and said, "Eighty." Mrs. Green, Director, also returned the call and said, "Sixty." At the next staff meeting the group bluntly attacked Mrs. Smith for her "failure." The staff turned on Smith, agreeing that she caused the Home's problems with communication. Mrs. Smith listened to the accusations. She did not return to the next two meetings.

What did the conflict represent for the larger system? Mrs. Smith delivered mail, memos and paychecks. She was associated with several instances of miscommunication and misplaced mail: "It's all your fault." She was a scape-goat for the group's anxiety about communication in general and the scapegoating also distracted them from their responsibility for solving the glitches in the mail and memo procedures.

Mrs. Smith was also the "oldest staff member." She often told her younger co-workers that "people near retirement age work best with the elderly." For the staff, Mrs. Smith was associated with fear of retirement and growing old. Psychologically, anxiety about old age was "controlled" by attacking Mrs. Smith sufficiently so that she felt pushed out of the staff meetings. In this way, the group as a system dealt with its inner tensions, though not in a healing manner.

• • • • •

Case Study #26: The Angry Mourner

This example of scapegoating comes from a ward meeting in a public mental hospital. David had been hospitalized for more than ten years. Finally, he was released. He got a job, found housing and had made some friends in a local church group. David was doing well!

The staff had put tremendous effort into moving David out and were proud of his success. He was invited back to the hospital to attend a ward meeting. The staff hoped he would encourage other chronic patients.

David's visit was a powerful event for that locked chronic ward. Clearly David now represented health and hopefulness for more than one hundred patients. He gave a progress report and left to go home. Halfway home he was hit by a car and killed.

The next day a ward meeting was called to discuss the accident. Staff and patients were crying and grieving. One patient was angry. Stephen kept shouting: "Why didn't he take care of himself? WHY?" Stephen was pissed off. The general response was: "That's a terrible thing to say." People attacked Stephen for expressing anger and "upsetting us even more." Stephen walked out of the meeting. Stephen had come to represent an unacceptable feeling, and the group moved to expel the perceived source of its tension.

What does the conflict represent for the larger system? Here, the group drives away the mourner who responds to death with rage. Stephen took weeks to recover from the rejection. He thought he had the wrong feelings because he was a bad person.

• • • • •

Summary. Scapegoating occurs when the group blames and attacks one or a few for the troubles of the whole. When faced with the discomfort of different viewpoints, groups "freeze out" the perceived source of tension. The group fixes blame rather than fixing the problem. As the case studies show, groups may attack people associated with anger, gentleness, silence, competence, peacemaking or old age. Scapegoating may be connected to multiple sources of conflict and interact with multiple patterns of conflict. Whatever the content, scapegoating is a destructive distortion of efforts to deal with variety and prevents the healing which occurs when groups learn from internal variety.

To list the issues of conflict is not to work them through. For this, we turn to models of conflict resolution, the topic of the next chapter.

WORKING GUIDELINES

Scapegoating occurs when the group blames one or a few for the tensions of the whole. Scapegoating includes the individual tendency to blame others for problems, and the group tendency to drive away the perceived sources of trouble. Scapegoating means the group destroys rather than learns from the internal differences.

Fortunately, individuals are not puppets of the group process. Scapegoating can be interrupted and channeled into creative problem solving through three steps:

1. Identify the Pattern. Scapegoating begins when somebody shows unusual thoughts, feelings or behaviors. The group response is fear and anger. The group attacks as if "the odd one" had caused the group's difficulties: "Your complaints are bothering us." The content of the conflict varies from setting to setting, but the process is always the same: the system blames one or a few for the tensions of the whole.

2. Stop the Attack. During conflict, group members can step back and describe behavior. For example, participants can ask for tolerance of different viewpoints: "I want to hear what Dianne has to say." Ignoring or attacking a group member is behavior which can be described. As attack shifts to analysis, a useful question is: What does the conflict represent for the larger system?

3. Analyze the Scapegoat's Contribution. The pattern of scapegoating is a two-way street. The victim of group-wide attack can soften or add to the battle. For example, when a group turns against a Fight Leader, he can respond with counter-attack or look at the chips on his shoulder and the quality of his anger. Self-study encourages analysis and peacemaking.

CHAPTER 8

PEACEMAKING:
Bringing Together

"The purpose of conflict is harmony."

Terry Dobson

Conflict is the opposition of forces. Peacemaking brings together opposing forces for creative problem solving. The most potent tool for peacemaking is face-to-face dialogue with a focus on the analysis and solution of shared problems.

Peacemaking begins by analyzing the issues and aims for consensus about action solutions. For the individual, peacemaking means people attack, withdraw, defend, observe, think, support, take risks and reach out. For the group system, each of these behaviors continually involves and connects with all other dynamics generating a field of psychological energy with a life of its own. The essence of group life is a fundamental rhythm of harmony. Peacemaking taps patterns of balance and rhythms of harmony across multiple levels of reality.

This chapter looks at six case studies in peacemaking, pauses to consider dreams as a tool of conflict management and concludes with ten key guidelines of peacemaking.

PEACEMAKING

THE BEHAVIORS OF PEACEMAKING

Pioneers. For almost twenty years, social psychologist Herbert Kelman has been designing Problem Solving Workshops for representatives of nations and cultures at war.[79] His workshops bring together men and women as private individuals, with the knowledge of high-level government agencies, for face-to-face communication with the enemy. Kelman-style workshops are facilitated by social scientists knowledgeable about conflict theory and group dynamics, generally meeting in a university setting.

Kelman has been strongly influenced by the "workshops in controlled communication" of John Burton, previously at the Centre for the Analysis of Conflict at University College, London and presently at George Mason University in Virginia.[80] Burton's early work was with representatives of the Greek and Turkish communities in Cyprus. Kelman often facilitates Palestinian/Israeli workshops; his colleague, Stephen Cohen, has facilitated Indian/Pakistani/Bangladesh workshops. Kelman also takes into account the work of Leonard Doob, William Foltz and Robert Stevens who designed conferences for representatives of an African border dispute between Somalia, Ethiopa and Kenya.[81] Doob and Foltz later worked with Protestants and Catholics in Ireland.[82]

These workshops analyze international and cross-cultural conflict. The theoretical foundation is the study of communication as a mutual process. In conversation, people voice their needs and perceptions while taking into account the other person's views, hidden agendas and cultural history. According to Kelman, face-to-face communication between enemies is a peace-seeking negotiation when participants attempt to accurately understand and describe the world-view and self-image of themselves and each other.[83] Under these conditions, potent solutions for social conflict emerge from a focus on shared needs.

Workshop Format. The participants in Kelman's workshops represent groups engaged in actual war, but they attend as private individuals. Participants bring their pain and passion to an encounter with the enemy, hoping to influence the prospects for peace. Kelman follows Burton's strategy of choosing representatives who do not have official policy-making positions but are quite influential in their respective communities. Participants include business or community leaders, educators and journalists. Kelman and Burton believe that unofficial but influential participants are less constrained by the public position, more open to new information and new insights, more available for change in thoughts and feelings and quite able to transfer workshop learning to political and diplomatic arenas. The workshop model would now be called track two diplomacy.

Workshop discussions are relatively unstructured but guided by social scientists in a third-party role who maintain an analytic and problem-solving stance. The social scientists structure the workshop experience, choose representatives and topics for the workshop and make comments during the discussions. The status of the social scientists as "professors," the use of the university as a setting and the **analytic** approach counter the usual hostile, blaming, legalistic tone of negotiations between parties in conflict. Kelman states that participants feel both obliged to and freed up by a focus on the analysis of conflict.

Topics for discussion must be relevant for group problem solving, such as regional economic plans, tourism, how school books portray the conflict and what kind of information each side has about the other. Or, topics may be issues closer to the fire, such as the drawing of national boundaries.

The comments of the social scientists during the workshop take three forms: (1) theoretical statements about conflict theory intended as conceptual tools for analysis; (2) content observations, including questions for clarification or statements of similarities and differences; and (3) process observations of the "here-and-now" behavior of workshop participants, especially those which reflect the dynamics of the political conflict.[84] The social scientists keep the discussion close to the ideas generated by the participants themselves. According to Kelman and Cohen:

> Certain solutions can only emerge from the mutual confrontation of assumptions, concerns and identities in the course of face-to-face communication. In other words, the parties need each other if creative new ideas are to evolve. (p. 290)

This problem-solving approach to international conflict is not an imposed solution. Genuine conflict resolution requires interaction.

For social scientists to serve as workshop facilitators, they require intense preparation. Kelman and Cohen believe requirements for such facilitation include:

> skills of a generalist in conflict resolution, familiar with the particulars of the case, [with] a sustained commitment to work in that specific conflict arena, knowledgeable about the internal complexities of each party, able to identify a broad range of potential participants, familiar with the political processes within and between parties and, above all, he must establish and renew his credibility with both sides over an extended period of time. (p. 296)

Workshop Events. The purpose of the workshop is analyzing conflict, though obviously conversations become quite emotional. Kelman uses pre-workshop sessions and then the problem-solving meetings.

The pre-workshop sessions strengthen cohesion and trust within national teams. These meetings allow participants to get to know each other and the workshop organizers and to present their views of the conflict.

The pre-workshop talk strengthens team identity in two ways. Discussion clarifies differences within each national group and allows comparisons with the official public position. At the same time, dialogue provides information to the organizers about topics for the problem-solving meetings. Kelman reports that cultural and religious explanations for the conflict and more volatile criticism of the enemy's cultural and religious values are more frequent in pre-workshop sessions than in the workshop itself.[85]

In Kelman's model, the workshop begins when the organizers introduce specific topics for discussion, but that is generally the only structure provided. As one might expect, the conversation quickly becomes quite intense. Simply "talking to the enemy" raises issues of survival, loyalty and betrayal. Discussion may bring out hatred thousands of years old. Nonetheless, the ground rules announced by the organizers lead to new learning: the goal is communication, not necessarily agreement; the focus is the analysis of conflict.

Kelman and Cohen concluded that the most useful and most difficult intervention from the third-party social scientists was observations and feedback of here-and-now group process. Feedback about group dynamics is powerful information for problem solving. Again, Kelman and Cohen:

> The parties will call upon their beliefs and attitudes about the adversary in an attempt to explain their workshop behavior to themselves and to respond to the adversary's words and actions. Such attitudes and patterns of response will necessarily reflect the images and perceptions rooted in their respective cultures and in the conflict between them, and are therefore ripe for intergroup process analysis. (p. 275)

In other words, the process of the workshop mirrors the dynamics of the international conflict, as the next case study shows.

Case Study #25: Enthusiasm and Fear

Kelman and Cohen have described a workshop where Pakistanis voiced fears about Indian designs on Pakistan and its territory. The Indians argued that this was an irrational fear. The disagreement continued unsettled until discussion turned to alternative futures for the region.

The Indians were quite positive about the vision of a united sub-continent. Then one of the social scientists asked a question, "Could this Indian enthusiasm [for unity] help explain the Pakistani fears [of invasion]?" (p. 295)

This comment helped shift disagreement and distance to curiosity and understanding. Discussion helped the Indians understand the Pakistani anxiety and helped the Pakistanis see that the Indian hope for regional peace was a higher priority than a united sub-continent.

ENTHUSIASM/FEAR is a group dynamic taking shape as a paired opposite embedded in a shared network of Pakistani-Indian history. The Facilitator who made the "enthusiasm-fear" comment helped workshop participants shift awareness from personal and national identity to understanding shared networks of relationships. This shift in consciousness moves the psychological system towards balance. The shift was a turning point.

• • • • •

Turning Points. Conflict shifts to problem solving through new learning and changes in perception or awareness. Turning points move the peace-seeking process along. They are often a single statement, beautifully reflecting the dynamics of the moment: "Could this Indian enthusiasm help explain the Pakistani fear?" Another example from a Kelman-style workshop was also a symbolic gesture: Pakistanis "hear" Bengali pain over atrocities and agree in theory to a war crimes trial. Kelman and Cohen concluded that symbolic gestures can have a tremendous impact, citing the positive Israeli reaction when Egyptian President Anwar Sadat visited Jerusalem. Within the workshops, symbolic gestures can become part of the "language of de-escalation" and contribute to the transfer of workshop learning to the larger political network.

The statements which become turning points may be the stirring words of a conference participant. State Department official Joseph Montville has written about the resolution of French-German hostility after World War II through the development of cooperative economic projects.[86] Significant discussions leading to economic agreements occurred during the summers of 1946 and 1947 in Switzerland, facilitated by an American Lutheran minister, Frank Buchman. Discussions were difficult; typically the French would leave the room each time a German rose to speak. The psychological breakthrough occurred in 1947 when Irene Laure, a heroine of the French resistance whose son had been tortured by the Gestapo, responding to a challenge from Buchman to describe her vision of a unified Europe, emerged from two days of solitude and addressed the plenary session: "I have so hated Germany that I wanted to see her erased from the map of Europe. But I have seen that my hatred is wrong. I wish to ask the forgiveness of all the Germans present." (McDonald and Bendahmane, *Track Two Diplomacy*, p. 17)

Political Scientist William Zartman links turning points to stages of development in complex negotiations.[87] Zartman defines three functions of the negotiations process: Diagnosis, Formula (such as the Israeli-Egyptian formula of security for territory) and Implementing Details. Zartman calls the shifts in learning which move dialogue along "the moments of seriousness":

. . . when both parties realize that it actually is possible to arrive at a solution to the problems by a joint decision, since their expectations are perceived to be within range of each other. . . the first turning point usually opens the formula phase. (Bendahmane and McDonald, *International Negotiation*, p. 3)

In the case studies which follow, the techniques, art and science of peacemaking are interwoven with hostility, turning points and shared decisions.

Summary. Conflict shifts to harmony through face-to-face discussion as participants voice and analyze problems, then take action on plans of consensus. Communication includes the analysis of conflict, the description of world views and self-images, and learning about shared networks of relationships. Since group behavior mirrors the dynamics of the larger political conflict, learning about "here-and-now" patterns of group relationships provides new information for problem solving and peacemaking.

In the next case study, a private citizen acted as a go-between in the Dominican Republic's civil uprising in 1965 at the request of the U.S. Department of State.[88] Dr. Bryant Wedge had a five-stage model for intercession in intergroup conflict: (1) establish contact with each party in the conflict, (2) define interests of each party and possible mutual interests of all, (3) bring together members of the conflicting groups on neutral ground to establish contact and communication, (4) give assistance in practical programs of cooperation and (5) terminate intervention when official negotiation is established. Case Study #26 is Wedge's version of events from MacDonald and Bendahmane's *Track Two Diplomacy*.

Case Study #26: Quelling Rebellion

On April 24, 1965, a group of young officers in the Dominican Republic army tried to overthrow a military-supported government and restore the previous president who had been deposed in a coup d'état. When senior officers tried to control the uprising by force, citizen and university violence broke out in the capital city. More than 700 persons were killed in four days and the country verged on civil war. At this point, the United States Marines landed and set up an "international zone" between the rebels (constitutionalists) and the junta loyalists.

On September 1, 1965, the U.S. State Department hired Bryant Wedge, a psychiatrist and professor of diplomacy, "to establish contact with young Dominican revolutionaries . . . to open communication between them and the U.S. diplomatic mission in that country—possibly to reduce the violence and killing that was taking place." (p. 36) Wedge negotiated a contract with the State Department that allowed him to act as a wholly independent consultant, "neither representing the U.S. government nor subject to official control, while the mission was entitled to disavow any responsibility for my work or findings." (p. 40) So began a track two intercession in violent intergroup conflict.

Wedge first made contact with the group self-identified as the Revolutionary Youth Movement, a combination of young military officers and university students and leaders who were mobilized by democratic ideals. The group had no dominant leaders, no clear structure of authority and operated through a powerful consensus process. Events were discussed until interpretation, position and decisions were decided through consensus. The revolutionaries resented the U.S. mission for bringing in the Marines and for implying a communist character to the revolution.

On the same day the deposed president had returned from exile, Wedge took up residence in a local hotel. After wandering the streets for six hours, watched but not talking to anyone, Wedge joined a group listening to Bosch and when Wedge raised a clenched fist "salute of the oppressed" three young men approached and asked, "Who are you?" Wedge explained he was a professor interested in the political psychology of revolution and had come to study their revolution and planned to stay for three weeks. He wanted to understand their point of view.

Dialogue began with a focus on social complaints and a sophisticated discussion of why people were participating in the revolution. Wedge thought they were a "thinking audience" committed to democratic reform who truly wanted him "to recognize the personal and social concerns and aspirations of their group." When the revolutionaries asked if Wedge was an intelligence agent, he said he was an independent scholar who was also having discussions with the U.S. embassy. Generally, such discussions led to Wedge's promise to do his "level best" to relay their positions and perceptions to U.S. officials. Subsequent mediation events circled around the opening of the Autonomous University of Santo Domingo under revolutionary auspices and a belief that transforming society would take knowledge and practical skills.

At the embassy, Wedge had more formal discussions. He met with the ambassador several days after making contact with the young Dominicans, and then the nine sections of the embassy that had concerns of any kind about youth affairs. According to Wedge, the U.S. diplomatic mission had, as a group, suffered a "traumatic experience" after working hard to encourage the stability and democratic development of a nation emerging from a radical dictatorship. The decision to bring in combat-ready troops was controversial at best. Wedge was brought in when the fighting had calmed down.

Listening to revolutionaries and the U.S. mission, Wedge concluded that each group had mostly hostile stereotypes of the other group and that he did better if he held to a role of trying to understand viewpoints not challenging them:

> ... it was soon evident that my firsthand knowledge of each side carried very little weight with the other, any challenge to the stereotypes was rejected, and it was clear that if I were to urge contrary facts and interpretations concerning either group on the other I would soon lose all credibility.... Each group asserted its belief that the other was unmitigatedly hostile to its purposes. (p. 44)

After the initial hostile phases, the groups tentatively asked whether the other side would ever offer any assistance for goals of social development. Wedge moved to the stage of identifying common interests—re-establish political stability, resume democratic institution building and make available technical and economic assistance. When the Autonomous University re-opened with the support of the revolutionaries, Wedge decided that would be the best context for the next phase of face-to-face dialogue. Although the University administration and the U.S. mission believed direct contact would damage credibility, both sides began speaking of cooperation and conditions for discussions. As Wedge's departure date drew near, he wrote a report for the U.S. government that recommended sponsorship of expert-to-expert and institution-to-institution contact for University development.

In March 1966, elections confirmed a reformist administration and soon the State department asked Wedge to put his recommendations about the University into effect. Eventually, experts in agronomy, chemistry, pharmacy, engineering, architecture, city planning and university administration were recruited from many different countries to act as technical consultants beginning in July 1966.

A turning point came during a luncheon for the visiting experts when revolutionaries accused the experts of solely assisting the conservative University. A Mexican professor of chemistry made a spontaneous and impassioned speech proclaiming that he was "no puppet" and that he believed the project to be "nonpolitical" and that "the life or death of the University depended on the quality of its work" and that it needed assistance regardless of the source. Within a few days, serious, cooperative work was established.

Eventually, at another luncheon in honor of the visiting experts, direct contact between the embassy and the University administration took place. The day after, Wedge observed:

> There was no change whatsoever in basic beliefs, nor would any participant from either side admit that he had learned any new facts or changed his interpretation of the facts which he had. But the members of each group now recognized their counterparts as serious and dedicated men who were sincere in their commitments to the development of a

better society no matter how much they might differ in social philosophy
and method. In brief, the two groups kept their identities distinct and
intact, and they remained at odds on many issues; but they now perceived
the "other" group as consisting of "men that you can work with" in
limited ways. Two days later, the American ambassador invited the
[university] rector for luncheon. (p. 49)

The mediation was completed after cooperative projects were worked out
between the groups. Wedge concluded that events support three main hypotheses: (1) contact and communication between members of groups in conflict
favorably alter the images or judgments of each other; (2) programs of limited
cooperation in pursuit of common goals result in further movements towards
less hostile images; and (3) limited cooperation and favorable changes in the
images between groups in conflict diminish the degree of violence. Wedge saw
his hypotheses as a theoretical and empirical basis for testing conflict reduction
procedures.

•   •   •   •   •

The following section also describes peacemaking in an international setting. Here, too, peacemaking emerges as participants tackle shared problems.

CAMP DAVID

From September 5–18, 1978 the American President Jimmy Carter,
Prime Minister Menachem Begin of Israel and President Anwar el-Sadat
of Egypt met in face-to-face dialogue at Camp David, Maryland, a country
retreat outside of Washington D.C.[89] Although the U. S. State Department and
National Security staff had modestly recommended the goal "to derive a
declaration of principles as a basis for future negotiating," the President made a
stronger statement of purpose: "a written agreement for peace between Egypt
and Israel, with an agenda for implementation of its terms during the
succeeding months."

Carter prepared for Camp David. He studied psychological analyses of
Begin and Sadat, considered several negotiating styles, heard briefing reports
from negotiation experts, Mideast ambassadors and policy advisers.

Carter defined his role as "mediator and active negotiator" who would
help opponents develop a mutually agreeable, written statement. Carter was an
active mediator who interviewed, wrote summaries, interpreted meanings,
relied on maps, dictionaries, thesauruses and the Bible, while facilitating
written agreement between leaders representing governments at war for 4,000
years. Most of the communication between Sadat and Begin was literally
carried by Carter. The Egyptian and Israeli leaders did not meet face-to-face
from *Day 3* until *Day 13*.

Carter had a strong wish to solve the Mideast problem before he was elected president. He visited Jeruslem in 1973 and was aware of the city's complicated history. He believed Christian, Jewish and Moslem visitors should have guaranteed and free access to their sacred sites. Like Sadat and Begin, he was a deeply religious man. Carter also believed in the philosophical and legal foundation of American democracy and pledged to uphold basic human rights—to vote, to assemble, to debate, to own property, to be free of military rule. As president, human rights were a central element of his foreign policy.

As early as March 1977, Carter had identified the three primary issues: Israeli security, Egyptian claims to the Sinai and self-rule for Palestinian refugees. He had strong emotional affinity for Israel, believed in self-rule for Palestinians, and called Sadat "a shining light on the Mideast scene."

Originally, Carter and Sadat tried to implement the U.N. format for a multinational peace conference—Arab and Israeli leaders with Americans and Soviets presiding. They were pledged to United Nations Resolution 242 (U.N. 242) which called for a just and lasting peace, an acceptance of Israel's right to exist, the withdrawal of Israeli forces from territories occupied in the Six Day War and a settlement of refugee problems. Carter's comprehensive plan for peace also included open borders, free trade, "a Palestinian entity" and diplomatic relations. Sadat basically agreed.

In part as a response to the breakdown in efforts to bring off a Geneva-type conference, Sadat made the historic visit to Jerusalem on November 19-21, 1977. Sadat's symbolic journey brought applause from most of the West and condemnation from his Arab neighbors. In January 1978, in a conversation between Carter and Brezinski, the idea emerged to invite Begin and Sadat to Camp David for extensive negotiations with Carter.

In *Keeping Faith*, Carter describes the thirteen days of dialogue at Camp David, 125 beautiful, wooded acres with an atmosphere of both isolation and intimacy. The Egyptian and Israeli negotiating teams each had nine members, the American team had eleven. Before negotiations began, the three teams prepared lists of goals, issues, areas of agreement and disagreement, and proposed solutions. Logistics mirrored the complexity of issues with three separate advisory, secretarial, communication, medical, security and cooking staffs.

Case Study #27: Camp David, September 1978

Day 1—Tuesday. At 2:30 in the afternoon, Carter and his wife Rosalyn walked to the helicopter pad to welcome the arriving Sadat, then the two leaders met briefly on the terrace of Carter's cabin. Sadat described his preference for a total settlement of the issues, referred to a comprehensive plan "here in my pocket" and said he was prepared to be flexible on all issues except two—land and sovereignty. He predicted difficulty negotiating with Begin, saying he had offered comprehensive settlement packages through third parties since 1971. Then Sadat, mindful of an earlier heart attack, left to go to sleep less than half an hour after he had landed at Camp David. In his notes, Carter thought Sadat "determined to succeed. . . therefore inclined to form a partnership with me in opposition to Begin." (p. 328)

Two hours later, Carter greeted Begin and his wife Aliza. Begin was thorough and methodical, asking details about schedules, procedures, the recording of sessions and number of aides. They decided Carter and Begin would meet after dinner, Carter would meet with Sadat in the morning, then all three would meet the next afternoon. Begin noted that the last agreement between Egypt and a Jewish nation was 2,000 years ago and he expected a focus on general principles not a total settlement. Carter objected, then said that Sadat had expressed a concern about Begin's preoccupation with details at the expense of the major issues, and Begin replied, "I can handle both." (p. 330) Begin left, agreeing to return after dinner.

That afternoon, Carter proposed an idea Rosalynn had studied in interfaith religious groups—that all three leaders issue a call for the world to join them in prayer for the success of the Camp David efforts. Sadat agreed immediately and after Begin reviewed the text word by word, they issued the first and last joint statement until discussions were concluded. In his notes, Carter wrote, "from the beginning, our differences were obvious, even in personal habits." (p. 331)

After supper, Begin and Carter met alone. Carter described his understanding of Israel's special problems, emphasized the importance of their meeting and clarified his third party role:

> I reserved the right, and had the duty, to put forward compromise proposals, and might on occasion merely adopt either the Egyptian or Israeli position if I believed it to be the best. I would not be timid but would not deal in surprises. (p. 333)

Begin demanded to see any American proposal before Sadat, following an agreement with President Ford. Carter "accentuated the positive," affirming the importance of Israel's security needs and praising Begin's proposal for Palestinian self-government and Begin's willingness to recognize Egyptian sovereignty in the Sinai. Carter listed the areas of agreement as he understood them and spontaneously made many comments about shared interests and common ground—the benefits of peace, consequences of failure and the desirability of a formally signed treaty.

They addressed the tough issues—security; Israeli settlements on Egyptian land; the interests of other Arab nations; a demilitarized zone in the Sinai; terrorism; Sadat's view that sovereignty in the Sinai meant a total absence of

Israeli settlements; U.N. 242, which Israel rejected saying it had a "right to occupy lands taken in its own defense;" (p. 336) and the problems of three Palestinians. After two and a half hours, the meeting ended at 11:00 PM.

Day 2—Wednesday. Sadat did not begin his official day before 10:00 AM. Carter described Sadat as

> punctual, calm and self-assured . . . brief and to the point in all his discussions. . . rarely dwelling on details or semantics, he spelled out his positions in broad terms with emphasis on the strategic implication of decisions . . . in other countries in the Middle east. (p. 338)

In his meeting with Sadat, Carter reviewed the prior night's conversation with Begin and they talked about Begin's personality—his formality, bitterness, inclination to look to ancient history rather than the present and future, and his fundamental integrity and honor. Then Sadat outlined Egypt's position emphasizing Arab sovereignty over occupied land. According to Sadat, Egypt had sovereignty in Sinai, Syria in Golan Heights and Palestinians in West Bank and Gaza.

Sadat agreed with Carter on the goal of a clear framework for peace but thought Begin was unable or unwilling to communicate effectively. Sadat then presented a written, strongly worded initial statement, stating his willingness to make major concessions leading to a final position. Sadat believed his negotiating strength depended on keeping the modifications secret. Sadat went on to outline solutions for key issues.

Although Carter was concerned about Sadat's harsh opening and Begin's inflexibility, at 3:00 PM the three leaders met. Sadat announced on arrival that he had just finished a good conversation with the Israeli Defense Minister. Begin began by talking about areas of disagreement, that technicians would need months to work out details and then shifted to questions about observance of Sabbath days—Sadat's special prayers on Friday, Christian services on Sunday and Jewish observance on Saturday. When the three agreed to refrain from working on Saturday, Begin replied, "We needed to start a new page and forget past disagreements."

Carter asked Sadat to respond to Begin's statement and Sadat said his peace initiative to Jerusalem had brough forth a new era, the era of war was coming to an end, and the three were gathered there to produce a comprehensive framework for peace and confront controversial issues. Begin wanted to deal with land issues but not Palestinian rights. Sadat and Carter wanted to settle the Sinai, West Bank and Palestinian issues.

Sadat read his "tough" statement after Begin agreed to discuss it with aides before responding. Carter ended *Day 2* concerned about Begin's perceptions of Sadat's harsh proposal—an impediment to progress or an opening gambit.

Day 3—Thursday. At 8:30 AM, Carter, Begin and advisers met to discuss the Egyptian document. Begin was irate about tone and content. Carter wanted to move on to modifications, while Begin wanted to analyze details. The two teams argued for two hours about the meaning of words—Palestinians, conquered territory, settlements and borders. These were heated and angry arguments, although Carter focused on the key question, what later would be called the security for sovereignty formula: Is Israel willing to withdraw from occupied territories and honor Palestinian rights in exchange for assurance of security? Sadat distrusted Begin because West Bank settlements were growing when Sadat wanted them dismantled.

Amid heated discussion of withdrawal from the West Bank, autonomy for Palestinians and Israel's genuine security needs, Carter accused Begin of subterfuge, a word Begin resented and remembered. Carter and Begin cooled down while advisers discussed home rule and a demilitarized Sinai.

At 10:30 AM, in Carter's study, Begin and Sadat faced each other across a desk while Carter mostly took notes. Begin began by attacking Sadat's initial proposal. Sadat, incensed, interrupted and the argument turned to defining "conqueror and defeated" in war. Carter calmed them down, saying "neither was claiming the other represented a defeated nation."

Talk shifted to the division of occupied territory, with Begin offering to return almost 21,000 square miles of territory (the Sinai) and postpone decisions about 2,340 square miles (the West Bank and Gaza). Sadat parried by suggesting an emphasis on general principles, not square miles. When Begin named conditions for returning the Sinai, Sadat pounded the table and shouted "Land was not negotiable... Security, yes! Land, no!" Through cycles of calm and anger, they debated settlements, waterways, U.N. 242, the West Bank, Lebanon, democracy and Egyptian forces in the Sinai. Carter described his role: "I acted as a referee and put them back on track, and on occasion explained what was meant when there was an obvious misinterpretation." (p. 353)

Before the break at 1:30 PM Carter reviewed the thirteen main issues: demilitarization, settlements, Palestinians, defense forces, military rule, autonomy, sovereignty, Jerusalem, the definition of peace, refugees, airfields, other Arab nations and mutual defense treaties. Although the list was long and depressing, all agreed they had made progress on defining the issues. They adjourned under considerable strain. By now Carter had adopted a negotiating strategy: "I would draft a proposal I considered reasonable, take it to Sadat for quick approval or slight modification and then spend hours or days working on the same point with the Israeli delegation." (p. 356) Carter went directly to Sadat for decisions and usually talked to Israeli advisers before discussion with Begin.

The afternoon session was the last meeting between Sadat and Begin for the next ten days. Argument erupted over airfields and military control, then Sadat stunned everyone with an eloquent speech:

> When Premier Begin says he will keep the Israeli settlements in the Sinai and defend them with force, it is an absolute insult to Egypt. I have tried to provide a model of friendship and coexistence for the rest of the Arab world leaders to emulate. Instead I have become the object of extreme insult from Israel, and scorn and condemnation from the other Arab leaders. . . I still dream of a meeting on Mount Sinai of us three leaders, representing three nations and three religious beliefs. This is still my prayer to God. (p. 358)

For a moment, Begin and Carter were speechless. Begin then described his risk inviting and receiving Sadat in Jerusalem. In 1973, Sadat had led a sneak attack which killed thousands of young Israeli troops. Begin invoked the image of Sadat's visit to Jerusalem, and the hospitality and peaceful wishes of the Israelis. Then Begin went on to reject the notion of "dismantling" thirteen Sinai settlements populated of 2,000 Israelis. Sadat responded with anger, declared a stalemate and in a flash the talks were breaking down.

Carter took action:

> They were moving toward the door but I got in front of them to partially block the way. I urged them not to break off their talks, to give me another chance to use my influence and analysis, to have confidence in me. Begin agreed readily. I looked straight at Sadat; finally he nodded his head. They left without speaking to each other. (p. 359)

Carter, Sadat and their advisers met from 10:30 AM until after midnight. Both the Americans and Egyptians agreed the Israeli settlements were illegal and should be removed. Sadat was clear: "I cannot yield conquered land to Israel." After discussing phased withdrawal, air bases, home rule, Jordan and Syria, the meeting ended with agreement to find a formula acceptable to both Egypt and Israel. Carter's notes about *Day 3* conclude: "During the brief times between discussions I craved intense exercise and lonely places where I could think and sometimes pray."

Day 4—Friday. Carter worked on a written compromise statement, and the American and Israeli negotiating teams met for two hours in the morning. Carter met Begin at 2:30 PM where familiar positions about the initial Sadat paper and the Israeli settlements were repeated. Carter was encouraged when Begin said, "I will never personally recommend that the settlements in the Sinai be dismantled." (p. 366) To Carter, this did not mean that Begin would never permit the settlements to be removed. A plan for Sadat to meet again with the

Israeli Defense Minister and for the Carters to join the Begins for dinner ended the conversation at 4:00.

In Sadat's cabin, Carter said an American proposal would be completed on Saturday and presented on Sunday first to the Israelis and then to Sadat. To work out differences on the proposal, Carter would "continue to meet individually with the two leaders, back and forth, until the best possible compromise had evolved, at which point the three of us, along with our advisers, would meet." (p. 368)

The meeting never took place because agreement was never reached. Carter and Sadat ended the day with a mutual pledge of friendship and fair settlement; the Carters and Begins finished the day with feasting and singing.

Day 5—Saturday. Carter had delegated most of the "routine administrtative duties of the Presidency" to the Vice-President and Cabinet officials. Carter, consulting with the American team, spent the day refining the American compromise proposal, trying to resolve some fifty interconnected issues. Sadat met with the Israeli Defense Minister. The American proposal, containing over twenty recommended actions and "American judgments on the most controversial issues" (p. 371) was ready for "final form" after midnight. Although Carter and his staff supported withdrawal of settlements, they decided "not to include this request in the first draft." (p. 371)

Day 6—Sunday. In the morning, after Church services and lunch, Sadat and Begin rode in Carter's limosine to the Civil War battlefields of Gettysburg, a few miles away, following the ground rule of no peace talk discussions and no talking to the media. The three leaders were military historians, familiar with the terrain, tactics and strategic circumstances of the classic Battle of Gettysburg. Begin was particularly excited visiting the site of Abraham Lincoln's famous address on liberty and equality.

In the late afternoon, Carter and three advisers presented the American plan to Begin and three Israelis. Carter consciously tried the positive view, touching on the hope of peace and the consequences of failure. Begin responded by requesting time to develop a third Israeli plan. After arguing about U.N. 242, "the problem of security also involves territory," (p. 374) the meeting was adjourned.

From 9:30 PM until 3:00 in the morning, the Israelis responded to the American plan paragraph by paragraph and sentence by sentence, beginning with the request to delete U.N. 242. Dictionaries were in demand to argue the meaning of words: "autonomy," "rights" and "sovereignty." A sharp exchange about self-government brought a small breakthrough—"We shall reconsider our objections." (p. 377) Carter was frustrated: "Begin was debating every point tenaciously, while Sadat had made it clear to us from the beginning that his document included extreme Egyptian positions on which he would not insist." (p. 378) When the session ended, Carter spoke with Foreign Minister Dayan and they created more options about Sinai settlements. As daybreak approached, Carter felt more enthusiasm and hope.

Day 7—Monday. In the morning, Carter met with Sadat, reviewed the amended American proposal, negotiated details about settlements, discovered differences about military forces, diplomatic recognition and Jerusalem—the no-win issue. In the afternoon and evening, Sadat reviewed the American proposal, while Carter met with Egyptian and Israeli advisers to look at battle charts, military zones, airfields and joint Israeli-Jordanian patrols.

In the evening, the Egyptian team requested an additional twelve hours to study the draft framework for peace. Israel's Defense Minister, preoccupied with a fallback position, asked Carter, "What are we going to do to prevent rapid loss of contact between Egypt and Israel when and if we fail at Camp David?" (p. 381) In the evening, there was good news. Begin was not going to reject the American proposal "out of hand" and had taken to referring to his own government for "final action." (p. 382) Later, Carter agreed to draft a Sinai document.

Day 8—Tuesday. In the morning, Carter met with Sadat, first reviewing regional Mideast and Persian Gulf issues, then Sadat shifted the tone: "Israel was not going to negotiate in good faith." (p. 384) After a worried conversation about adverse Arab reactions to wording in the framework, Carter left to write out terms of an Egyptian-Israeli treaty. Sadat approved the wording in a twenty-minute meeting. At 8:00 PM, Begin made an impassioned statement to Carter about his fears of using U.N. 242 in the Framework for Peace. Carter ended the heated discussion and accused Begin of giving up peace "just to keep a few illegal settlers on Egyptian land." (p. 387)

Day 9—Wednesday. Carter and Secretary of State Vance met with the Israeli Attorney General and the militant Egyptian Under Secretary of Foreign Affairs to refine the Framework for Peace. After eleven hours, trading words and phrases back and forth, agreements were reached on language about U.N. 242 and Jerusalem, although differences remained on settlements, open borders and diplomatic recognition. Although Begin said late in the day that he "could not accept any language that called for Israel to remove its settlements," Carter ended the day pleased with their progress.

Day 10—Thursday. Carter joined Sadat for his early morning walk at a rapid military pace. Sadat spoke of the need for material and spiritual healing after a time of war, citing America's Civil War, Vietnam and the Mideast. Throughout the afternoon, one impasse remained: the settlement issue. Egypt wanted Israelis out, Israel wanted the settlers to stay. No agreement, no signed

Framework. Carter went to sleep unable to end the deadlock, preparing to terminate negotiations.

Day 11—Friday. In the early morning, a heartbroken Carter planned a final report that summarized agreements and differences. All participants felt pressure to take care of business back home. When Sadat announced his immediate departure, Carter, whose hopes for a harmonious departure were fading and who now imagined the worst in Mideast power shifts, prevailed on Sadat to stay. The staff developed "failure plans" while Carter reviewed the Framework and Sinai document. That evening, Carter, Mondale and Sadat watched the world's heavyweight boxing match. Calmer, they spoke of a document all could sign.

Day 12—Saturday. In his morning walk with Sadat, Carter reviewed the Sinai settlements impasse. The topic continued as a focus throughout the day as a contrast to the other agreements being made. Finally, Begin made a small but significant concession; he would submit to the Israeli Parliament the question: "If agreement is reached on all other Sinai issues, will the settlers be withdrawn?" (p. 396) Carter's response: "Breakthrough!" This was an agreement about Sinai that all parties could sign. Then, reviewing the whole text of the Framework for Peace, making "insignificant editorial changes to overcome significant objections," and outlining agreements about Palestinians, Jerusalem and an end to new West Bank settlements, an agreement for a written Framework was reached.

Day 13—Sunday. Carter reviewed final proposals with Sadat, made another full revision, talked with Israelis, resolved two serious last minute crises, then wrote the final draft, the twenty-third version of a Framework for Peace. Carter, Sadat and Begin flew to Washington by helicopter, landing at the White House for a signing ceremony and press conference at 10:15 PM.

Carter's final notes are telling. He thought everyone got to know each other well, except Begin and Sadat. Only later did they feel friendship and respect. Still, the result was two steps forward—the Framework for Peace in the Middle East and the Framework for the Conclusion of a Peace Treaty between Egypt and Israel.

For the mediator and peacemaker, what are the technical lessons of Camp David? It can be seen how a written statement drives the machinery of a diplomatic conference and that the skills of a third party mediator include visioning a hopeful outcome and balancing content and process. Personality styles, cultural differences and negotiating strategies may help or hinder agreement, while faith holds people to the task of conflict resolution. Analysis of the Camp David strategies continues below.

∙ ∙ ∙ ∙ ∙

STRATEGIES OF MEDIATION

Robert Blake and Jane Mouton have been organization consultants for more than thirty years.[90] In "Overcoming Group Warfare," published in the *Harvard Business Review*, they describe two strategies for resolving intergroup conflicts. In the interpersonal facilitation approach, a neutral **facilitator** writes compromise proposals and moves between groups in conflict to help opponents identify areas of common ground. In the interface conflict-solving approach, a neutral **administrator** helps opponents deal with each other directly as members of whole groups trying to solve problems and achieve an ideal relationship. In the first approach, the facilitator may become involved in the discussions themselves. In the second approach, the administrator is uninvolved in content and acts principally as a guide to the process.

The first approach is similar to the Harvard Negotiation Project, President Carter's approach at Camp David and Terry Waite's strategy for freeing hostages in the Mideast. For example, the previous pages show President Carter as facilitator—actively writing proposals, confronting participants, agreeing, disagreeing and otherwise involved in content. The second approach is more like Burton, Kelman, Wedge and the model presented in Chapter 1. Wedge, for example, followed a five-step model and mostly interviewed and listened. Blake and Mouton suggest that the interpersonal facilitator usually starts out as the objective mediator and moderator: "When we got underway, I stepped back from the discussions because I wanted them to speak to each other directly. Soon they refrained from talking to me or even attempting to draw me into the conversation." (p. 100) When talk breaks down, the facilitator jumps into content and process. Blake and Mouton describe an industrial mediation where the facilitator's words sound similar to Carter's early observations at Camp David:

> Eventually, the argument bogged down when each began to repeat himself and to ignore the other. By the end they were both talking at once. My attempts to change the subject were futile. As they moved toward the door I got in front of them to block the way. I urged them not to stop these conversations but to give me another chance to use my influence. (p. 100)

In the Blake and Mouton example, the facilitator then became more active, first as a referee to put the discussion back on track, then as a "go-between" and finally an "intermediary who formulated positions and developed compromise proposals." When talks threatened to break down again, the facilitator pressed one participant to reconsider his "unrealistic, rigid position" and the confrontation was a turning point which produced some concessions.

When Blake and Mouton describe an intervention with union and management teams, the facilitator stayed out of the content and focused on procedures and processes. They describe a series of meetings composed of six top managers and six union officials, with an outside consultant hired as administrator. The consultant defined a procedure to shift a destructive union-management relationship based on suspicion to a problem-solving relationship based on respect. The procedures were four steps:

1. Each group separately writes out the characteristics of an ideal, effective relationship and chooses a spokesperson to present its statement.
2. Each group separately writes out the characteristics of the actual here-and-now union-management relationship.
3. Together the two groups generate a combined statement of union-management problems.
4. The two groups together identify steps to improve the relationship with specific plans for follow-up evaluation.

In their example of the "administrator" approach, management in particular was shaken by union perceptions of lost dignity and destroyed incentive. The first turning point came as the management team struggled to understand the union's experience of "despair and hoplessness." The plant manager, in particular, requested feedback from his team and learned they perceived him as shifting from "open, forthright and honest" to "using force, no discussion, no alternatives, no involvement, pure force." The plant manager accepted the feedback: "You're right."

The union team was totally surprised when management explicitly acknowledged a previous win-lose orientation, a present wish to change, a need to convince the union of this hope for change, a recognition that other managers need to change their attitude and the desire to resist resuming the win-lose position. Had hell frozen over? A break for small group discussion and then back to the general session. The union response to the management initiative: "We'll cooperate in any way to bring about the change."

The recognition of shared goals reduced the tension between the groups and specific plans were developed to solve old problems. In the several years since the consultation, ten joint union-management task forces have facilitated problem solving: there have been no strikes; both sides judge the factory "tops in problem solving;" and the plant had moved from Number Eleven to Number One in financial performance for the company.

Comparing the two approaches, Blake and Mouton acknowledge that the interpersonal facilitator model is a popular variation of a lawyer working an out-of-court settlement between conflicting parties. This is also similar to the Camp David model, where Carter mediated, facilitated, developed proposals, and consulted to both content and process. Blake and Mouton conclude that this model is most useful when only two people are involved, there is little common ground and personal chemistry has blocked communication.

The "whole group" model is more appropriate when many are involved in the conflict, when change must be based on understanding (rather than compliance) and when there is sufficient time to allow changes in perceptions and develop appropriate solutions. In these situations, Blake and Mouton conclude that success is more likely when managers use the interface conflict-solving model rather than a mediator or interpersonal facilitator who gets involved in content and compromise proposals. They identify the powerful elements of their interface model—the attractiveness of rational problem solving, the vision of an ideal relationship and the peer pressure to honestly confront perceptions and illusions. They believe risk taking is a function of felt need—when the pain of conflict is greater than the pain of honesty, then the candor necessary for realistic problem solving surfaces. A comparison of the two approaches can also be made in the next case study.

SYSTEM-WIDE CULTURAL CHANGE

This section describes a complex consultation from the author's private practice. This is long term, multi-level intervention in a large public hospital. The hospital provides health care for primarily geriatric and chronically disabled patients and has an excellent city and national reputation. The hospital is basically a healthy system as measured by self-report and external ratings of quality, productivity and general success.

Case Study #28: System-Wide Change

The contract between the senior consultant and the hospital administrator was to introduce the 10∗STEP^{SM} team-building, problem-solving model to four hospital levels to improve communication generally and to specifically provide training and attention to an often ignored group of employees—the Housekeeping staff.

Eventually, the training model was taught to nine members of the Executive Team in a two-day off-site retreat, to twenty-eight Department Heads in a three-day workshop; to seventy-five Housekeeping staff (mostly black, Hispanic and Asian-Pacific porters) in four two-hour segments over four days; to six Housekeeping Supervisors in a half-day meeting; to twenty-six Activity Therapists in a one day workshop; and to twenty-four head nurses in four half-day meetings. At different times, six consultants (three white, three black) were involved in the project which lasted about sixteen months. There is still a positive professional relationship between the senior consultant and key hospital managers and employees.

Executive Retreat (Two Days). In Summer 1984, in the first morning of a two-day off-site retreat, the Hospital Administrator and eight of his ten senior staff were asked to generate a philosophy statement: "What is the primary mission of this hospital and what shared values support this mission?" As they worked on a statement of consensus, they easily identified the primary purpose: "To create and maintain excellent quality of health care, quality of life and quality of caring for all patients." A small disagreement about the difference between quality of medical care and quality of psychological caring was resolved and led to a second goal of: "the staff has unity of purpose and demonstrates leadership in a changing industry." About here, the Hospital Administrator noted, "In talking about our differences, we evolved to a higher level of agreement and a broader perspective."

The discussion turned to the values of participatory management and differences turned to conflict. The Administrator had a traditional, directive management style and held a tight lid on information and decision making. The executive staff wanted more information and more input into the decision-making process. There was no clear consensus about the degree of "participation" appropriate for the executive team. The phrase "strive to speak and listen effectively in a setting which [emphasizes] participation" was added to the philosophy statement with the word "emphasizes" in brackets. The philosophy statement ended with the sentence, "There is recognition that all parts contribute to the whole."

Personality Styles. After a break, the executive team moved to the next workshop segment which focused on individual differences. Through the Myers-Briggs Type Indicator, the group of nine learned they were six "intuitive thinkers (NTs)" (including the hospital administrator), two "sensing judgers (SJs)" and one "intuitive feeler (NF)." The two consultants (two women, one white, one black) were intuitive feelers (NFs).

Discussion helped the executives recognize different styles and understand their internal dynamics. They observed about themselves their comfort with "complex ideas" and discomfort with "feelings and process." While individuals applied their findings to their work and life, the whole team considered the typical NT difficulty giving and expressing appreciation. Making a commitment to show more appreciation, the group recessed for a shared lunch.

In the afternoon, the group brainstormed a list of strengths and challenges. The strengths included:

STRENGTHS

1. Sincere interest in patient well-being
2. Patient and people centered
3. Rich texture of history in community
4. Lead institution in some computer projects
5. New and expanded programs
6. Strong community support
7. Outstanding geriatric facility
8. Stimulating work environment—something's always happening
9. Increasingly identified need—the right place at the right time
10. High-level intelligence, efficient executives & dept. managers
11. Overall objectives met
12. Relatively high level of organizational loyalty
13. Executive staff have wait and see attitude—don't mess in others territory unless help is asked
14. Strong political support
15. Highly motivated care-giving staff
16. Increasing scope of outreach programs that bring patients in touch with community
17. Participatory management style with adequate forums for discussing issues
18. Quality of staff
19. Parking space

When the group turned its attention to problems and challenges, a list of twenty-nine was generated. There were seven items requesting more training, including management, computer and cross departmental. Six environmental items including references to cumbersome public bureaucracy, city politics, the pace of health care change and increased requests for services due to successful new programs. Six purpose items related mostly to the expanding role of geriatric hospitals, new links to universities and increased expectations about new successful programs. The eight policy items were about allocation of staff, supplies and resources. The two key process comments were about communication on the executive team and the need for greater group input about institutional policies.

Clearly, even the list of "problems, isssues or challenges" reflected a strong sense of accomplishment in this hospital's successes. The group ranked the twenty-nine issues and chose Item #5 for analysis: "There is a need for greater and more effective communication among the executive team." The senior consultant introduced the 10∗STEP<u>SM</u> Model and the group moved through problem solving. Both consultants wrote out key phrases and ideas on paper taped to the wall:

Identify the Problem: There is a need for greater and more effective communication on the executive team, more group input, participation and clearer communication about priorities.

Define Problem Clearly: There is a need to improve participation and communication in executive meetings which can be accomplished by clarifying purpose, format and norms for disagreement; more in-depth problem solving; more honesty, less avoiding, less sidestepping; less assumptions about each other; AND MORE SUPPORT.

Analyze the Problem: Causes and contributing factors include:

1. Too much sidestepping
2. Assumption—your problem isn't mine
3. Too much after-group discussion
4. Unclear purpose of meeting: to get sense of issue or solve it now
5. Unclear expectations of what to do when someone raises issue
6. Unclear how and who made decisions about agenda
7. Unclear responsibility for priorities when not part of decision-making process & what to do when something goes wrong
8. Ground rules unclear—who decides agenda and time limits
9. Everyone has different perceptions of what's happening at executive meetings

Here, the group paused to analyze perceptions of the executive meetings.

MINI-ANALYSIS:
PERCEPTIONS ABOUT EXECUTIVE MEETINGS

- The Boss gives information, then requests input from each person, everyone is free to participate
- The format is a barrier
- Some people don't feel free to raise any issue (e.g., housing the students)
- Group norm—we stifle discussion by interrupting, cutting it off: "I don't want to talk about it, it's your problem."
- Information given is limited, as needed, reflects trust issue
- We only raise issues when we know The Boss's position first
- People reluctant to speak up, we get shot down
- Sometimes people walk away feeling blamed
- Incomplete communications
- REMEMBER: There are good dynamics—most people participate in go-arounds. There is a lot of listening, giving of information.

With some discussion, *Day 1* ended here. The two consultants left feeling great about the progress of this terrific group. The hospital administrator left angry that his staff was discussing his style and particularly angry at the senior consultant.

Day 2 started with a vague discussion about group process, then returned to structured problem solving. The focus was to clarify the format, priorities and purpose of executive meetings. The group reviewed the data of the previous day's discussion, then brainstormed solutions:

SOLUTIONS: IMPROVING EXECUTIVE MEETINGS

1. Learn each other's priorities, roles
2. Have a better agenda
3. Summarize conclusions, check on follow-up, report back to group about closure
4. The Boss could use notes to review actions, clarify decisions, check follow-through
5. ASK for what you want—attitude of getting what you need
6. Balance departmental and hospital-wide topics
7. Use more discretion, some issues are personal
8. More clarity especially about priorties
9. Clarify process for negotiating expectations, priorities

The group then decided to brainstorm solutions to another aspect of their communication: "How can we share more information?"

SOLUTIONS: HOW CAN WE SHARE MORE INFORMATION

1. Develop better network for gaining information—within and outside the executive group
2. The Boss could give more information
3. People have different needs for different levels of information
4. Learn how to manage ambiguity
5. Bug his office
6. Don't personalize it
7. Adjust and operate in given framework (it's less than perfect)
8. ASK for more information
9. REMIND group and Boss of continuing importance of effective communication and teach consequences
10. Model better communication—share information with subordinates
11. Respect confidentiality
12. Get closure on decisions
13. Discuss operational issues
14. Discuss macro-health issues

Somewhat on a roll, the group brainstormed solutions to another aspect of the problem:

SOLUTIONS: DIFFERENCES IN LEADERSHIP STYLE

1. Appreciate complexity
2. Use this workshop to appreciate differences
3. Appreciate diversity
4. Appreciate leader's direction
5. Don't personalize—emphasize objective analysis

With time approaching for the closing activities, structure broke down. A few people got angry and several sensitive comments were made to the Hospital Administrator. The senior consultant made a strong statement to the Administrator, "There is a clear consensus from the executive team that they want more information from you." Silence, and the co-consultant moved to sit near the Administrator; more silence and then a shift to a brief discussion about evaluating change.

There was a break, then a closing ritual about appreciation. The consultant asked each person to give a statement of appreciation about each group member. The Hospital Administrator was asked to give his statements of appreciation last. The two consultants started and each made many comments about people's honesty, integrity and courage getting right to the key issues. When it was the Administrator's turn, to the relief of the senior consultant, the Hospital Administrator made a series of astute, personal and very positive feedback statements about each person in the room. It was a bit stunning and a fine ending to the retreat, with the Hospital Administrator re-asserting leadership and gaining respect. The consultants looked forward to the follow-up meetings with the executive team, but this collection of individuals would never reassemble.

Department Managers. Two weeks after the executive retreat, following a discussion about breaking or maintaining the consultant contract, a three-day training workshop began with all department managers in the hospital, except two on vacation.

Day 1 began with discussions of primary purpose, especially "What is the purpose of the department managers meeting?" The afternoon focused on individual differences. Most of the department managers were "sensing-judging" types who were great with details, multiple regulations, closure and structure.

Day 2 focused on problem solving. First, the department managers brainstormed a list of seventy-three positives with "I love it here!!" from a surprisingly large number. Then they brainstormed a list of "Problems or

Issues" and ranked them to chose one for discussion. Like the executives, the managers got right to the point, they chose for analysis: "Improving Inter-departmental and Departmental/Executive Team Communication." The managers were asked how they felt about the lists and despite some angry exchanges, a very strong sense of mission emerged.

More easily than the executives, the department managers could and did talk about their support, affection and loyalty to the hospital. In discussing morale, several mentioned "loyalty to a tradition of service" and "the challenge and creative work of assisting the city's frail and elderly." They experienced a "genuine impact" on city needs and belonged to many departments that had received "national recognition" for outstanding service in the rapidly changing field of geriatric health care. The managers were proud of the excellent quality of care, the professional opportunities for growth and a decades-long history of accomplishment.

The department managers, many of whom were twenty-year veterans of the hospital or city system, could also talk about commitment more easily than executives. Unlike the outward-looking, systems-thinking executives, more embedded in political dynamics, the department managers were dutiful, detail-oriented achievers who voiced commitment to the hospital, the city, their careers, their colleagues, their patients. Many used the word "love" to talk about their work as managers of major departments in a respected institution of an admittedly special city.

Some managers went on to voice support, affection and loyalty to the Hospital Administrator and his executive team. The group acknowledged the improve-ment, successes and outreach efforts of the executive team under the new leadership of the Hospital Administrator, including his success in moving the hospital into the modern age of computers. So discussion continued in a context of strong support for the hospital and its leadership, though some department managers were angry about the Administrator's style.

The 10∗STEP^{SM} technology was then introduced and applied to the topic of Communication. For *Day 2* and *Day 3*, the managers discussed in pairs, small groups and as a whole workshop, the essence of their communication patterns and strategies for improvement. One key issue was the structure, purpose and membership of the Department Managers' Meeting. Every other Friday after-noon, more or less, department managers who supervised more than ten people met with the executive team for announcements and reports. There was discon-tent with this meeting and some anger surfaced about the hospital administra-tor's demanding style and his tight control on information and decision making.

The department managers were divided into four problem-solving teams who chose to focus on improving communication, morale and the Friday meetings.

In the afternoon of *Day 3*, after small groups reported back their recommendations. The managers delegated the task of writing a draft statement to the senior consultant. Her best faith effort had mixed reactions.

The report had four sections, each one summarizing the recommendations of one of the small groups. The introduction to the report included a sentence describing an "affirmation of support, affection and loyalty to the hospital and its leadership," intended to invoke the department managers' team spirit. Some thought this "honey-coated" requests and covered up anger.

The report began by stating that the department managers' workshop focused on mechanisms to improve communication. The main conclusion was that the primary structures for effective cross-level and interdepartmental communication already existed, but that these structures needed to be opened up for better communication. The report itself had thirty-six recommendations briefly summarized below:

Part 1: Purpose, Roles and Structure.

1. The major functions of the Friday meeting include: sharing information; reporting activities and events; presenting and solving problems, especially interdepartmental issues; and providing a forum to add management input into administrative policy discussions.
2. The Friday meeting be expanded to include four kinds of meetings: department managers; division meetings; Problem-Solving Task Force Meetings; and Open Forum meetings quarterly or twice a year.

Part 2: Improving Communication at Friday Meetings.

3. People increase depth of information shared
4. The meeting day be changed—Fridays is awful
5. Standing committees report regularly
6. Information be shared about "external forces" and "political realities"—e.g.., the Mayor
7. More problem-solving opportunities
8. More manager input on issues affecting them
9. Clarification of who attends Friday meetings
10. UPDATES on important events/changes/projects
11. Agenda set prior to meeting, sent out ahead of time
12. Minutes of meetings sent to managers to share information with staff
13. More discussion of hospital mission, goals, major policies, changes, etc.
14. Mechanism for coordinating interdepartmental problem solving—i.e., Quality Circle Coordinating Committee
15. Review purpose & membership of hospital committees

---

16. POLICY: meetings have clearly-defined director or chairperson or facilitator; more thought out agendas and membership; agendas sent out early; mechanisms for follow up; and published minutes
17. Some form of managers policy committee to address issues of concern
18. Does Administrator's role include negotiating changes in city, state or federal rules [when requested by staff], e.g. job security issues
19. Staff clarifies its support and respect of the chain of command and encourages staff to use the chain of command first
20. Regularly scheduled Division Meetings be held
21. Division directors share more information
22. Rationale for clustering departments in present divisions be re-examined
23. More use of agendas and printed minutes
24. Interdepartmental problem solving for common interest task forces
25. An Open Forum held 2–4 times a year, for all staff, community members (maybe patients)—on mission, goals, projects, etc.
26. A mission statement be issued
27. Print weekly Bulletin of activities, meetings
28. More executive/mid management interaction
29. Executives do more MBWA—manage by walking around
30. More xerox machines, better intercom system

Part 3: Goals and Objectives.

31. Managers participate in developing clearly defined "management by objectives" (MBOs) for all departments including goals as defined by: City Hall, Health Department, the Hospital, Divisions, Departments, and Sub-Departments and that there be a comprehensive follow-up.

Part 4: Improving Morale, Support and Cooperation

32. Staff at all hospital levels be congratulated for a strong atmosphere of cooperation and accomplishment.
33. Executive and departmental managers make a concerted effort to guarantee that issues of concern be discussed in non-threatening atmosphere.
34. Executive and department managers share responsibility for modeling a friendly, smiling interface with patients and staff.
35. This new step in improved communication begin with dialogue about mission, goals and culture.
36. Follow-up discussions specifically focused on improved communication efforts be scheduled for some time in the future—perhaps every 6-8 weeks.

About the time the Administrator received the report (known as the "Lynn Kahn Draft"), he took some time off. When he came back, he was in some ways a new man. His executives reported that he now listened more carefully, asked everyone for their opinion more frequently, gave more information and more decisions over to his team and turned out to be a skillful and effective facilitator who could often bring the group to consensus on important and difficult issues. Reportedly, he was freer with praise and positive reinforcement for outstanding work. Executive team members reported their "amazement" and some could more easily talk about his political skills as a city official. For the executive team, the honeymoon was on.

Life was more difficult for the consultant. In a debriefing session with the senior consultant, the Administrator reported his concern (the consultant heard "anger") about "opening the can of worms" and the "demands" of the department managers. Did he have a rebellion on his hands? The consultant's response was to discuss the balance of power between department managers, executive team and Hospital Administrator. She emphasized that the managers wanted information and input into decision making, not authority to make executive decisions. They wanted to run their departments, executives could run the hospital and the boss could stay in charge.

The Administrator's response to the "Lynn Kahn Draft" was to give the department managers two meetings a month to run by themselves, developing their own leadership, agenda, structure and procedures. The department managers were stunned. The Administrator gave more than they asked for.

Meanwhile, executive team members were adapting to the Administrator's transformation. He was reportedly more approachable, the executive meetings were more effective, problems were getting solved and important hospital projects were turning out extra successful. Except for one or two very difficult relationships, there was improvement in communication and morale at the executive level. The executives were happy.

Housekeeping. The week after the department managers' workshop, the scheduled training for hospital porters began. The porter supervisors (due to scheduling problems) would be trained one month later in October. This, it is to be recalled, was the Administrator's primary interest: "To give the least recognized staff some attention and training."

From Tuesday through Friday, from 10:00 to 12:00 noon, five consultants met with about seventy-five porters to do problem-solving, team-building training. On *Day 1*, the porters divided themselves into four teams and then moved through the **10∗STEP**<u>SM</u> problem analysis and found solutions by consensus. Each of the four groups had the services of an outside facilitator (three blacks, one white) plus the senior consultant.

Again, typical of this institution, the multi-racial, multi-ethnic staff of house-keepers and porters went directly and honestly to the heart of the issues. The four teams chose to analyze and solve the following problems:

Group 1 chose as their problem "Seniority, Respect and Equality." These porters thought there was a lack of respect and equality in the system. They defined equality as: "When people are treated the same." They brainstormed solutions, many aimed at improving relationships with the porter supervisors:

SOLUTIONS: SENIORITY, RESPECT AND EQUALITY

1. Administration needs to reinforce equal treatment
2. We all need to stop prejudging people
3. Supervisors need to learn how to relate to people:
   a. Make clearer evaluations of our actions
   b. Get some management training
   c. Get some communication training
   d. Improve academic skills, reading, writing
   e. More effective evaluation of employees
   f. Better notification of testing for supervisor
   g. Get some motivation training
   h. Orientation/training of new staff by supervisor and not porter
   i. Supervisor should know all job functions and responsibilities
4. Identify systematic process for advancement, promotion in system
5. Have preparatory courses for Civil Service Test
6. More interaction with upper management, rap sessions and tours
7. Increase staffing to cut workload
8. Investigate high turnover rate
9. Develop efficient system for job assignment (splitting up wards)
10. Allow new staff time to adjust to new environment and job
11. Get uniforms, workers design uniforms
12. Have alternate holidays off
13. Work in job classification (i.e., not exchange porters with laundry)
14. Have respect for each other's work, especially porters and nurses

---

Group 2 chose as their problem for analysis "Keeping Wards Cleaner." They brainstormed a list of six solutions:

SOLUTIONS: KEEPING WARDS CLEANER

1. Clearer supervision of work done by "floaters"
2. Porters cooperate with each other and with floaters
3. Post a "What to do daily" list—no excuse for not cleaning
4. Methods of communication between porters and supervisors must be improved!
5. Supervisors only get involved in operations when necessary and without harrassment
6. Management should recheck porter assignments and priorities. There are easy-to-maintain wards and hard-to-maintain wards. If a porter must be assigned two wards, management must be aware and sensitive to ward condition. Assign one hard and one easy!

Group 2 went on to offer solutions to thirteen more problems, including recommendations about annual leave, sick leave, emergency phone calls and supervisors (e.g, "supervisors should get facts from porters;" "supervisors shouldn't low-rate porter in front of others, especially outside the department").

Group 3 was the angry group. They chose as their problem for analysis "Double Standards." They defined the problem clearly: "Double standards occur when formal or informal rules are applied differently to different people, including areas of unequal discipline, sick leave, vacations and late pay-checks." They brainstormed seventeen solutions:

SOLUTIONS: DOUBLE STANDARDS

1. Get new supervisors
2. Test supervisors' knowledge of job
3. Supervisors agree on procedures
4. Porters have one supervisor
5. Supervisors stay in assigned areas
6. Supervisors not give orders to porters out of area
7. Get a relief supervisor
8. Supervisors respect porters—not treat them as children
9. Supervisors conduct themselves as professionals
10. Supervisors stop harrassing porters
11. By seniority, ask porters one-on-one in January when they want vacations and settle it early
12. Don't insist or threaten porters to work holidays
13. If work one holiday, ASK if porter wants to work other holidays
14. Ask who wants to work holiday
15. Clarify "if stationed, you work holidays" policy
16. Can people scheduled off be allowed to work holidays?
17. Pay holiday and overtime pay on time

Group 4 chose to analyze the historical and sticky relationship between porters, orderlies and nurses. They focused on "How to Get Cooperation with Nursing Department." They brainstormed four solutions:

SOLUTIONS: HOUSEKEEPING & NURSING COOPERATION

1. Housekeeping supervisors and nursing supervisors meet at least quarterly to discuss each area of responsibility and let nursing supervisors know our supervisors back us 100%
2. Porters and aides meet as often as supervisors meet
3. Porters and porter supervisors meet to make sure our supervisors know what happens to us, each department knows their responsibilities, our supervisors back us and we know what's been agreed upon with Nursing Department
4. Give us more training and orientation: "Who does what job?" "What are differences between porters and orderlies?"

Finishing early, Group 4 went on to solve another problem: "How to get payroll checks on time, including on days off." Again, the supervisors were the target of a lot of anger. The solutions included: "Supervisors get off power trip, don't treat us like kids, give out checks when they are ready and give to people who have day-off without waiting for everyone else." The porters also complained that the kitchen personnel and nurses were taken care of better: "Their supervisors give them their checks when they come in."

On *Day 4* of the training, the porters reassembled. Each of the four groups reviewed its analysis and recommendations then chose two representatives for follow-up meetings. The Hospital Administrator came into this last meeting for a twenty-minute dialogue affirming his support for their problem-solving efforts. This symbolic gesture had a tremendously positive influence on subsequent events.

Follow-Through. The Housekeeping Manager (then acting, now permanent) got immediately into a series of follow-up and training meetings with his employees and the porter supervisors.

The Manager met with the eight representatives every Monday for one hour until everyone felt satisfied that each issue or recommendation was dealt with appropriately. Line by line, each group's report led to clarification and shared understanding. The street-wise Manager of Housekeeping also met with the porter supervisors for some home-spun training in communication, listening, honest evaluations, respect and clearer policy guidelines. At the same time, hospital executives provided more support for clarifying limits about discipline problems (e.g., absenteeism). The porter and porter supervisor meetings continued as a regular communication forum in the Housekeeping Department.

Porter Supervisors. Four weeks after the porter training, six porter supervisors met with two consultants for four hours to learn the problem-solving technology. After discussing their role as black supervisors, working with black, Hispanic and Asian porters, they chose for attention "Absenteeism." They defined the problem clearly. Staff are absent or AWOL because: lack of self-motivation, job not pleasant enough, job is embarrassing, drug abuse and alcoholism; also when there is not enough follow-through on disciplinary action, there is an increased workload causing doubling up, shifting assignments, more accidents and more absenteeism. They brainstormed solutions:

SOLUTIONS: ABSENTEEISM

- More upward mobility
- A rehabilitation program
- Training for dealing with personal problems at work
- Show employees we care/support them
- Give information about other jobs and promotions in the city
- Act quicker on disciplinary actions
- More meetings to communicate and share information
- Have a porter of the month
- Acknowledge who works hard

At a preannounced time, the three next levels of management (the Manager of Housekeeping and two executive team members), came into the meeting to discuss results. There was a strong sense of accomplishment. Later in the hallway, one executive team member said that he was "surprised those men could analyze and solve problems so effectively."

Follow-Up. The consultant's first follow-up meeting was with the department managers. About three months after the workshop, in a laborious two-hour meeting on a Monday afternoon, the department managers decided to turn down the Administrator's offer of meetings on their own. Opting for a more traditional balance of power, in addition to more information and quicker assessment of the Administrator's position, the department managers wanted the Administrator back in meetings. They also had specific recommendations for the Friday meetings. Three department managers took a week to write a memo to the Administrator, which read in part:

To: The Administrator

We met with Lynn Kahn on November 19 from 2–4 PM. Many items were discussed, especially the "Lynn Kahn Draft." Although items in the draft letter are concerns of the committee, they do not necessarily indicate our position. Our recommendations follow:

The purpose of the extended staff as we see it is to present and solve problems, especially interdepartmental issues; provide a forum to add management input into administration policy; pass information from Executive Administration to Departments and from Departments to Executive Administration; and report activities and events.

First and foremost in our structure, we desire biweekly meetings composed of department managers (as defined by those in the management session) and Administration (Executive Administrator and Executive Committee Members) with the proposed features:

1. A quarterly rotating chair/facilitator be appointed by Administration. [We have appointed the first chair.]

2. The agenda will be as follows:

   A. Review previous meeting's minutes.
   B. Hospital Committee Reports (as needed).
   C. Administration Update—on changes affecting us internally and externally.
   D. Old Business—items left unresolved from the prior meeting.
   E. New Business—items submitted from the membership by 12:00 Noon, Thursday prior to the Monday meeting
   F. Problem solving
   G. Department Overview for staff to become aware of functions of other departments (five-minute presentation followed by five minutes of discussion).

3. Monday afternoons have been a successful time for meetings.

We acknowledge your efforts in seeking our input into the structure of this meeting, problem solving, conflict resolution and team building. Your reception of our proposed input was well received by most of those in attendance. With our suggested changes outlined in this memorandum, we look forward to continuing this dialogue and forum, which we anticipate will provide for discussion of differences in a nonthreatening and cooperative environment.

Yet to be resolved is the membership composition of the Friday meeting, which is a difficult issue. This will be our first problem-solving effort.

We feel that a review of the aforementioned purpose and structure will be necessary after a three-month trial period.

Again, thank you for your support. While this is only the first step in the long process as defined by Lynn Kahn's "Draft" statement, we look forward to a positive, productive relationship which will enhance the lives of our patients, clients and employees, as well as perpetuation of the deep feelings we all share for the Hospital.

Sincerely,

Your Department Managers

The Administrator and consultant, on moderately civil terms by now, decided the Administrator did not have a revolt on his hands at all. The Administrator had given them more freedom than they wanted and was willing to go with the recommendations, though he did not particularly want someone else to facilitate his department managers meetings, now often scheduled for Mondays.

Porter Supervisors Follow-Up. Two months after the porter training, a two-hour follow-up meeting with the porter supervisors showed great progress. Fourteen new porters allowed a better distribution of work. Most porters no longer had two wards; most were now responsible for one specific ward. Following the porter requests, the supervisors made ward assignments. Porters felt more personal responsibility for the cleanliness standards of "my ward," according to the now smiling supervisors. Following porter requests, the schedule was rearranged so more porters had more weekends off.

The supervisors reported more rapport between themselves and the porters: "we're listening better so there's more trust." They thought they had become better mediators in Housekeeping/Nursing conflicts: "We stand up for our porters, we don't cave in to Nursing." They discussed the relationship between mostly white nurses and mostly black porters; they reported, "It's getting better here." Later, an executive team member told a story about a porter at a ward's annual Christmas Party. He had been singled out for appreciation and acknowledgment when the ward Head Nurse reviewed the previous year's accomplishments. The porter's pleasure was obvious.

The supervisors also thought the porters were working better: "Their attitude is better, they come forward and tell us problems. There's more honesty. There's a common effort. The hospital is cleaner." The discipline problems— especially the serious abusers of sick leave—were being dealt with quicker: "The bad eggs are out, so there is more respect for administration. The attitude has changed. You can't do nothing and get away with it." There were still issues to be resolved, such as requests for more technical training and still some concerns about Nursing.

The best part of this follow-up meeting was conversation about "the turn-arounds." Some porters who had had "bad attitudes" were now better workers, more responsible, and the supervisors thought the porters were proud to work for this hospital. Follow-up data for six months after the porter workshops, showed dramatic improvements in absenteeism and days lost to industrial accidents.

One Year Later. In the summer of 1985, the consultant had follow-up meetings with the Hospital Administrator, three members of the executive team and the Housekeeping Manager. The meeting with the Administrator was in a delightful French restaurant. In response to the question, "So how's it going?" the Administrator reported:

I'm very happy. I'm very proud of my team, they're terrific. There's a lot of cohesion and team effort and creative work going on right now. Communication is excellent. It's the best team on the city payrolls. The hospital just won some more national awards for geriatric care and we all feel great. Our problem team member left the executive staff and there's less conflict at our staff meetings.

The consultant responded that the new executive team member, an articulate, successful black man was a "healthy choice" and bound to have a good impact at all levels of the organization.

Talk turned to the department managers. The Administrator reported that they had recently decided to go back to meetings with the executive team present. It seemed that the first department manager to take the role of facilitator had wanted to rotate the role to someone else and no one so far had volunteered. The administrator thought that the department managers had improved the structure of their meetings, that more information was now shared, there was less anxiety about speaking up and more open dialogue. However, there was no emerging leadership and the group wanted the Administrator back in their meetings. The consultant commented that the Administrator's energy and leadership in large group meetings was missed by the troops.

The conversation then turned to the Housekeeping Department. The Administrator reported that he was pleased with how the hospital looked, that it was noticeably cleaner and that the porters were more pleasant, their attitude had improved and they seemed to feel part of the hospital team as a whole. He knew the Housekeeping Manager had been meeting with his supervisors, they had cleaned up some personnel problems, the supervisors seemed more professional and the department was doing well. He had just given the Housekeeping Manager an assistant—a young white man.

The meeting with the three executive team members revealed some positive changes. They reported that the Administrator was giving more information and more support. The Housekeeping Manager reported improved communication and more access to the executive team and their decision-making process. In her meeting, the Nursing Director reported: "Terrific!! Staff feels great, there's a lot of communication and we're talking about some ways to celebrate how well things are going." In the fall of 1985, the senior consultant worked with all hospital Head Nurses (see Case Study #12).

In 1986, the senior consultant attended several hospital social functions and had informal follow-up conversations with key hospital managers, executives and employees. The consensus seemed to be that there was better communication among peers— executives talked more frequently and freely to each other, the department managers and the Head Nurses were more likely to meet formally and informally to solve cross-departmental and shared problemsand House-keeping was doing well. Several suggested that the next consulting focus would need to be cross-level communication—information flowed freely and effectively within levels of the hierarchy and for the most part across departments, however, more attention was needed on cross-level interaction (especially between department managers and the executive team). In 1987, the Administrator left the hospital for a university position.

* * * * *

Change. Time passes, people do make efforts. People don't really change personalities but they do learn to listen better, to communicate more easily, to work more attentively in groups, to give more appreciation and to strive more clearly toward excellence and quality in products and services.

INTER-GROUP CONFLICT

The next case study makes three points: groups in conflict can be turned around in a very short period of time; the key to genuine change is follow-up and maintenance of solutions agreed upon in the heat of consensus; and there needs to be a clear structure when large groups break off into small groups to problem solve and then negotiate with each other. When conflict resolution involves many small groups, and it is time for the groups to report back to the conference as a whole, typical directions might be:

I want a Representative from each problem-solving team to report back to us your group's analysis, solutions and recommendations for action. Please also say something about your group dynamics. Each group has ten minutes to report back. There will be time for anyone to ask a clarifying question after the Representative's report.

Usually, the group leaders or organizational authorities sit near where the consultant stands. After each Representative's report and any clarifying questions, the consultant reviews each item on the recommended solution list one at a time and asks the boss if he or she wants to agree or disagree on the spot or think the suggestion over. This item-by-item clarification is especially useful with people who have a strong need for closure. Most often, the majority of the suggestions are obvious next steps to improved communication (e.g., meeting twice a month or for fifteen-minute huddles at change of shifts). Typically, most of the report back is a list of suggestions easily agreed to by the boss. When suggestions are tabled for further discussion or delegated to a task force, it is useful for the consultant to ask for a specific time and place for the next discussion or first task force meeting. In summary, the consultant goes through the list of solutions to clarify the action plan which is usually the weakest part of the Representative's report back.

Sometimes solutions require the agreement of peer groups in conflict. For example, if all the departments at the plant need to share information better, then sub-group negotiations can be scheduled—for right then, the next meeting or between now and the follow-up session. The consultant might suggest that each of the following pairs of groups meet for one hour according to the following schedule to talk about improving communication:

Transportation and Marketing	1:00 - 2:15
Production and Sales	1:00 - 2:15
Transportation and Production	2:30 - 3:45
Marketing and Sales	2:30 - 3:45
Transportation and Sales	4:00 - 5:15
Marketing and Production	4:00 - 5:15

Experience suggests that most of the small groups report back solutions which authorities often agree to or are at least willing to support a task force for further discussion. In this approach, about 95% of small group requests are agreed to by organizational authorities. Most of the rest of the Solutions are to be worked out in task forces or between sub-groups.

Case Study #29: The One-Day Turn Around

The Vice President of Sales asked the consultant to "do conflict resolution with our managers about the problems between the sales managers and Quality Review. You can have the third day of a four-day All Managers Meeting for twenty-seven division, branch and group managers."

At the appointed time, the VP welcomed all the managers and introduced the consultant who said:

I have been asked to design today's session to improve communication between sales managers and Quality Review. I have designed some activities to teach you problem analysis and problem solving. We will spend about three hours on general activities, then an hour sharing perceptions about the two groups in conflict, then two hours to generate a strategy and plan to improve commnication between Sales and QR.

The next three segments were Introductions, a Warm-Up Game and discussion of Myers-Briggs personality types (see Chapter 2).

At 10:25 AM, the consultant introduced a segment called "Sharing Perceptions." The twenty-seven managers were divided into their five naturally occurring sub-groups: Sales Groups #1, #2 and #3 Quality Review (also known as QR or Group #4) and Group #5 the clerical managers. From the

Sales perspective, Quality Review was an unpopular inspection team. QR sent memos and made telephone calls when the Sales staff submitted forms or reports which missed rigid, detailed legal and procedural standards. Once in a while they sent "Commendatory" memos. On the other side, Quality Review genuinely wanted to be "helpful, providing assistance." Group #5, clerical managers, were neutral co-workers.

The five groups were given these directions: "Each group answers these four questions, writing their comments on large paper to be reported back at 11:00."

1. What are your perceptions of your group?
2. What are your perceptions of Group #4?
3. What do you think Group #4 thinks of you?
4. How would you describe the Field-Quality Review relationship?

The consultant and the VP wandered around, checking in on the group discussions, which revealed some angry accusations and inflammatory language. Meeting in the hallway, the consultant checked in with the executive: "How are you doing?" He replied: "Well, it's angrier than I thought, but I think the discussions are productive." At 11:00 the groups came back to the large conference room. The consultant said:

> Each group selects a representative to read off the answers to the four questions. The ground rule is: THERE IS NO DISCUSSION OF THE ISSUES. THERE IS ONLY READING THE LIST OF PERCEP-TIONS AND ASKING CLARIFYING QUESTIONS.[91]

Each representative had about three minutes to read responses to the four questions. The lists revealed anger about evaluation, frivolous negative memos, power struggles, productivity standards and expectations about the quality of work. The admitted irony was that the Sales department was in fact quite effective and successful, as measured by district, regional and national production reports. They produced a lot of quality clients and one person called the problem "perfection in paperwork."

The lists were read out loud, the participants took it all in, few questions were asked and then the consultant said, "Now each group huddles in a corner and spends four minutes coming up with a one-sentence response statement. How do you feel, what is your reaction to what is being said here, to the perceptions being shared?" The groups huddled and responded:

> - There are common themes in our perceptions
> - A lot is similar
> - Relieved to get it on the table
> - Shocked at intensity of anger toward review
> - Seems like we all want to solve the problem

The consultant then said, "I want everyone to take a few deep breaths, and as you exhale imagine all the negative feelings and images are released from your body, and imagine as you exhale that you blow these images into the middle of the room, right over there, where I'm pointing. Let go of the negative, put it in a little dust pile in the middle of the floor. Breathe, breathe fresh air, have a pleasant lunch and we'll reconvene at 1:00." People walked outside mostly in small clusters and almost everyone ended up in the same large restaurant known for a wonderful salad bar.

At 1:00, the consultant asked, "Anything happen at lunch that related to the morning events, anything important left over from earlier discussions?" There were few responses, so directions for the next event were given: "We will spend until 2:30 solving the problem: How can we improve the relationship between field agents and review staff? You have been divided into four groups, mixing up all the sections. A person has been designated as facilitator, and one person from Group # 4 is in each discussion group. The facilitator will not give opinions about the issue. The facilitator role is to help the group move through the **10∗STEP**$^{\underline{SM}}$ problem-solving model. The first step is given: improving the field-staff relationship. The discussion rooms are posted. If no questions, go and report back at 2:30 with an action plan for improving the field-staff relationship."

At 2:30, the groups reported back their analysis, lists of causes and many overlapping solutions to the problem. The emphasis was more information and training about procedures and standards, more communication between QR and the Sales groups, discussion sessions so field and staff could know who each other are, and better use of a newsletter announcing changes in procedures ("So QR helps educate us and stops playing "GOTCHA!!!"). There was a lot of discussion about review memos with a stronger attitude of wanting to educate, provide information and solve problems.

The consultant asked for clarity about the NEXT STEP. After ten minutes of discussion, the consensus emerged that the manager in charge of Group #4 would be responsible to coordinate a task force to summarize and implement the solutions. The task force would include one sales manager, one salesperson and one QR analyst from each geographic area. The task force would meet within the next twenty-five days.

After discussion of applying workshop learning to their role as manager, and time for each person to give a closing statement, the workshop ended at 3:00 PM.

· · · · ·

Perhaps the two most useful lessons of Case Study #29 are (1) when the conditions are right, most conflict can be turned around in a relatively short period of time and (2) follow-up attention with details about next steps is the key to long-term resolution.

COMMENTS ABOUT COMMUNICATION

When work groups brainstorm lists of problems, or "What do you want to change around here," more often than not, COMMUNICATION appears on the list. Often, there are requests to improve communication in many ways—top-down, bottom-up, between departments, between executives and mid-level managers, between similar functions in different geographical areas and between peers and co-workers.

A useful team-building or conflict resolution strategy is asking the group to focus on the one issue of "Improving Communication." When there's not been enough time for pre-session preparation, interviews or surveys, and many other times when it's simply a good idea, the group can use the 10∗STEP^{SM} Model on the problem of "Improving Communication."

There are four general trends in the analysis and solutions given:

1. Changing the structure of existing meetings (e.g., more often, less often, fifteen minutes every morning, once every three months, more agendas, less agenda items, agendas ahead of meetings or agendas created at the meeting, managers meet monthly and informally on their own time to get to know each other better). Sometimes groups of people doing similar or related work admit they have never met and decide to begin meeting; or groups with a history of meeting one-on-one or "as necessary" decide to meet on a regular schedule.

2. Changing the content of the group meetings (e.g., more time for departmental updates, more focus on inter-departmental issues, less announcements and more interaction, less repeat discussions and more time for closure and action plans).

3. Changing the dynamics of group meetings (e.g., less scapegoating, more appreciation, more listening, more use of consensus, less use of consensus and quicker decisions, more awareness of sexist remarks, more awareness of cross-departmental issues, managers accept more responsibility for information they need).

4. Changing the context of group meetings (e.g., agreeing on a philosophy statement, values statement or culture statement with items about respect, participation and support).

It is most useful to ask groups to focus on internal communciation before dealing with cross-departmental or other organizational issues.

INTERRACIAL PEACEMAKING

Can a problem-solving approach bring peace where there is racial or ethnic tension? Can dialogue and self-study change perceptions influenced by centuries of ethnic conflict? The answer is YES.

Perhaps the most successful approach to cross-cultural and interracial conflict resolution is the training model of Dr. Price Cobbs, co-author of *Black Rage*, and a management consultant with twenty-five years experience as a conflict mediator.[92] Dr. Cobbs has written and lectured extensively on the dynamics and effect of racism on the victim and the perpetrator. He has developed a clinical model, Ethnotherapy, capable of changing attitudes and assumptions that arise from racial, ethnic, cultural or value differences. This section describes Cobbs' model in a consultation set in America's Deep South. The senior consultant is Dani Perkins, certified to use Cobbs' model.

Perkins is a petite, 34-year old, dynamic, effective, black organization consultant. In this two-day workshop, she and a white co-consultant are leading twenty-one white, male, southern managers through Cobbs' model. The men are all managers for a chain of grocery stores and their participation has been required by corporate leadership who wanted the store managers to understand where racism and sexism block teamwork. Corporate headquarters had decided that financial success depends upon a manager's ability to work with women and minorities. Into the room of whiteness, filled with images rooted in slavery, entered Perkins and her partner.

The interview questions to Perkins were: Describe a racism workshop. Visualize the best one! What do you do? What are the segments of your program? What's your theory, approach and model? What are the critical turning points? You know there is a lot of anger and rage and hate at first. How do you turn it around? What are the major issues? Who says what?

So Perkins described a Management Effectiveness Workshop. The stated purpose was "to increase the majority manager's effectiveness in managing multi-cultural, multi-ethnic work teams; to raise consciousness about race and gender issues, including how you respond to people who are different, and how you impact individuals, subordinates and the system; and to begin the process of changing behavior."

Case Study #30: The Legacy of Slavery

In the morning of *Day 1*, Perkins started with an introduction about Cobbs' model, stating the purpose of the workshop and its Ground Rules based on openness, honesty, candor, feedback and confidentiality. She outlined the conceptual operating framework: personal and external forces influence your style in the organization and your way of valuing minorities. She stated, "Your managerial challenge is to define racism and for the first time explore the racial messages given and received in your work." She goes on to talk about affirmative action and the costs of racism. Here, the managers started to resist, complain or ignore her, but she continued with a statement about the phases of racism: overt, covert and systematic. For the rest of *Day 1*, they play Free Association. Perkins asks "What have you heard about black women? Fill in these lists with your free associations: Blacks are . . . Women are . . ." They discuss the issues and the nature of sterotypes until the end of the first day.

On the morning of *Day 2*, Perkins began:

> The Deficit Model views "differences" as "less than." Anyone different than the majority manager is perceived and categorized based on external differences rather than who they are as a person and without personal interaction or relationship development.

> So, where do you buy in? Are differences less than, equal to or better than expected. How do these images influence evaluations? Budgets?

Perkins then talks about black realities of corporate life. The deficit model is the basis of why minorities may experience isolation, loneliness, a double-bind on aggression and overscrutiny. According to Perkins, mistrust lies between blacks and whites as a barrier to authentic relationships and effective teamwork. Some blacks believe they work twice as hard while struggling to maintain ethnic identity in an organization that continually questions their loyalty. White managers struggle to understand their role in shaping a multicultural organization.

In the workshop, Perkins challenged the white managers:

> What are your underlying assumptions about who is lazy, ambitious, entitled, irresponsible, dumb, insensitive, untrustworthy, oversexed or violent? What is your gut level response? What is happening between managers and employees in your stores? What is happening at the corporate level? What is the impact of historical images? Where is racism operating in your work setting?

Perkins then talked about *Black Rage* and the impact of race on evaluating a subordinate's performance. The consultants guided the group through discussions of how people react to race and gender and what pushes people's rage buttons.

According to Perkins, the Cobbs' model builds a shared reality through discussion. The consultants start from a place of distrust and after discussion about unconscious assumptions, parental influence and black realities, the group starts to appreciate what they are learning and dialogue flows easier.

Perkins could recall some dialogue that was a genuine turning point for one group. The action included lots of anger, then honesty, then relief, openness to the message, then respect and affection.

John: I see affirmative action as reverse discrimination. The Bakke decision shows there's discrimination against white men.

Tom: Yeah, we're promoting unqualified people.

Perkins: How can you say that? Examine the numbers. The numbers show underrepresentation of minorities and females. Everything points to your resistance. Do you know any situations when someone has been promoted in this system that's not qualified?

Ed: Yeah, but you don't know a job walking into one.

Mark: If you examine job qualifications or job specifications and most appointments, seldom does anyone meet specifications.

Tom: Those actions are o.k. unless it's a minority or female. Then we scream.

Jack: I've hired a white male without qualifications because it was a political decision.

Mark: Yeah, I was recommended for a promotion and didn't understand why I got it and someone said you must have been at the right place at the right time so don't worry about it.

Perkins: So you could promote minorities and females. If racism is so expensive and costs so much and affirmative action is a solution to the problem, why are the numbers off and why do you have emotional responses to these issues?

About here, the attitude has changed. There is open discussion. The problem is discussed on its merits. According to Perkins, the racism and sexism issues are (1) fear about job loss and (2) fear about giving up vested interest of seeing minorities as less than, which is giving up a way of life.

In Perkin's words:

The shift is when you see what the costs are in training and recruiting. Bottom line measures are underlying currents. There's lots of resistance, so the positive view of the highest ranking managers helps them confront the issues honestly.

• • • • •

WORK-RELATED DREAMS

A common pattern in the case studies of this chapter is that transformation occurs when the pain of the conflict outweighs the pain of honesty. The role of dreams is less clear and more personal.

Dreams are among our most powerful personal tools for problem solving and conflict resolution. This problem-solving view of dreams is expertly described in Gayle Delaney's *Living Your Dreams*.[93] Dreams help restore psychological harmony and promote individual growth. The images and actions of our dreams spring from inner wisdom and contain needed information to balance our waking life. Whatever role we play in the dramas of conflict, dreams work to restore harmony. Dreams always point towards the path of wholeness and well-being. Even nightmares are intended to help, pointing out the need for attention to troublesome parts of our lives. According to Delaney, it is important to approach the study of dreams with curiosity and avoid judging dream events as good or bad.

The study of dreams is as old as history. Since ancient times individuals and whole cultures have used dreams for problem solving. The Iroquois of America, the Asclepians of ancient Greece and probably the Senoi of Malaysia used their dreams for guidance concerning tribal problems.

This problem-solving approach is a sharp counterpoint to Freud's view that dreams are masked statements of pathology and mechanisms to disguise and discharge "unacceptable" sexual and aggressive impulses and conflicts. Freud also described dreams which repeated early traumatic events to control psychological damage.

Unlike Freud, Jung emphasized the healing aspect of dreams. Jung believed that dreams integrate conscious and unconscious needs, moving the dreamer toward harmony and wholeness. Jung described how dream symbols represent universal images, touching the human need for spiritual meaning.

According to Delaney, you are the producer, director, writer and star of the movies of your mind. You created the whole show to deliver a message. Understanding your dream message moves you toward well-being.

Delaney describes how to "ask your dreams" for help with a specific problem or conflict. Since antiquity, people have used conscious intent to focus dream energy on specific topics. Delaney calls this "dream incubation" and recommends the following steps:

Step 1: Choose the right night—not too tired, no alcohol, drugs or pills.

Step 2: Day notes—write out a few sentences about the events of the day.

Step 3: Lights!!—before sleep, discuss the specific issue with your self, writing down important ideas: What are the causes of the problem? What are alternative solutions? Does living with the problem feel safer than solving it?

Step 4: Incubation Phrase—write a one-line sentence that describes what you want or need.

Step 5: Focus! Camera!—turn off the lights, close your eyes, repeat the incubation phrase and let yourself fall asleep.

Step 6: Action!—write down dreams as soon as you awake. Write down any associations to dream elements or the dream as a whole.

The dreams you produce in response to a request for help or the spontaneous dreams you produce each night may need some thought before the dream message is clear. Delaney's method of dream interpretation is called dream interviewing. You the Dreamer interview You the Producer by asking key questions about the elements and events of your dreams. You wrote the script so you are the best available expert on the meaning of the dream.

You will have interpreted your dream in a meaningful way when you have an "AHA" response. Something "clicks" with the right interpretation. You understand something you did not know before. The new understanding often includes ideas for action regarding a waking life situation.

According to Delaney, appreciating dream puns, metaphors and the creative playfulness of your dream life will help you in the adventure of learning from your dreams. She recommends an attitude of patience, curiosity and acceptance and reminds us that dreams always offer help, showing our weaknesses with humor and our strengths with beauty.

Work-Related Dreams. Dreams contain information to put together the puzzles of work-related problems and conflicts. Sometimes this happens spontaneously and straightforwardly. For example, toward the end of Chapter 3, I had spent the evening sorting out my thoughts about Group Roles and that night I had this dream:

I am telephoned by a women who tells me she works in a Chicago convent. She requests my services as a consulting psychologist. I ask "What are the important issues?" She responds "I've been trying to get authority to call you for a year. The problem is that there are fixed rules for rotating the roles. We don't have any choice. It's terrible."

First, the dream reminded me that Chapter 3 did not clearly state how important it is to rotate the roles of Facilitator, Recorder, Process Observer, Representative and Timekeeper. I also understood the dream to be a reminder of the theme of sharing psychological roles—anger, support, analysis and so on. Theoretically, group maturity means sharing reponsibilities on many levels of participation. Associating to other dream elements I remembered I went to college near Chicago and writing this book was like living in a convent. Only several years later did I see the dream as questions to myself about my authority and leadership.

Sometimes dream messages come through with great impact. A mid-level business manager described a dream which convinced him to make a major life change:

> In the dream, I was in the elevator shaft of my office buiding. I was on top of the elevator between the roof of the elevator and the top of the building. The elevator moved up. I got smashed. I woke up, shaking.

When asked, "What did you think the dream was about?" the manager replied, "My job was dangerous to my health. I resigned soon after."

Obviously, not all dreams are warnings of impending doom. A mid-level manager in a large high-technology corporation told a graduate business class about the following dream. She had just that week finished writing a manual about a computer-based system for co-ordinating technical, financial and administrative information.

> Some man is trying to print something from the computer when the paper jams in the printer. He can't fix it. I take the machine apart. The paper is crooked by seven holes on one side. I straighten out the paper until it matches perfectly.

For this manager, the dream was a message that her manual matched the needs of the system perfectly. She asked for (and got) a raise and a promotion.

The above dreams were spontaneous. Incubating your dreams also produces results. An organization development consultant and colleague of the author asked her dreams for help with a consultation in a large hospital:

> In this dream I am called in to consult to a school. The problem is that the children do not complete their work assignments. I am asked if there is something wrong with them. I look around. The teachers are marching in and out of the classroom, interrupting the work.

The consultant started transferring her understanding of the dream to her hospital work:

> The problem is not the quality of care. The hospital staff have the ability to 'complete their work assignments,' but the administration is too chaotic. Roles and policies are not clear enough. Also, I need to look at how my work interrupts. Maybe I've been giving too much advice and need to listen more.

The consultant decided to focus her energies on developing a strong relationship with departmental managers and suggested meetings to clarify roles and responsibilities.

Sometimes dream images are quite vivid, but the message is not clear for a long time. Here is a dream whose full message is still out of my grasp. I had this dream the night after I served as Process Observer at an Interdepartmental Task Force for Women meeting at The White House in Washington, D. C. during the Carter administration. This was a very exciting time for me. The meeting was in the Roosevelt Room next to the Oval Office:

> In this dream I am back in the Roosevelt Room setting up chairs for a Cabinet meeting. I set up two extra chairs and mark them with two signs: Secretary of Success and Secretary of Failure.

Using typical Gestalt techniques, I tried to identify with every element in the dream. I was drawn to the paintings on the walls, especially the picture of Teddy Roosevelt charging up San Juan Hill. My associations ended with images of my generally enthusiastic and sometimes impulsive personality along with thoughts about success, failure and political power. The dream alluded to the structure of cabinet offices and associations led to thoughts about successful teamwork at the federal level, separation of powers, interaction and cooperation. This book is in part a response to the questions I asked myself after this dream.

WORKING GUIDELINES

Ten key points about peacemaking through dialogue can be made from the examples in this chapter:

1. Peacemaking is problem solving—the primary focus is the analysis of specific conflict issues, such as diplomatic recognition or policies about paychecks.

2. A neutral third party can facilitate dialogue between opponents. Consultants design the structure of dialogue meetings, encourage participation, manage angry exchanges, interpret, summarize, report observations and make recommendations. Neutrality seems to mean supporting the views of all sides, unafraid to display passion in the pursuit of peace.

3. Underneath positions in conflict are shared needs and compatible interests. Despite the anger, participants in conflict resolution generally want to improve communication and the ability to work or live together.

4. Peacemaking occurs as differences in perception become a source of curiosity not conflict. This is a conclusion Kurt Lewin reached over forty years ago when he studied the social psychology of racial conflict. Conflict resolution begins as opponents recognize that different people see the same event in different ways. "I brought the issues up before" and "I had no idea" are different perceptions of the same event: previous discussions. Peacemaking includes the learning that different human beings perceive, experience and respond to the same event in different ways.

5. Peacemaking surfaces individual differences in values, personality, motivation, style of handling conflict and typical group behavior. In one conversation, Henry is angry, Kate feels invisible, Susan is hurt, Jan is afraid and Sarah is supportive. Peacemaking means we learn to identify, appreciate and channel the differences among us.

6. Peacemaking through dialogue presses us to voice our perceptions, pushing us to clarify our sense of SELF identity. Peacemaking is a confrontation with the truth of our individual social and psychological reality: What is this fight about? What side are my friends on? Who's right and who's wrong? What is important to me now? How do I know the truth? Jung used the term "individuation" to describe this journey of self-discovery. Peacemaking through dialogue is strongly connected to our individual struggles with meaning, maturity and identity.

7. Individuals joined together for dialogue generate a larger system of psychological relationships—the group process and its network of connected interactions. Stepping back, the dynamics of the group-as-a-whole can be observed—such patterns as hostility toward authority, scapegoating, support and analysis.

8. Group behavior may be observed and reported as feedback for self-correction and problem solving. The most valuable contribution of third party mediators is feedback about group-wide dynamics: "The main issues right now are trust and betrayal."

9. All patterns emerge from a shared field of energy. President Carter's mediating comments explicitly tapped the shared field of energy at Camp David. He often spoke of areas of agreement, consequences of failure, the value of a signed treaty, the benefits of peace and the opportunity of the moment.

10. Peacemaking taps patterns of balance and rhythms of harmony across multiple levels of reality. This is the conclusion of the chapters which follow.

Technically, peacemaking is the rational analysis of shared problems peppered with inspired insights and interventions. Psychologically, peacemaking is a transformative process which changes fundamental perceptions. Participants move from the classical perspective of You versus Me to an organic worldview where even enemies share systems of relationships. The art of peacemaking blends the techniques of creative problem solving, an awareness of individual differences and the ability to give feedback about group process.

Chapter 9

SUPPORT:
Holding Together

Yet everything that touches us, you and me,
takes us together as a bow's stroke does,
that out of two strings draws a single voice.
Upon what instrument are we two spanned?
And what player has us in his hand?
O sweet song.

Rainer Maria Rilke

Support is caring about the well-being of each other. Support is the behavior generally called friendship and it potentially emerges in all face-to-face dialogue. Support is complicated, it includes: belonging, affection, loyalty, nurturance, sensuality, sexuality, creativity, intimacy and spirituality.

Social science research shows that dialogue strengthens the patterns of support. Talking about different viewpoints and common ground moves people through cycles of testing, sharing and trusting. Continued dialogue brings new learning and shared identity. Even when the group experience has been difficult and filled with conflict, individuals accept face-to-face discussions as a valuable opportunity for learning and problem solving. Along the way, people feel closer. This closeness both helps and hinders the progress of peacemaking.

This chapter shows that dialogue strengthens support and continued dialogue brings new learning and shared identity.

SUPPORT

BEHAVIORS OF SUPPORT

Support is connecting, caring and holding together. Support is just one of the forces which attracts people to a particular group, or keeps them together when the going gets tough. Cohesion is the sum of the forces to be in a group minus the sum of the forces to be out of the group. Cohesion is the balance of rewards and costs of group membership, the balance of belonging and being alone.[94] Some of the forces of cohesion are charted below; support is a personal reward of group membership.

COHESION: ATTRACTION TO THE GROUP

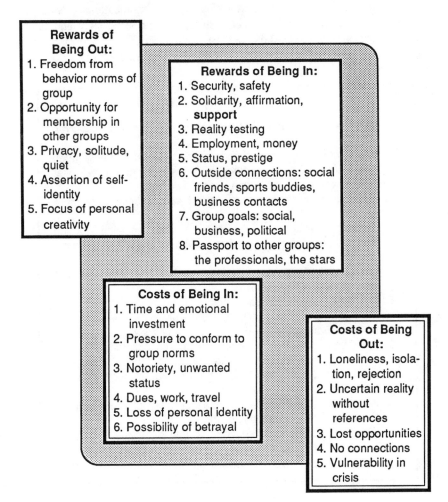

Rewards of Being Out:
1. Freedom from behavior norms of group
2. Opportunity for membership in other groups
3. Privacy, solitude, quiet
4. Assertion of self-identity
5. Focus of personal creativity

Rewards of Being In:
1. Security, safety
2. Solidarity, affirmation, **support**
3. Reality testing
4. Employment, money
5. Status, prestige
6. Outside connections: social friends, sports buddies, business contacts
7. Group goals: social, business, political
8. Passport to other groups: the professionals, the stars

Costs of Being In:
1. Time and emotional investment
2. Pressure to conform to group norms
3. Notoriety, unwanted status
4. Dues, work, travel
5. Loss of personal identity
6. Possibility of betrayal

Costs of Being Out:
1. Loneliness, isolation, rejection
2. Uncertain reality without references
3. Lost opportunities
4. No connections
5. Vulnerability in crisis

Genuine communication (learning about each other, giving and receiving feedback) brings awareness and closeness. As people learn about each other's viewpoints, they pause for self-study and learn more about themselves. The authoritarian plant manager and the controlling hospital administrator learn that employees suffer from their demands; they think about their style, change some behaviors, feel vulnerable at first and then stronger as employee morale and effectiveness improve. Or, white men confront their stereotypes: assumptions and beliefs about blacks and women. They are perhaps stunned into awareness, then relieved as old tensions lessen, and the world makes more sense. A context of support encourages healthy change.

In a Business School's graduate course on Human Behavior, class members had met for fifteen sessions and a Weekend Communications Workshop, with a classroom structure that mixed lecture, team projects, large and small group discussions. On the last day of class, the teacher asked, "How have you changed over time? Have you been a support group for each other?" They responded:

A SUPPORT GROUP:

1. We have been sharing time and space together. This has given us identity as a group.
2. The level of involvement has increased. No matter how much you talk or the way you talk, you show more of yourself over time. Everybody has become more involved.
3. There's more trust, more comfort with silence and more support.
4. Support is giving information to each other, knowing you can ask for information, giving encouragement and showing appreciation.
5. We learned about groups, roles and what happens when our energy level is high or low.
6. We're more open with each other.
7. I understand individual differences better.
8. It's okay to be yourself—very quiet or very active.
9. We communicate and perceive with less distortion. We've learned to look through the windows of perception. Everyone looks through the windows differently, or through different windows.
10. We give each other more accurate feedback with more support. We want to help, and we know how.
11. We have become a group. We share an identity.
12. There's still testing the water. We look to see how the conversation is going, what's important, do I want to jump in or not.

> 13. There are specific events we shared together—when we re-
> belled against the consultants during the Weekend, when Jack
> walked out of the meeting, when Jason changed his leadership
> style, when Jon discovered group process and when we pre-
> sented our team projects. We have a history that gives our
> group meaning.
> 14. There's more acceptance of individual differences.
> 15. There's different kinds of membership—belonging to the whole
> class, the team projects, the small groups and the secret
> meetings.
> 16. There's more support, because we spent time together and
> talked to each other.

When individuals join together for genuine group discussion, support naturally emerges from the time spent together. When dynamics become difficult, these alliances hold the group together. Ultimately, this holding together is the source of achievement, friendship and self-discovery. In any group setting, the patterns of support are always present.

Words of Support. The AU Research Groups led to four conclusions about support:[95]

1. Support comes alive through words. Support is talking about "positive" thoughts, feelings and behaviors:

"I appreciate your opinion."
"Thanks for saying that."
"I feel taken care of in here."
"I didn't know you wanted to be hugged by me."
"I want to move us four closer."
"I like gentleness and peace."

2. The more time people spend working together, the more words of support they use. A statistical procedure called a trend analysis showed a significant increase in AFFILIATION words for all groups over time. Over eight 90-minute sessions, people spoke a statistically significant increase of support words.

3. Support implies increasing trust and increasing discussion of personal thoughts and feelings. There are three main types of support and affiliation words:

• Positive statements ("I appreciate that").
• Kinship words (mother, father, wife, son, daughter, grandparents, etc.).
• Belonging words (we, our, us, ours).

When a group starts using the phrase "our group" a powerful shift in identity has occurred. The two words are a subtle reflection of emerging patterns. The next chapter shows how the phrase "our group" balances personal pain and needs.

4. Support increased in quantity and changed in quality over time. Early support was very general: "Our difficulty is confronting the consultant." Early support was also often about external people and events: "My father was like that".

Later, support was more personal, more direct and more likely to be about a here-and-now event: "Our group is in a certain way like a marriage." Later it also showed more balance between self concern and concern for others. For example, later support included the questions: "How are you feeling about that?" "You look upset." Or, "You've been quiet for a while, what do you think?"

In summary, dialogue brings more words of friendship, increased self-disclosure and more words about group identity. Belonging and loyalty emerge from participation as people learn to care for each other. These changes in the quality of support demonstrate that group behavior evolves over time. This topic of group maturity will be discussed at the end of this chapter.

Patterns of Support. In face-to-face dialogue, the potential for support is **always** present. Support develops as any group works together on a particular problem or issue. Support interacts with conflict to encourage our potential for unity. Support appears as group members test the water, share perceptions and feelings, learn, solve problems and then show appreciation. This network of testing, sharing and trusting defines the support pattern.

Support interacts with other dynamics of dialogue: risk, share, pull back, reveal, describe, give, care for, argue, ask about, protect and guide. All of these mobilize, and all of this is growth. Sharing information creates connections. When this information includes feelings and observations of the moment and when there is understanding about each other, the connections are strong indeed. From this foundation, individuals become "us" and "our group," and shared identity is stronger.

Dialogue brings identity, support and often an affection or feeling of unity that can be frightening. A recurring theme in all eight research groups linked affection with sex and fear. Some form of this question appeared in all eight groups: "How can we be intimate without being sexual?"

Intimacy is linked to sexuality through vulnerability. Listening to others very well can be moments of lovely tenderness. The softness of the moment sometimes has a physical, sensual quality. This sensuality may blend into a sexual feeling. If the group has learned that there is a difference between having a feeling and acting it out, then group members may enjoy a caring for each other of great complexity.

Support patterns contain caring, trust, affection, vulnerability, intimacy, sensuality, sexuality, strength, power, cohesion and group identity. The support patterns influence all behavior whenever any collection of individuals joins together for any purpose in any setting.

MALE NURTURANCE

Human beings require support from others for survival and problem-solving teams are a valid source of social support. While the source may be there, many people struggle to satisfy the need. The wish for intimacy is accompanied by the fear of connections. Resistance to peacemaking is built on this fear of intimacy.

At first glance, anxiety about intimacy may pass for a male trait not a female trait. In the AU Research Groups, women used more words of support than the men. The men talked less than the women about families, group belonging and positive thoughts or feelings. Their conversation about support showed more caution. The men were aware that showing their "soft" side could be dangerous: "Gentle men are ostracized."

Looking closer shows the difference between quantity and quality. The women may have talked more about support, but the male conversations about mutual support were powerful and substantial. In the AU Research Groups, there were no apparent male-female differences in risk-taking, vulnerability, emotional support and intensity of involvement.

In the following transcript, the men of Group 2 raise the question of support in the last session of *Day 1*. In Chapters 3 and 4, Group 2 talked about dependency and rebellion. Here, Group 2 discusses sex, support and intimacy:

Case Study #31: Nurturance

Group 2 (Male Members, Male Consultant)

Session 4: The Question of Support

Donald: I've been listening to you, and I've been wondering. Are you saying that one of the things you would like to improve in skill is being able to talk about intimate relationships with the male population at large, or your male friends?

Chuck: My male friends, yes.

Donald: Right. And I think that's something that I would like to be able to do better, too. I think that's probably something everybody here would like to do better.

Chuck: That's what I'm trying to check, and he's not saying that.

David: I agree with that, that I would like to do that, too.

Donald: And I think where we're at is how we can start to do that without threatening each other.

David: Yeah, how can we do that with each other? That's my question, too. Do we want to do that with each other? I would agree that I would like to do it with my male friends, but you are not my male friends. You are people I met this morning, and admittedly under unusual circumstances.

Donald: So the question is, do we want it at all?

David: That's my question.

Chuck: Yeah, I started off saying this is something I do want to talk about.

David: Do you need a consensus of opinion? Do you need the group's approval?

Chuck: No, I'm just getting reactions. Like you said, this is the question. I'm putting my vote in.

David: Well, it might be that if you started off relating a story it would evoke something in me that I would want to respond to on the same level.

Sam: It's like playing chicken. Who goes first?

Chuck: Now I'm getting maybe not competition, but something going on.

David: I saw you trying to work on something in a non-abrasive way, not competition.

Chuck: My whole feelings about the group are changing.

Robert: We all agreed that we wanted to give each other feedback.

Chuck: What about this business of sharing sexual experiences on an emotional level?

David: I think that we would find if we were to share such experiences that we would all probably be much more supportive of each other than we might expect, but it's nevertheless going to be difficult to proceed.

Chuck: Rationally, I would expect a lot of supportiveness, but I don't have any models to go on.

David: Let me ask this question. As a result of all this preliminary conversation, working up to a goal, do any of us, do all of us, how many of us have specific things about sex that they want to talk about?

Later: The Topic of Touching

David: I've never hugged a male. I don't equate hugging with not touching. I touch men all the time, but it's kind of, you know, tap on the back; maybe I rest my arms momentarily on a man's back. I've never felt comfortable hugging a man.

Robert: I've been to a lot of group sessions where it's okay to show physical affection or concern or feeling for a male, and you feel like, well, this is a proper place and time for that. But you get back to the work setting, and if a male comes up to you and puts his arm around you, you tend to say, "Well, what's with this guy?" You get back. You lapse into the old cultural thing. I would hesitate. I want to express friendliness with this male, but people might misinterpret it, so I don't.

David: I don't have those feelings about what other people think.

Robert: I do.

Chuck: What about this. This is an experience that happended to me when I was in the Army on an escape and evasion course. You have nothing with you except a poncho, and a poncho liner. There was this guy, my buddy, and this was in Ranger School. You're out there, the two of you. You have to spend the night. The way you spend the night is underneath the little skinny poncho. And it's cold. And I remember feeling really bad about I wouldn't touch this guy. And I wouldn't get up against him the way I would if it were a woman. Even if it were a woman I didn't know. It was to the point of not having enough poncho to cover both of us, having part of me sticking out, freezing.

Robert: Did you each have a poncho?

Chuck: Yeah, one goes on the bottom and one goes on the top, so that you're not on wet ground.

David: I would have reacted the same way.

Chuck: Yeah, what I'm saying, there's a case where it's clearly not to my advantage to do that, it's a panicked response to the cultural thing. There was just the two of us, out in the woods with no-one to be accountable to at all. Another factor was that he and I got into a very close relationship. There's alot of pressure, it makes you close. But I think that was another thing. In a way I don't want to get this close.

Donald: These are uncomfortable questions. My anxiety is much higher.

Chuck: I respect the fact that you brought it up.

David: I'm not uncomfortable touching men. I mean, extended bodily contact. There are things I feel comfortable doing, obviously, shaking hands, and putting an arm relatively briefly around a man's shoulder. But, hugging a man, being in a situation like you were in the army, I wouldn't feel comfortable with any of those things and that doesn't bother me.

Donald: Well, I do feel uncomfortable at times.

Chuck: You know, prolonged physical contact. I wouldn't feel comfortable with a woman if it were not appropriate, and that doesn't bother me. What does bother me, for example, is this situation in the army when there was real reason to do it, when I was cold and shivered the whole night, and when it was the logical thing to do. It is a fact that another body will keep you warm. For me, that's been my experience, and yet I wouldn't do it.

David: That would have been for me, too. My response would be the same.

Donald: Me too, definitely.

Chuck: I'm glad to hear that.

Donald: What would be most difficult for me would be someone I didn't know from a hole in a wall. A stranger that I have to have physical contact with, I wouldn't like that. But people who I know and trust, I don't mind. Like, if a friend of mine, a male, who I hadn't seen in a long time or even in a not so long time, but someone who is close to me or at one time was very close to me, and I was happy to see and wanted to see, I would consider hugging, "How are you?" And that's more than shaking hands or a pat on the back, yet it's restrained. I would hope the person would say, "He's happy to see me. He doesn't want to have sex with me. He's happy to see me."

David: The thing you said was that you'd consider it. I would do it.

Donald: Yeah, I have done it.

David: But, it would be conscious, kind of.

Donald: Definitely. It would be a conscious process of watching the reaction, because if I offended you I would never do it again.

Day 2—Session 6: Understanding

Chuck: It's like another situation I've been confronted with is that if I'm admiring a guy's body, and I like to think I have an appreciation of bodies, male and female, I'm very reluctant to express it with males. On a few occasions I said, "Well, dammit, you really ought to express it," and I've been only able to do it in the most round-about way.

Donald: Yeah, I do that too. I mean, like, I wanted to tell you that you look exceptionally tired. But I didn't.

David: Today?

Donald: Yeah, you look terrible. But I withheld that. I've taken notice that his eyes are black. He's not looking as alert as yesterday, and I don't know if you're feeling that way. I mean, when he walked in the room I looked at him. I evaluated him. I looked at his body, and I thought the reason I didn't say that to him was because I thought it might offend him.

David: It doesn't.

Chuck: To me, that's a different category because society says you can say, "How are you?" or even "You look shitty today, your eyes look bloodshot," or whatever. But not "Your body is aesthetically pleasing to me."

Donald: I think I could do that.

David: I have the feeling that women talk about each other in a much more open way. That may not be true.

Donald: I don't think women are any more comfortable expressing their feelings toward one another than men are.

Chuck: My feeling about all this is that homosexuality is one issue, touching is another, there are others. They inhibit my relating to men in some cases on the level at which I feel I want to relate. It's one of those things that puts up stop signs that I want to get through. I want to understand more about what's going on inside of me, about exactly where the stop signs are, and whether I want them to be there or not.

David: To talk about intimate sexual matters, for example, or any other intimate matter. I guess that's a process one goes through to decide at any given point whether one's willing to be intimate. It is not an ultimate decision that one makes.

Chuck: That brings up a point. Why is intimacy equated with sexuality? I see that as sort of a cultural convention. Most people do equate intimacy with sexuality. And maybe this is what's in my mind when I have my hang-ups about relating to men on an intimate level. How do you be intimate without being sexual? Does it matter?

David:　I think there are many kinds of intimacy.

Chuck:　Yeah, I think so, too. I'm trying to think and check my own feelings, my anxieties about relating to men. It's how to be intimate without being sexual.

David:　I feel that we're using intimacy maybe in two different ways. You're talking about sexuality of a process of relations with men, your relations with other men, as somehow being intimate and being somehow difficult. But, I'm talking about not the process so much as various subject matters which may be considered intimate, one of which is our subject of sex, which men I don't think share in an intimate way, in a caring, non-competitive way.

Chuck:　Yeah, I'm saying that I agree, but I'm saying for me, one of my problems, I guess, I connect it with sexuality.

David:　But I see you as an open person and as a sharing person and as a person who to an extent as great as anybody in the group is willing to put himself out on the line and give us a kind of intimacy which couldn't be classified as sexual. I don't consider it so.

Chuck:　Yeah, that makes me feel good to hear you say that. As I was saying before, when Donald sat there and said, "I enjoy being with men," it struck me that I wouldn't say that because if I said that I would . . . my mind would be working, like, "What would people think?" I mean, I was just impressed with the way he sat there and said it very comfortably. I'd say it in some roundabout way. I think I'm very good at saying things in some roundabout weasling way, where I don't accept full responsibility for it. And as a result it doesn't have the same effect. It has the effect of putting up stop signs. I'm saying to the other person, "You gotta be careful about being too direct."

David:　Did it make you uncomfortable when Donald said that to you?

Chuck:　No, it made me feel good.

Donald:　I like being with men, like it's rare that I'm only with men. A lot of the people I work with are women, and sometimes I get tired of being with them.

Chuck:　If I were to sit there and say that "I like being with men," just like that, my little anxieties in the back of me would come up and say,

"How's somebody gonna interpret this? Are they gonna think I'm one of 'those guys'?" And yet it didn't seem to bother you at all.

Donald: No. I can make the statement that I feel comfortable with men because I do. I wouldn't have sex with a man, but I like to be with men.

Chuck: What about sharing sexual feelings or, that is, not feelings of attraction or anything, but feelings about other events?

Donald: Oh, if there are men that I can relate my thoughts to on intimate levels, I would definitely be happy to do that. I think it's important to me to realize that people are intrinsically the same. I mean, we can feel the same things, and that's amazing to me. But some people put up stop signs. They're not willing to share. They won't say, "I can hurt, too."

Chuck: Or the other thing that gets me is when they say, "I know how you feel. I was in such-and-such a situation." And they describe the situation and it's completely different.

Donald: People generally don't listen well, and if I can find someone who listens well I'll talk to them. And I've grown more and more comfortable dealing with men on more and more intimate subjects other than sports and politics.

• • • • •

Process Review. Group 2 teaches us about trust and the fears associated with mutual support. The conversations about sexual topics raise anxiety and then curiosity about intimacy. For some, the sexual topics are the "stop signs" that block a deeper relationship with male friends. Ultimately, this fear of intimacy and these questions about sexuality block peacemaking. This theme was raised in all eight research groups: where does intimacy meet sexuality? David's description of two kinds of intimacy—feeling close and talking about personal matters—helps his group understand that the affection that often accompanies honesty is not necessarily erotic.

Mutual support is multi-dimensional. On the level of content, there are difficult issues—conflict, anger, perceptions, values, analysis, solutions and actions. On the level of process, sharing and support bring "a kind of intimacy," belonging is strengthened by self-disclosure, understanding adds to group identity, all of this interacting in a spiraling fashion.

In most cultures, the Male Role is associated with competition, aggression, striving for success, domination, independence, control and rational analysis. At the same time, as the transcript shows, men are sensitive to their capacity for caring, concern, affection, encouragement and vulnerability.

Male leaders who speak out in favor of peacemaking, cooperation, active listening, shared problem solving and spiritual motivations may generate support or panic. This "soft" behavior stirs up conscious and unconscious questions about the Male Role. The perception that Jimmy Carter was "weak" was influenced by this group dynamic. South African Prime Minister Botha's comment that "Negotiation is not a sign of weakness" also shows the impact of these unconscious dynamics.

Men are aware that nurturance, intimacy and peacemaking are not traditionally associated with male identity. Peace-seeking men may stir up the anxiety and anger of difficult change.

Psychiatrist Terry Stein studied a variety of all-male groups, including those meeting to discuss the male role.[96] He concluded that three issues make change difficult for men who want to show support and nurturance, rather than domination or aggression. First, power and authority are attributed to men simply because they are men. So men are reluctant to change in general. Second, male identity is partly established as boys learn **not** to be like their mothers. Change requires men to work through the fear that nurturant, expressive, caring and cared-for is "being like a woman" and negative.[97] Third, Stein believes that inappropriate guilt troubles some men. Stein encourages men to freely examine what actual responsibility they have for oppression, domination and aggression.

Men and women are currently re-evaluating their social roles and finding new identities. Dialogues for problem solving and peacemaking are also struggles to balance achievement and support, aggression and intimacy, masculine and feminine values.

GROUP MATURITY

Support is the pattern which holds us together. Support emerges from participation and develops over time, changing as the group matures.

In conversation, we describe perceptions of ourselves and the world around us. This exchange of information connects us to each other. Though the linkage may be angry, the connection is always present. When we listen for understanding, the linkage is supportive, and we create belonging and a shared group identity.

The connections between us are holding us together. In the physical sciences, research inside the atom shows that particles hold the nucleus together through interaction. These forces of holding together are the strongest in the universe. In face-to-face groups, individuals hold the group together through interaction. This holding together is a powerful source of achievement, identity, nurturance and creativity.

An "older" group is different from a "younger" group. A group that has shared time and learning now shares and coordinates information more effectively, talks about internal tensions more easily and genuinely respects the knowledge found in different viewpoints. The more mature group is less likely to search for causes and reasons, more likely to observe and describe connections, patterns and strategies for change.

Over time, a group holds together with stronger links and develops a culture with special language and shared folk tales or myths. Group theorists John Hartman and Graham Gibbard state that any theory describing how groups mature over time must account for group myths. Myths are shared fantasies built up out of group events—like the "stop signs" of Group 2.

Hartman and Gibbard describe a very common category of group folk tales—the myths of unity.[98] For example, *Mystical Fusion* is the fantasy of merging with the group, often described as similar to the mother-infant bond. *Utopia* myths suggest that members feel unconditional love and universal harmony, with conflict denied and evil projected outside the group or onto authority. *Messiah* fantasies are a wish for a savior to prevent or repair internal damage, often strongest when two group members are paired together.

Hartman and Gibbard conclude that shared fantasy is essential to group formation. They believe that myths of unity play a crucial role when people join together to create a face-to-face group, a social system or a political entity.

The myths of unity are a source of both inspiration and anxiety. Individual, group, community and international dynamics are influenced by this wish for and fear of unity. A mature system learns to balance individual identity and group belonging, so unity is less terrifying.

Group maturity is the increased sharing and coordination of information, roles, power, patterns and responsibility. A mature group balances the needs of individuals and the reality of unity, influenced by the fundamental rhythm of separating and belonging. It takes some time for a face-to-face group to learn these skills of balance, which is essentially a spiritual experience.

Spirituality. When sharing is in a group setting, personal boundaries shift back and forth. The following comments describe a consultant's experience of boundaries in an intimate group discussion:

When you and I first communicated, my boundary was "around me" and "between us." After a while, when we could describe, agree, disagree, laugh, cry and discover, the boundary "between us" became lighter. The boundary "around us" became stronger.

Soon, as a group, our conversations created a boundary "around all of us," and that was a very safe and nourishing place to be. Within our group, we found ourselves both apart from and within each other. We played our individual roles and saw universal patterns. And the moments when we spoke from the heart and felt the same rhythm, saw the same dream, when I felt most connected to whatever it was we had created among us, those were the moments beyond self. That was for me a spiritual experience.

And so the force which holds people together emerges from their interactions, follows the rhythms of separating and belonging, and meets our needs for achievement, support and meaning. Peacemaking combines a search for support and unity with our needs for spirituality.

WORKING GUIDELINES

Support has many forms: encouragement, affection, intimacy, trust, vulnerability, sensuality, sexuality, strength and team spirit. As previous chapters have demonstrated, the patterns of support are interwoven with patterns of conflict, peacemaking, analysis and problem solving. The patterns of support are visible in activities, conversations and attitudes.

Activities. Problem-solving teams and working organizations are sources of social support. People meet important needs for friendship and affiliation through relationships at work. Fortunately, many work organizations actively encourage a variety of support networks such as staff newsletters, lunch-time meetings with invited speakers, talent shows, basketball teams, company teams, "sunshine clubs" (cards and flowers to seriously ill staff) and training programs where experienced staff (mentors) consult with younger employees about career development. These programs promote well-being. Other support programs may include weight loss clinics, stop-smoking meetings, pre-paid legal services, alcohol, drug and personal counseling. In-house training programs may teach the skills of effective listening, participatory management, constructive confrontation or team building. Sometimes support networks in large organizations bring together individuals doing the same work—such as the Women Lawyers in Federal Government Thursday Lunch Support Group. These activities strengthen team spirit and mutual support.

Or, a staff group may meet with the specific purpose of answering the question: "How can we create a more supportive work environment?" For example, group members may be asked to "describe three special skills you have," or "describe something you did this week and felt good about but no one noticed." Here, support merges with healing, a pattern considered in the next chapter.

Support is visible in the activities of an organization. Support also means talking to each other in a certain way.

Conversation. Verbal appreciation for good work and strong efforts conveys support and concern. Words of appreciation include "thank you" and "you did a great job." Support includes genuine interest in the perspectives of each other. In conversation, support means listening until you understand the other and asking questions when you don't understand: "Is this what you mean?"

Support includes a genuine interest in the well-being of another. This means voicing concern when you see something is not quite right: "I noticed you haven't said anything since John got angry. What's going on with you?"

Sharing information builds mutual understanding and connects us to each other. When conversation is aimed at understanding, that connection is supportive. Support is strengthened when dissent and disagreement are openly expressed, worked through and channeled into creative problem solving. Support requires trust that anger will be listened to and worked through.

Some aspects of support may seem frightening to particular group members. Trusting and expecting encouragement may be new experiences for some. For others, tapping into the patterns of group life may feel too chaotic. Group activity may be associated with past embarrassment, manipulation, exploitation or betrayal. Here, support means giving individuals enough room to find a comfortable place in group discussions.

Attitudes. In organizations which understand and value human resources, productivity rests on emotional support. The effective work organization values the well-being of employees. The work group is a family for eight hours a day. Keeping the family together takes conscious effort. Management supports this effort based on the belief that respect for human resources contributes to the quality of products or services and the quality of work life. A supportive environment contributes to creativity, productivity and well-being.

In summary, support is the holding together which emerges from participation, including encouragement, caring, trust, affection, nurturance, intimacy, sensuality, sexuality, strength, identity and spirituality. At all times, small groups show movement along all pathways of the network called support.

Chapter 10

HEALING:
Repair and Growth

*"Something we were withholding made us weak,
Until we found it was ourselves."*

Robert Frost

    Healing means to restore health by making whole. Psychological healing includes problem solving, emotional discharge, support, a clearer sense of self-identity and a stronger connection to the rhythms of the universe. The dynamics of peacemaking and healing cannot be separated. Both are movements through pain and opposition to a third position of balance, harmony and integration.

    Face-to-face discussion activates the patterns of healing across many conscious and unconscious levels. Talking to friends or counselors can ease or repair personal damage. Community healing occurs as citizens and local service agencies join together to deal with domestic violence, unemployment or drug abuse. National healing occurs as feuding sub-groups join together to strengthen domestic health. Global healing occurs as separate political systems join together to create regional peace and solve global problems.

    This chapter looks at patterns of renewal for individuals, groups, organizations, communities and nations.

HEALING

PERSONAL HEALING

Healing means to restore health by creating harmony and making whole. In *The Turning Point*, Fritjof Capra viewed the human organism as a living system, then concluded that illness and pain are not the result of an attack by external forces.[99] Illness is the disharmony and imbalance of internal resources which makes people more vulnerable to external influences. We heal ourselves by looking in the mirror and finding harmony in body, mind and soul.

Health is more than the absence of disease. Health is the dynamic balance of relationships across multiple levels of reality. According to Capra, a healthy system is characterized by dynamic flexibility and creative adaptation to a continually changing and challenging environment. Health is the harmony of physical, emotional, social, spiritual, community, ecological and global needs.

The transformation of opposition to creative movement connects participants to the fundamental rhythms in nature. Peacemaking is inherently a healing and spiritual practice, where individuals, groups and institutions evolve to a higher level of adaptability and creativity, and hopefully divert some energy to larger global problems.

Awareness. Kenneth Cohen has compared the healing practices of Taoist and Native American medicine.[100] Both traditions are rooted in the same consciousness—respect for the planet earth. In both Taoist and Native American medicine, the student of healing often begins training by assuming the postures and actions of animals such as bear, deer, cat and eagle. Both believe that healing begins with awareness.

Both Taoist and many American Indian traditions describe healing as opening up energy centers located in the spine and both use deep breathing to enhance the flow of this vital energy. The Taoists call this energy Ch'i which is not a specific substance but rather an image of our internal essence in interaction with the universe. Ch'i is the flow and fluctuation of the human organism. This flow of energy is always cyclical, matching the movements of nature at the center of life where opposing tensions Yin and Yang generate rhythms of harmony. Throughout the ages, spiritual enlightenment has often been described as the direct experience of this universal rhythm.

Attention to breathing and the flow of personal energy awakens the forces of renewal. Awareness balances the needs of body, mind and self-identity by reaching into a deeper, inner wisdom. Both Taoist and American Indian cultures use song, dance and meditation to bridge this deeper source of knowledge to everyday social reality. Gradually, awareness brings out a central consciousness and a sense of self with clarity about visions, values, needs and priorities.

Psychologist Barry McWaters calls this self-awareness "the coordinative center"or the "I" which actively participates in healing by placing and withdrawing attention, then accenting and creating.[101] McWaters believes that any inner tuning of individuals occurs with an alignment to the whole, the consciousness of Humanity. There is no inner healing without attention to the larger field of energy, the planetary consciousness.

For the individual, healing means restoring health by bringing the parts of self into balance and bringing the whole of self into harmony with the environment.

Case Study #32: The Author

I believed the only way I could manage all my anger was to write a book about peacemaking and so I learned about healing. In 1987, I can look back and say "In 1981, I arrived in California hurt, angry, moderately depressed, broke and barely employed and now I feel healthier."

For me, healing began by confronting my pain and talking about my turmoil. I felt frustration, rage, ignored, betrayed, torn apart and scattered. Naming those patterns was not a great deal of fun, so I learned to avoid by hiding in my confusion. Avoidance and denial took up a few years. That's where I met my Shadow and learned about cowardice, deceit, envy and vengeance. Self-pity only works for a while. Eventually, I found myself learning from past mistakes and opening up to present opportunities. Accepting responsibility for my feelings was a big step forward. The love and encouragement of family and friends supported me throughout this time. Pain went away. The play of all the patterns brought balance. The combination of old friends, new friends and new events, new projects and new jobs, thinking and meditating, writing and rewriting, sunsets and ocean sounds, all helped me balance love and work in a more harmonious fashion.

• • • • •

The next sections describe healing between and within groups, institutions and nations, where healing always accompanies peacemaking.

THE THERAPEUTIC COMMUNITY

The therapeutic community is a residential treatment center which uses psychological models based on group techniques.[102] Psychological damage is healed by learning new skills in a setting which values personal responsibility and mutual support. The therapeutic community model has been used successfully with alcoholics, drug addicts, delinquents, child abusers, chronic schizophrenics and even the "not guilty by reason of insanity."

The basic principle of a therapeutic community is participation. Doctors, nurses, aides and patients share decisions. Leadership is based on ability not status. All parts of the psychiatric environment and all interactions are seen as potentially healing. Patients are called clients. Clients are involved in the welfare of themselves and each other through participation in group therapy, psychodrama, family meetings, community meetings and patient self-government. Staff move from doing for the client to teaching clients to do for themselves. Personal, social, vocational and community living skills are taught in a direct way, with clear expectations and rewards. In hospitals, patients (called clients) do as much of the every day work as possible, including cleaning, clerical and recreational activities.

In traditional psychiatric hospitals, clients are called patients and policies generally keep patients dependent upon staff and institution for food, clothing, shelter, quality of care and daily schedules of events. In traditional psychiatric hospitals, well-intentioned staff may reinforce this dependency by lighting cigarettes, cleaning up after patients and planning all their activities. Over time, mastery of skills is lost. As Mrs. X once told me, "I used to have beautiful writing before I came here. But the nursing students have been writing my letters for so many years, I'm sure I couldn't remember how to do it myself. So I can't send a Get Well card to Norma." In traditional settings for the chronically disabled, the dependent relationship with the institution is so strong that discharge leads to great anxiety about separation from a structure representing security.[103]

Healing. Psychiatrist Richard Almond has studied health care systems in cross-cultural settings and concluded that a healing community is a universal phenomena.[104] The norms of a healing community are a set of beliefs about the nature of change. When a newcomer enters a therapeutic community, the initial focus is a pragmatic, problem solving approach to the presenting complaint: What is the problem? What are the consequences? What are your options? What makes choice difficult? Rather than encountering the traditional expectation that the patient is sick, helpless, dangerous or uncontrollable, the norms of the therapeutic community insist that the patient be treated as having the competence to bring problem behavior under control and the capacity to have interactions with peers that promote health.

In a therapeutic community, self-discovery and new behavior take place among peers who have been through similar struggles. They offer support, though not always gentleness. For example, at Synanon meetings, where residential treatment is offered for former heroin abusers, analytic interpretations are avoided and aggressive confrontation pressures individuals to give up a lifestyle based on manipulation and verbal game-playing. These peer counseling models have been used in jails and prisons which have shifted from punishment to rehabilitation. When peers approve healthy behavior and ignore or criticize destructive behavior, pressure to conform encourages change.

Problem solving does not deny the need of people in pain to voice emotions. Group meetings intensify the here-and-now experience. The discharge of rage, grief and terror may seem explosive but the sudden release of blocked or denied psychological energy brings renewal. Discharge of emotion brings the clarity necessary to make healthy life choices. Of course, the group system must be "ready" to hear the discharge of feelings or the exploder will be ignored or possibly scapegoated.

Almond believes that healing and change are related to both individual and group dynamics. The individual makes a personal choice when crossing the boundary to enter a treatment system. Immediately, the newcomer is enmeshed in a social setting which values the public description of problems, supports positive change, and ignores or challenges negative behavior. According to Almond, in this natural process of behavior change, the sufferer becomes the healer. Therapeutic community members learn to promote health in each other.

At the level of group process, Almond attributes healing to two group qualities: "Communitas" and "healing charisma."[105] Communitas is belonging or group spirit. Communitas includes commitment and faith in the program.

Charisma is the magical quality of specialness, the capacity to evoke an image of Self beyond the ordinary: "I am more than I thought." Healing charisma focuses on health-promoting activities and Almond believes the central leader's capacity to voice consistent and genuine faith in the skills of all community members is crucial for success. Staff and patients are not the objects of the charismatic process but active participants in it.

Healing brings balance by raising problems to conscious awareness and allowing interaction to free up blocked energy and generate new knowlege and choices. When this takes place in a group setting, there is a special quality of friendship and support you do not have if you try to do it alone. Personal and group healing are the core of institutional healing.

ORGANIZATIONAL HEALING

In the 1980s, corporations and government agencies have been looking inward, asking the difficult questions: "What business are we in? How can we encourage innovation and quality? How can we maximize human resources? What is our culture and what are our spoken and unspoken values and assumptions? How do we relate to ecological concerns? What are our social responsibilities?" As business and public organizations answer these questions, they embark on a course of peacemaking that often leads to healing.

As managers and employees learn the technology of group problem solving, they develop an appreciation of individual differences along with respect for the wisdom of group creativity. As divisive issues are raised and resolved, the disruptiveness of disagreement decreases. Information and energy flow more freely. Conflict more regularly turns to creativity. The parts of the organization fit together with greater harmony; the parts become aligned. In self-reflection, organizations are developing awareness.

As problem-solving teams go about solving shared difficulties, the patterns of healing are activated. Conflict resolution through dialogue brings learning, meaning, belonging and group identity. As the discord subsides and the players realign themselves in a more harmonious fashion, the system repairs itself and becomes more whole. The groups have moved to the point of conflict through opposing tensions to a third position of balance.

Healing Burn Out. Working the wards of a public mental hospital, where the job requires workers to encounter "the psychotic experience" on a daily basis, is an exceptionally stressful occupation. Staff may become frustrated, angry, tired, then withdrawn, detached and apathetic. "Going through the motions" is a common coping mechanism when job conditions are psychologically overwhelming. The next case study shows the healing of burn out.

Case Study #33: The Therapeutic Community

In 1978, a therapeutic community that aimed to treat chronic psychiatric patients by teaching personal, social and community living skills, began when the staff learned "Peer Counseling."[106] The goal of the course was learning basic counseling skills to be used with hospital patients. The procedures of the class had staff practicing these counseling techniques among themselves.

In the first session, the staff was asked to describe something done in the past week which felt good but which no one else had noticed. After a few minutes of embarrassed silence, one nurse spoke out and then the whole class joined in. Everyone could describe at least one event that week where a special effort "not in my job description" had gone unnoticed: "No one appreciates what I do here." At the end of the meeting, the group agreed to "pay more attention and say kind things to each other."

In the next class, we learned that emotional discharge—crying, shaking, bellowing—can heal. We learned that staff members can encourage this natural healing process by active listening. As we practiced listening, sharing and risking involvement with each other, we became more cohesive and more confident about our ability to provide mutual support. Simultaneously, there was more energy available for the task at hand.

One year later, the evening and night shifts were sending representatives to day shift staff meetings. On their own time, the staff had developed a program of community trips for the long-term disabled patients. The staff held bake sales to earn money to hire teachers from the Community College to come on the wards and give classes to patients in reading, writing, art, dance and personal hygiene. Young student interns from the city were brought in to help out. Eventually, all patients were divided into small groups where they began to learn specific skills necessary for living outside the institution, as they became ready, and should they be lucky enough to find a place to live.

The most personally touching moment occurred a few weeks after the college teachers had started the reading classes. It was on the locked ward, in an evening community meeting. The patients voted to end the meeting by singing "My Country 'Tis of Thee, Sweet Land of Liberty."

· · · · ·

DOMESTIC VIOLENCE

Stress is a signal that demands attention and requires action. The symptoms surround us, touching every one of us.

Illness is an indicator of stress turned inwards. Listening, we hear stress in the body: headaches, backaches, ulcers, colitis, irregular heartbeats, high blood pressure and feeling tired. Or, we hear stress of the psyche: anger, depression, anxiety, fear, loneliness, nightmares, alcoholism and drug addiction.

Violence is an indicator of stress turned outwards, against others. Psychological tensions fueled by social and economic fears may erupt in movements which act against the community. Like a steaming tea-kettle with the lid on too tight, something somewhere explodes. The family system is a typical arena for violence in part because our most primitive connections are with family members.

Violence in the home and crime on the street are related dynamics: internal stress erupting destructively. Child abuse, street crime, racial or ethnic hatred are outward indicators of internal stress.

The irony of domestic violence is that THE KNOWLEDGE IS IN THE SYSTEM. Our educational, health care, social service and government agencies fail because they deny the skills of teachers, nurses, doctors, social workers and public employees. The talent necessary to revitalize our social institutions and restore domestic health exists within the ordinary people who work in schools, hospitals, clinics and jails, but bureaucratic structure represses these human resources.

Organizational structure contributes to the cycle of domestic violence by failing to provide formats for communication, cooperation and creativity. When policies and procedures are built on rational analysis alone, social institutions cannot succeed. Often, frustration flows from rigid policies and achievement occurs despite the rules.

The failure of institutional logic abounds in health care. Hospitals, medical clinics, social service agencies and other healing systems often need time and energy to look inward, realign and heal themselves so they can provide quality service.

As modern organizations are discovering, group problem solving brings renewed vitality and more effective activity. The benefits of dialogue can also be found in local neighoborhoods experiencing citizen and self-help movements.

Self-Help. Since the 1960s, especially in the United States, community health has been strengthened by the dramatic growth of self-help groups. The self-help group is a collection of sufferers with similar problems, such as the Brain Tumor Support Group, Gamblers Anonymous, Mothers Against Drunk Drivers or Parents Anonymous (for parents who have abused their children). There are support groups for parents without partners and support groups for children of single parents. Many of these groups have been influenced by the peer counseling approach of Alcoholics Anonymous which relies on group meetings for problem solving and encouragement.

The self-help movement demonstrates a grassroots belief that face-to-face discussion includes the patterns of healing. These groups believe that honest communication, mutual support and sharing problems with those who know because "I've been there, too" is a healing experience. Communication among peers relieves and repairs psychological damage.

Domestic Health. The second generation of self-help groups seem to be those which combine healing and problem solving to manage neighborhood conflict. A fascinating form of social healing is the "victim-offender" approach which gives first-time or juvenile offenders the opportunity to avoid jail by accepting responsibility for their crimes and making restitution.[107] In Elkhart, Indiana, a program called PACT (Prisoners and Community Together) had 80% of the offenders successfully make restitution. In Quincy, Massachusetts, 95% of juveniles and 70% of adults made restitution to victims in a program called EARN IT: "You have no second chance unless you earn it."

As offenders answer for their crimes, the most powerful changes often occur as the offender meets the victim face-to-face and acknowledges "I did wrong." Individuals who act out their anger or other emotions against the community can change problem behavior by taking responsibility, making restitution and forming a relationship with a community system which clearly defines appropriate behavior.

Other examples of community healing include the coordinated parent-teacher-student-administrator efforts to deal with drug abuse and violence in schools, or the business-community-government efforts to teach basic job skills to the chronic unemployed. Town hall meetings can be excellent settings for starting and monitoring such projects in problem solving and community healing. These projects can successfully reach into and transform the core of rage and stress which are the underside of domestic violence.

All self-help projects are founded on the same basic assumption that has fostered therapeutic communities and participatory management: THE KNOWLEDGE IS IN THE SYSTEM. This is the assumption that can repair the psychological damage of war because peacemaking and healing are interwoven across all human systems.

Communities torn by crime, violence, ethnic hatred or racial conflict can apply the technology of problem solving to domestic violence. Dialogue is a tool for dealing with neighborhood conflict and regional rage. Peacemaking heals. The resonance of patterns and rhythms of participation bring renewal and wholeness across multiple levels of social systems.

HEALING THE PLANET

The dynamics of aggression include rebellion, splitting, scapegoating and destruction of the Earth's natural resources. Although content and intensity may vary, the dynamics of conflict and peacemaking are the same for all levels of living systems. Conflict is the opposition of forces; peacemaking and healing bring together opposing forces for balance and wholeness.

According to Barry McWaters, the internal rhythm of living systems connects individuals to the movements and balance of the planet Earth.[108] McWaters believes that personal and institutional transformation inherently lead individuals to an alignment with the collective mind of all humanity and the consciousness of the planet Earth. McWaters has drawn out the psychological implications of the Gaia hypothesis.

Gaia is the Greek name for Earth Goddess. The ancient Greeks as well as other early civilizations revered the planet Earth as a living, spiritual being. *The Gaia Hypothesis*, published in 1975 by James Lovelock and Lynn Margulis, used scientific evidence from geophysical research to conclude that the planet Earth is a living, self-regulating organism.[109] For example, for the past two billion years, the Earth's temperature has remained relatively constant, despite increases in solar radiation. The oxygen content of the atmosphere has remained rich and constant, in just the right proportion to sustain life, and the chemical composition of the atmosphere and the salt content of the oceans has also remained relatively constant.

McWaters believes that the biosphere actively controls atmospheric conditions with the well-being of life in mind. Gaia, at mid-life, is drawn toward fuller harmony, pulling the parts of her system together toward greater integration. Individuals and institutions who move toward greater harmony by solving problems and reaching into a deeper consciousness also become aligned to the inner wisdom of planetary rhythms.

People joined together for problem solving and peacemaking embark on a journey of personal and institutional transformation—healing themselves, their institutions and communities. The maturation of peace-seeking diplomacy suggests arms limitations or improved trade relations must go hand-in-hand with cooperative action and ecological problem solving.

The notion of global healing and regional peace are images to guide actions. Solutions and strategies emerge more clearly from a systems point of view. The interdependent cluster of climate-related problems—destruction of tropical rain forests, drought, crop failures, the greenhouse effect, glacial changes, increased carbon dioxide in the air—demonstrate two strategies for peacemaking. First, critical ecological problems requiring emergency action offer regional leaders of cultures in conflict an opportunity to cooperate on shared needs. Secondly, the single action of re-foresting land would solve a global problem of unemployment, slow the release of CO_2 in the air and strengthen other ecological resources.[110]

People joined together can heal the planet. Perhaps the most inspiring examples of global healing are the rivers and waterways, such as the upper Hudson, the Willamette and the Potomac Rivers, which were once unbearably polluted and now are clean and healthy.

Part III

THEORY

Chapter 11:

A SCIENCE OF PEACEMAKING

Chapter 11

A SCIENCE OF
PEACEMAKING

"We can begin to build a science of what I would unashamedly call peacemaking."

Bryant Wedge

An effective theory of peacemaking must account for behaviors, values and perceptions while making a connection between conflict and unity. In this book, systems science is the framework, problem-solving technologies are the muscles, Jungian psychology is the heart and quantum physics is a metaphor describing group energy and the dynamics of peacemaking.

As technologies turn problems to solutions, General Systems Theory shows how individuals form networks of relationships. Problem-solving teams are living systems with purpose and meaning, self-renewing and self-transcendent. As systems seek balance, psychological change occurs on four levels: individual style, group dynamics, organizational procedures and cultural values. Jung's theories about personality, archetypal images, the interplay of opposites and synchronicity help shift the analysis of conflict from assigning blame to describing meaning and solutions.

As problems turn to solutions, concepts are needed to describe the transformation from conflict to unity. Quantum physics describes opposing forces emerging from shared fields of energy. Quantum theory provides metaphors, models and mathematics for the young science of peacemaking. From the perspective of space-time, individuals joined together in dialogue tap patterns of balance and rhythms of harmony across multiple levels of reality. The fundamental rhythm of the universe is the unity of opposing forces.

This chapter outlines the principles of a science of peacemaking.

TECHNOLOGY

Peacemaking through dialogue is built on the technologies of creative problem solving. The basic steps are problem identification, problem analysis, brainstorming solutions, designing action plans by consensus, evaluating procedures and giving feedback about progress and process. Other tools may include warm-up games, personality tests, pre-workshop surveys, sub-group negotiation, humor, written statements, visualization or whatever it takes to mobilize and focus the attention of opposing parties on the need to solve shared problems. Third party consultants may prepare briefing statements, design the structure of meetings, encourage participation, manage angry exchanges, interpret, summarize, report observations and hold the participants to the task of communication and problem analysis.

When these techniques are integrated into a series of meetings, a peace conference has come into existence. The sessions may be called negotiation, team building, mediation, treaty verification or creative problem solving. Psychologically, they are all peacemaking events. Technically, they share many similar activities: opening ceremonies, introductions, problem solving, negotiation, conflict resolution, joint (written) statements, action plans, follow-up, celebrations and closing ceremonies.

Despite the anger and hurt, opponents talking about problems generally want to improve communication and the realities of working or living together. Negotiators William Lincoln, Roger Fisher and William Ury look below the surface for the common ground that holds participants to the negotiating process and paves the way for success. They negotiate underlying interests rather than initial, public positions. The technologies introduce the first four principles of peacemaking:

1. Conflict is the opposition of forces.
2. Peacemaking brings together opposing forces for creative problem solving.
3. A neutral third party can facilitate peace-seeking dialogue.
4. Underneath positions in conflict are shared needs and compatible interests.

Technically, peacemaking is a collection of tools and strategies for creative problem solving. Psychologically, peacemaking is a transformative process where opponents share perceptions and move from the classical split of YOU VERSUS ME to an organic world view of shared relationships, YOU AND ME. Theoretically, the rhythm of quantum fields unifies matter and energy, while the rhythms of dialogue unify the needs of opposing sub-groups. The systems view puts all this in perspective.

SYSTEMS SCIENCE

A system is any whole with interacting parts.[111] Atoms in a molecule, parts of our bodies, trees in a grove, members of a problem-solving team, divisions of a large corporation and nations on the planet Earth are systems with interacting parts. General Systems Theory describes how parts of a whole relate to each other with concepts common to different academic disciplines. For example, the principle of feedback is found in the studies of biology, psychology, engineering, communications, political science and peacemaking. Systems science bridges the physical, social and psychological sciences and is the foundation of an evolving "unity of science."

Modern systems thinking began in the early 1900s when biologist Ludwig von Bertalanffy first described living organisms as whole systems. The body is not a machine, it is an organic whole. Survival means we coordinate information from the environment (for example, the weather) with information from all parts of our human system—circulatory, respiratory, neurological, hormonal, muscular and memory. Coordination of the parts is guided by feedback loops. Feedback is information about performance: if body temperature falls to ninety-five degrees, alarms sound!! Boundaries are guidelines which separate parts from each other and separate people from each other.

The application of systems concepts to management and the organization of work has been traced to the Russian philosopher Alexander Bogdanov in the early 1900s, about the same time as Bertalanffy's first lectures.[112] The workplace is a system whose purpose, policies, people, in-house norms and environmental demands form an interdependent network embedded in a larger social/economic/political community.

Beginning with Kurt Lewin in the 1940s, social psychologists have used systems concepts to describe the interpersonal behavior of human groups.[113] Lewin viewed social groups as a field of forces where roles link people to the organization and the larger environment. In 1979, James G. Miller published *Living Systems* and showed similar scientific concepts operate across all system levels from the cell, organ and organism to the group, organization, society and supranational systems.[114] The intellectual stage is set for applying systems concepts to the dynamics of peacemaking.

Systems science is an elegant framework of concepts to describe groups in dialogue and the dynamics of conflict and peacemaking. For example, the concepts of feedback, boundaries and sub-systems clarify our understanding of conflict management. Through feedback, individuals and group systems learn to make internal self-adjustments that improve communication. Clear boundaries—especially starting and ending meetings on time—help participants feel safe enough to explore difficult issues. The influence of the surrounding culture and environment makes sense when we view living systems as part of larger systems and composed of smaller sub-systems. For example, South African political, economic and social systems are influenced by global attitudes toward apartheid and business decisions about investments.

More than a collection of concepts, systems science provides a perspective for understanding group, organizational, political and global dynamics. The systems view shifts observations from individuals-in-the-group to the group-as-a-whole where interaction, patterns of relationships, underlying order, creativity, evolution and the unity of opposing forces are understood. The systems view is a lens for reviewing and refining the practice of conflict management. From systems science comes the next five principles of peacemaking:

---

5. Groups are living systems composed of individual people who interact through conversation and action, influenced by surrounding conditions.
6. Groups can be observed at the levels of action (having a meeting), content (topic of conversation), process (patterns of relationships) and rhythm (tempo).
7. Groups become self-correcting and self-healing when behavior can be reported as feedback for the group system: "The group is sitting in a circle, but only talking to the General."
8. Group behavior shows synergy or combined energy—the whole is more than the sum of the parts. The group has a life and logic of its own.
9. Boundaries are the guidelines which separate individuals from each other and group systems from each other.

The behavior of the parts can be observed and the whole has a meaning different from the simple addition of parts and departments. The living organism has a creative mind, seeks meaning and struggles with identity, bringing us to the realm of psychology.

PSYCHOLOGY

Technology refers to procedures, systems science refers to a framework for analysis and psychology refers to underlying process and emotions. In conversation, content is **what** you talk about—job demands, budgets or arms control. Process is how you talk about it—dependent or rebellious, supportive or dominating, trusting or deceitful. Process contains individual, group and cultural dynamics.

Individual Differences.   Personality can best be understood as our general way of behaving, believing, gathering information and making decisions. Jung identified four dimensions:[115]

1. EXTROVERT/INTROVERT (E/I) — does your energy come from people or solitude?

2. SENSING/INTUITIVE (S/N) — are you more pragmatic or intuitive?

3. THINKING/FEELING (T/F) — are your decisions more logical or emotional?

4. JUDGING/PERCEIVING (J/P) — do you prefer events scheduled or not scheduled?

Awareness of individual styles and understanding without making judgments improves the chances of creative problem solving. At Camp David, methodical, pragmatic SENSING Begin often clashed with a conceptual INTUITIVE Sadat. After some bumpy starts, Carter worked out a strategy: he talked with Sadat about overall plans and with Begin about details.[116] In Geneva, Reagan and Gorbachev's instant rapport was the connection of two EXTROVERTS who enjoy good-natured story telling, two INTUITIVES who prefer fundamentals to details and two FEELING types comfortable with strong emotions. Their similar styles eased communication.

Group Dynamics. When people join together for discussion, each carries along a unique combination of personality, family history, ethnic heritage, cultural values and typical group behavior. As discussion moves along, personalities meet group process. Psychologists agree that individuals take on group roles reflecting both personal experience and the dynamics of the group system. All behavior shows this duality—the individual/group connection.

For example, anger is voiced by Fight Leaders, encouragement by Support Leaders, action words come from Soldiers, concepts from Analyzers, pain from the Scapegoats and metaphors from the Philosophers. Individual styles and group patterns are like particle and wave—two sides of the same coin. You listen to individuals and hear the group process.

Consider some conversation from *Day 6* of the Camp David peace talks. This is a drama of Support, Negation, Action, Hostility, Wants and Concepts. First the dialogue, then **Table 2** analyzes each sentence: who spoke, words spoken, individual roles and group patterns. The edited conversation occurred after Carter has presented a compromise treaty to the Israelis. This meeting was a statement and discussion of their response. The segment opens with the familiar "Yes. . . but" gambit.

Day 6, Camp David:

Begin: Parts of the document are deeply appreciated and positive . . . but we have a proposal for some changes.

Barak: First, to delete all references to United Nations Resolution 242 [to deny the legitimacy of territory acquired by war].

Carter: This is not the time to beat around the bush. . . . If you don't espouse 242, it is a terrible blow to peace.

Begin: I am willing to respect it, but not as a basis for what follows in your proposal.

Carter: Our document makes clear that borders have to be negotiated. . . Sadat genuinely wants an agreement with you.

Begin: We speak here of the very existence of our nation.

Weizman: Let's move on. . .

Carter: What you want to do is make the West Bank part of Israel.

Vance: The whole idea is to let the people govern themselves.

Begin: We want to keep the right to do so [have authority over the Palestinians] but we don't intend to do so.

Carter: No self-respecting Arab would accept this. It looks like a subterfuge. You are not giving them autonomy if you have to approve their laws, exercise a veto over their decisions and maintain a military governor.

Begin: Autonomy doesn't mean sovereignty.

Weizman: We want to have a time factor, to give the idea a test.

Carter: Sadat will not negotiate on the details you have proposed.

After spending time with dictionaries and looking up meanings of words (such as sovereignty, autonomy and rights), a breakthrough occurs voiced by Dayan: "WE SHALL RECONSIDER OUR OBJECTIONS." There is more disagreement amid tiny progress toward small compromises, but that night a helpful alliance formed between Carter and Dayan. The above dialogue can be organized into a chart similar to **Table 1** in Chapter 3: ROLES (see page 54). Only the stakes are higher.

In **Table 2** below, Begin's "appreciate . . . but" sentence made him a Supporter and Denier voicing the group patterns of *Support* and *Negation*.

Table 2

WORDS, ROLES and PATTERNS

Person	Words	Individual Role	Group Patterns
Begin	appreciate, but	Supporter, Denier	SUPPORT, NEGATION
Barak	delete	Actor	ACTION
Carter	don't, terrible	Denier, Fighter	NEGATE, HOSTILITY
Begin	respect, but	Supporter, Denier	SUPPORT, NEGATION
Carter	negotiate, wants	Actor, Discloser	ACTION, WANTS
Begin	existence	Philosopher	NATURAL PROCESS
Weizman	move on	Mediator	ACTION, MEANS
Carter	want, make	Discloser	WANT, ACTION
Vance	idea	Thinker	CONCEPTS
Begin	want, but	Discloser, Denier	WANT, NEGATION
Carter	no, subterfuge, approve	Denier, Fighter, Actor	NEGATE, HOSTILITY, ACTION
Begin	autonomy	Conceptual Analyst	CONCEPTS
Weizman	want, time	Discloser, Thinker	NEED, NATURE
Carter	not negotiate	Denier, Actor	NEGATE, ACTION
Dayan	shall reconsider	Thinker, Actor	CONCEPTS, ACTION

Table 2 shows group patterns voiced by individual role specialists: Begin is Discloser, Denier and Analyzer. Carter stimulates—he is Denier, Fighter, Actor and Discloser. Vance and Weizman are Thinkers whose concepts further analysis. On *Day 6*, the roles and patterns brought balance. The segment was one of those turning points that moves peacemaking along. Dayan voiced the breakthrough: "We shall reconsider our objections." Interaction brought balance.

Throughout, there were undertones of archetypal energy. When dialogues are meaningful and reach a certain level of intensity, individual roles shift to archetypal images: Good Parent, Hero, Weak One, Wise Old Man, Earth Mother, Soldiers. An archetype is a compelling, wordless psychological image. Archetypes active during confict and peacemaking may also include the Hero, the Terrible Parent, The Fool, Death, Dreams, Nature, Animals and Spirit. Ultimately, the interaction of the patterns, archetypal images and the unity of opposites brings balance.

Paired Opposites. We live out many opposing patterns in our everyday life: sleeping and waking, thinking and feeling, male and female, life and death. Jung believed archetypes always constellate along with their opposite. Opposing patterns occur at the group level, too. Research shows group dynamics are made of paired opposites and the interaction of the pairs bring balance.

Group dynamics such as dependency, rebellion against authority, scapegoating or cooperative achievement are made of basic building blocks—such as hostility, analysis, support, pain, action or perceptions. The basic building blocks contain smaller dynamisms of energy—the paired opposite such as HOSTILITY/ANALYSIS or PAIN/SUPPORT. The paired opposites are mechanisms of balance—Hostility attracts Analysis or Pain attracts Support.

In 1982, twenty-two paired opposites were identified when data from the AU Research Groups was re-evaluated, and factor analysis results were re-interpreted. Factor analysis was born in 1888 when Scotland Yard called upon a researcher named Galton to design a mathematical model to classify and identify criminals. Factor analysis lumps together clusters of data based on positive and negative correlations. A factor analysis generates a continuum with positive and negative poles. For example, in this research Factor 1 is STRESS/CONCEPTS. The positive pole contains words of emotion, arousal, pain, questions, submitting and negativity; the positive pole is named STRESS. The negative pole has words of abstract analysis such as overstate, abstractions, evaluation of others; the negative pole is named CONCEPTS:

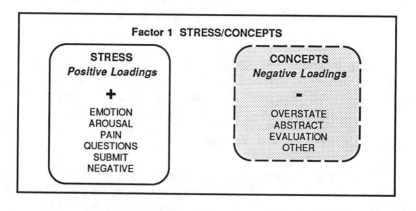

In the 1970s, Dexter Dunphy used a factor analysis on General Inquirer data to study group roles and he interpreted the poles as the words **used** and words **avoided** for each role type.[117] The interpretation presented here looks at the used and avoided words as simultaneous opposites.[118] Although unrotated data is normally ignored, it is presented here because the statistical procedure yielded clinically useful and intuitively valid data. **Table 3** shows patterns of group life composed of pairs which may seem to be opposing concepts yet actually fit together to form a creative whole.

Table 3

PAIRED OPPOSITES

Day 1	Day 2
(Rotated)	*(Rotated)*
STRESS pairs with CONCEPTS	STRESS pairs with ACTION
GENDER pairs with SOLUTIONS	PERCEPTION pairs with SUPPORT
REBELLION pairs with YOU	NATURE pairs with SOLUTIONS
SUPPORT pairs with ACTION	HOSTILITY pairs with Support
PERCEPTION pairs with DISTINCTION	CONCEPTS pairs with DISTINCTION
(Unrotated)	*(Unrotated)*
ACTION pairs with YIELDING	PAIN pairs with SUPPORT
BELONGING pairs with PAIN	SUPPORT pairs with SOLUTIONS
GROUP IDENTITY pairs with NEED	NATURE pairs with CLASSIFYING
WEAK pairs with SELF-ASSERTION	WEAKNESS pairs with AROUSAL
	CONCEPTS pairs with HOSTILITY
	POWER pairs with RELATING
	HESITATION pairs with NEED

Table 3 shows group dynamics take shape as paired opposites—STRESS/CONCEPTS, HOSTILITY/ANALYSIS or PAIN/SUPPORT. Words avoided by one individual create a vacuum which pulls forth the opposite from another group member bringing balance to the larger psychological system—STRESS attracts CONCEPTS, HOSTILITY attracts ANALYSIS, PAIN attracts SUPPORT. The basic building blocks of group life are dynamic pairs with the potential for balance.

Table 3 gives a strange, mathematical summary of the dynamics of eight groups as a whole over two days of face-to-face dialogue. On *Day 1*, STRESS attracted CONCEPTS, GENDER awareness brought social SOLUTIONS, REBELLION required BONDING, SUPPORT brought ACTION, PERCEPTION brought DISTINCTIONS. On *Day 2*, STRESS brought ACTION, PERCEPTION brought SUPPORT, DREAMS showed SOLUTIONS, REBELLION brought SUPPORT, and more CONCEPTS brought more DISTINCTIONS. What is most appealing about the pairs is the extraordinary potential for psychological balance.

The unrotated data (normally tossed out) are presented here for discussion purposes only, since the computer generated pairs, although mathematically suspect at this time, are clinically and intuitively verifiable. The unrotated data show, on *Day 1*, ACTION paired with YIELDING, BELONGING balanced PAIN, GROUP IDENTITY balanced NEED and WEAKNESS brought SELF-ASSERTION. On *Day 2*, PAIN brought SUPPORT, SUPPORT brought SOLUTIONS, NATURE brought CLASSIFICATIONS, WEAKNESS attracted AROUSAL, CONCEPTS paired with HOSTILITY, POWER found RELATING while HESITATION paired with NEED and NATURE balanced NEED. In general, the pairs are the internal balancing skills of group life.

The specific patterns and pairings are not predictable. The pairs can interact in any order—her PAIN can attract his statements of BELONGING or her discussion of BELONGING can activate the PAIN of his loneliness. They take shape according to the needs of the moment, influenced by context and external events. This is particularly important given our newer understanding of the power of organizational culture. There are no guarantees. PAIN may attract CONCEPTS, ACTION, BELONGING or SUPPORT, depending upon what is necessary for balance. Or, as a Vietnam veteran said when discussing this data, "Sometimes PAIN attracts SUPPORT but in the prison camp PAIN attracted more PAIN." The data presented here are just a sample of the uncounted patterns of group life which attract and repel each other in an internal dance of balance.

Culture may support the potential for balance in group dialogue or may work against it. The values and vision of top leadership are crucial. They may shape a culture which reinforces interaction or obedience. Peacemaking emerges when a culture reinforces genuine interaction and the free flow of honest communication.

The specific pairings are less important than the conclusion that the basic building blocks of group life are dynamic pairs which contain the potential for psychological balance. The ancient Taoist notion that form and process in nature take shape as the interplay of opposing patterns Yin and Yang gives added credence to this research finding. Several examples show the potency of these pairings:

(1) The Kelman example (see page 131): "Could the Indian enthusiasm [for unity] help explain the Pakistani fears [of invasion]?" is a comment about ENTHUSIASM/FEAR, which shifted conflict to curiosity, separation to shared relationship.

(2) In Geneva, Gorbachev rejected Reagan's negotiating package and at the same time declared "we must continue to talk" voicing an opposing pattern of REJECTION/CONTINUING.

(3) A pairing from an all-female group in the AU Research Groups shows NEED triggering HOSTILITY/ANALYSIS:

Barbara: I like to feel protected. . . I like to feel security. . . I think
spiritually it's men's responsibility [to protect women].

Enid: I really hate that point of view.

Anna: I want to open doors for different viewpoints rather than attack
points of view.

The movement from Barbara's NEED to Enid's HOSTILITY to Anna's
ANALYSIS was a sequence of movements bringing balance. In this brief
interaction, relationships were changed when discussion showed that different
individuals perceived the same event in different ways.

Cultural Values. Groups, organization and the surrounding environment and larger social-political community all have typical styles, norms and
assumptions. Values are our core beliefs—both conscious and unconscious.
Groups and organizations differ according to how feeling, analytic or action-
oriented they are. For example, comparing the strongly intuitive animal keepers in a zoo with the pragmatic, detail-minded officials in a bank illustrates how
corporate values and personality style combine to create a unique work culture.

An example of the impact of cultural values on conflict and peacemaking
occurred at the Geneva Summit. Reagan was aware that the word "compromise" had negative connotations to the Russians and implied weakness or
giving in on principles. Significantly, the more delicate conversations (human
rights) took place with little press coverage.

Individual styles influence group dynamics and the patterns of conflict
and peacemaking. When personalities meet process and culture, we grapple
with the nature of time.

Synchronicity. Jung believed that archetypal patterns relate to each
other through meaning not causality.[119] Jung had already moved away from
Freud's emphasis on childhood causes of pathology and instead focused on the
meaning of relationships. He used the term "synchronicity" to describe how
psychological patterns connect with each other.

Synchronicity means "meaningful connection," separate events may
have a compelling relationship without one causing the other. Jung said that
the archetypes were the contents of consciousness and that "synchronicity" was
the concept that described how archetypal patterns relate to each other.[120]

For example, Ira Progoff tells a wonderful story about a synchronistic
event in the life of Abraham Lincoln.[121] It occurred when Lincoln still lived in
a frontier town, with little access to the books of law, economics, history,
philosophy and the other tools he would later need. One day, Progoff tells us, a
stranger came to Lincoln to sell a barrel of odds and ends, asking for a dollar.
Lincoln did not think the barrel worth a dollar, but saw the man was needy and
paid the price. When he opened the barrel he found an almost complete edition
of Blackstone's *Commentaries*. Lincoln's legal education had begun.

One small research finding supports this observation about non-causal events.[122] In the AU Research Groups, in eight face-to-face groups meeting for two days, the CAUSAL pattern almost disappears and certainly loses its statistical significance from *Day 1* to *Day 2*. At the same time, the SOLVING, CLASSIFYING and CONCEPTS patterns emerge more strongly. In other words, as individuals and groups learn about behavior, they stop using words of causality ("because," "effect," "consequence" and "fault"). They shift to words of analysis, observation and naming. Group dynamics is rarely a cause-effect universe, so it is more useful simply to observe, report and give feedback. Progoff also concluded that synchronistic events are more frequent in highly emotional situations.

If the patterns of group life have a synchronistic and not causal relationship, then peacemaking is not a matter of assigning blame since one psychological event does not cause another. Rather, peacemaking is creative problem solving. The psychology of individuals, groups and cultures brings nine principles of peacemaking:

---

10. Group discussion surfaces individual differences in values, personality, motivation, style of handling conflict and typical group behavior.
11. Individuals joined together for dialogue generate a larger system of psychological relationships—the group process.
12. Large patterns such as dependency and rebellion, cooperation and healing are composed of basic building blocks such as anger, analysis, pain and support.
13. Individual role specialists voice group patterns such as the Fight Leader voicing anger, showing the characteristic of duality (the dual individual/group connection).
14. The roles and patterns of group life may have an archetypal intensity.
15. Peacemaking occurs as differences in perception become a source of curiosity not conflict.
16. Group dynamics take shape as paired opposites containing the mechanisms for balance.
17. Cultural style and values influence group behavior.
18. Patterns occur at or about the same time without one causing the other; they show synchronicity.

When Jung looked for principles to describe the interactions of the archetypes, he found parallels between the physical and psychological sciences. For Jung, the interactions of particles in the nucleus of the atom was similar to the interactions of archetypes. The metaphor holds for the interaction of individuals within the patterns of face-to-face dialogue. The patterns of our physical and psychological reality show stunning parallels and reveal nature's internal unity. Quantum physics gives us words to describe peacemaking.

QUANTUM REALITY

Physics is the ancient search to find and measure our fundamental physical reality.[123] Physicists study matter, energy, light, sound, time, space, magnetism, electricity, gravity and radiation, among other events, generally as numerical formulas. Physics, from the Greek word "physis" meaning "essential nature," was originally the province of Greek philosophers and magicians in the 5th century B.C. who sought to understand "the essential nature of all things."

In classical physics, all the material stuff of this world—from people to trees to birds—was thought to be made of atoms, the "basic building blocks." Atoms were solid, indivisible, indestructible particles which moved in empty space, through the purity of time and in accordance with the laws of gravity. Many of these ideas held sway for 2,500 years, influenced by Cartesian philosophy, which divided mind from body ("I think therefore I am") and demoted consciousness, the observing mind and intuitive knowledge to the non-scientific.

The 20th century changed all that. We now know that atoms are not solid, space is not empty, time is not pure and activity follows the logic of internal needs. Furthermore, the observer helps create reality.

The atom is not "solid" but composed of hundreds of subatomic particles in constant motion, described as multiple, simultaneous patterns of interactions, or bundles of energy. The particles are surrounded by space, but space is not "empty." Space is inextricably connected with fields, such as magnetic and gravitational fields.

As physicists studied these fields, they were confronted with conflicting observations, especially about the nature of light. Einstein concluded that light can be understood as both particles confined to a small space or waves spread throughout a region of space. Particle or wave depends upon your perspective (what equipment you use to take measurements) and neither can be understood apart from the other.

The particle/wave duality is the foundation of quantum theory and a fruitful source of guidelines to understand the individual/group connection. Quantum theory shows the dynamic connections and dual aspects of parts and wholes, particles and waves, and individuals in group dialogue. You and I are the particles, the group process is the wave.

In 1905, Einstein published his article on quantum theory and his famous article about relativity theory, drastically changing our notions of space and time. It has alway been common knowledge that dimensions in space are relative: what is right or left, up or down, depends on who is doing the describing. Einstein extended this relativity to dimensions in time. A charming metaphor attributed to Einstein easily teaches the concept of relativity: "Two seconds on a hot stove is an eternity, two seconds with a pretty girl is but a moment." Specifically, time slows down as the observer or the observed approaches the speed of light. In modern physics, time is no longer pure.

Relativity theory showed that time and space form a fundamental, four-dimensional reality, called "space-time." Particles emerge from and dissolve into quantum fields existing in space-time. The particles are best understood as bundles of energy.

A closer look will help. Like face-to-face groups, the subatomic world is a realm of ceaseless, simultaneous, overlapping patterns of interactions. Pions collide with protons creating neutrons and kaons. The lambda decays into a proton and a pion. Photons are spontaneously created from the energy of motion. From the perspective of the quantum field, matter and energy are two sides of the same coin. In the words of physicist and systems thinker Fritjof Capra:

> Atoms consist of particles, and these particles are not made of any material stuff; when we observe them, we never see any substance. What we observe are dynamic patterns continually changing into one another—a continuous dance of energy. (Capra, *The Tao of Physics*, p. 188)

Most importantly, space participates in this dance of energy. Space is an all encompassing energy field. Particles are local condensations of this field, concentrations of energy which come and go. Einstein's famous equation, $E=MC^2$, where C is the speed of light, shows the equivalence of matter and energy.

In modern physics, the fundamental physical reality is the quantum field, interlocking networks of energy where order emerges from interaction and duality is commonplace. Such opposites as particle and wave, mass and energy, matter and space, space and time, destructible and indestructible are unified through rhythm and relativity theory.

Relativity theory describes the perspective of the quantum field (four dimensional space-time) where concepts in conflict are different aspects of the same underlying reality. Matter and energy are two sides of the same coin. Participants always define the window of balance for any system in conflict. Relativity theory is the conceptual proof. Relativity theory unites concepts in conflict by focusing on a shared field of energy. Quantum theory and relativity theory are the sources of at least six more principles to talk about group life and peacemaking:

19. Individuals joined together for any purpose generate a shared field of energy.
20. Patterns take shape with a dual particle/wave aspect.
21. All patterns and roles live in all players; all individuals have the potential to play in any pattern, including Anger, Analysis, Need, Support and Vision.
22. The same pattern can be perceived differently by different observers, including observations of sequence in time.
23. Concepts in conflict are different aspects of the same underlying reality.
24. A focus on the shared field unites concepts in conflict.

Quantum theory provides words connecting individual differences (particles confined in space) and group dynamics (waves spread through a region of space). Relativity theory describes the unifying movements of a shared field of energy. Bootstrap physics raises principles of order, logic, rhythm and consciousness. (Yes, I still remember that a lambda is like a photon but Pain is not Joy; entropy describes the distinction, while metaphysics provides the perspective.)

Entropy. In the engaging words of physicist Heinz Pagels, "Entropy is a quantitative measure of how disorganized a physical system is, a measure of its messiness." (p. 101) In a closed system, entropy increases. "Everything eventually falls apart—buildings crumble and fall into ruin; we age; fruit rots." (Pagels, *The Cosmic Code*, p. 102)

Entropy, the messiness or wasted energy of a system, is a useful metaphor for the Shadow motivations—the darker, destructive motives and impulses. In a closed human system, entropy grows. Without a continuous exchange of energy and information, and a concern for the well-being of others, violence and waste grow. Without feedback from the environment, systems wind down and die. Entropy is contained within Principle #14 Archetypal Energy and is the opposite of Principle #7 Feedback. As the discussion below shows, feedback imports energy and exports entropy by tapping the dynamics of self-organization.

Order. Order means how patterns connect with each other. Traditionally, observers such as Ira Progoff talked about three types of connections:[125] (1) Causal relationships mean one pattern is the result of another. For example, if I punched you in the nose and you said "ouch!", your words are probably the result of my action. (2) Goal-seeking relationships mean patterns are connected in the service of some purpose. For example, behavior may be motivated toward meeting a specific need such as hunger or thirst. Fundamental needs drive people toward survival and then beyond. (3) Simultaneous relationships mean patterns are connected through a shared participation in the flow of events. If this connection has a quality of significant coincidence or even magical effect, then the patterns have a synchronistic connection. Synchronistic means meaningful connection.

More recently, discussion of "order" in living systems has included physical chemist Ilya Prigogine's work on "order through fluctuation" and Erich Jantsch's writing on the "dynamics of self-organization." In 1967, Prigogine confirmed the existence of "dissipative structures," which are the new structures generated when some chemicals are added to others and certain conditions are met—similar to the snowflakes which emerge from cooling water.[126] These structures are open, dynamic, self-renewing systems maintained by a continual exchange of matter and energy with the environment.

For Jantsch, the existence of dissipative structures describes a new ordering principle and provides a metaphor for creativity.[127] When interaction spontaneously generates a new structure, a system is creative: "the role of fluctuations . . . renders the law of large numbers invalid and gives a chance to the individual and its creative imagination." (p. 8) Jantsch sees creativity and self-organization reflected in the interconnectedness of natural dynamics at all levels of nature. According to Jantsch, the characteristics of the physical and social universe are self-determinacy, self-organization and self-renewal. The open system is neither emerging nor decaying, nor is it predetermined; open systems are creative and self-organizing.

All face-to-face groups contain this internal capacity for self-organization. In dialogue, what might appear to be "controlled chaos" is a living network of dynamics with an internal logic—order emerges from interaction. HOSTILITY attracts SOLUTIONS which pair with DENIAL which stimulates more HOSTILITY and draws out PAIN which brings forth SUPPORT and room for ANALYSIS before ACTION. All groups contain this potential for balance, renewal and creative fluctuations.

The patterns of peacemaking are dynamisms emerging from internal networks of communication across multiple levels of relationship influenced by fundamental rhythms of harmony. People speak their words and generate a field of energy where universal images and their opposite tensions are communicated across multiple levels of meaning. The patterns take shape as pairs according to the dynamics of self-organization, following a logic of their own.

Logic. Gregory Bateson defined the fit between patterns of relationships as complementary or symmetrical.[128] Complementary relationships are mutually exclusive, dissimilar pairs which fit together to form a whole, such as MALE/FEMALE. Symmetrical relationships are similar pairs that fit together so that more of one brings out more of the other, such as the ARMS RACE. Complementary and symmetrical are useful ways to distinguish between individual and group behavior. Both kinds of activity (individual differences and group dynamics) have their own logic.

The research data show that patterns take shape as dynamic pairs. The pairs seem to operate differently for individuals and the group process. The pair STRESS/CONCEPTS shows this difference. For the individual, STRESS and CONCEPTS have an exclusive quality. When voicing stress and anxiety, people are not likely to be intellectualizing and using words of conceptual analysis. For the individual, the paired opposites mean the presence of one is associated with the absence of the other, though the potential for shift is ever present. The pairs are complementary.

For the group system, however, the presence of one is associated with the presence of the other. STRESS and CONCEPTS may attract each other, occurring at the same time. Anxiety and its opposite, analysis, appear together, one draws out the other. For the group, the paired opposites bring balance. They are symmetrical and include the complementary logic of individuals. Transported across nonlocal and multi-levelled channels of interaction, archetypal images and opposing patterns always contain the potential for balance. The two points to be made from these data are that group patterns take shape as pairs and group behavior, with a life and logic of its own, is a separate level of relationships different from individual behavior.

Awareness. Group life appears to have knowledge, consciousness and mindfulness. Systems theorists Gregory Bateson, Erich Jantsch and Fritjof Capra essentially agree about the criteria which define "creative mind."[129] Capra notes that mind implies a certain complexity and refers to Bateson's six criteria for mind. Mind shows characteristics of:[130]

(1) the transfer of information about differences,
(2) along channels of communication,
(3) emerging from an internal reservoir of energy,
(4) as patterns of relationships,
(5) with meaning and context, and
(6) with the capacity for self-correction.

Any system that meets these criteria shows the activities we associate with mind—such as thinking, learning and remembering.

Group life satisfies Bateson's criteria for creative mind. The patterns of group life emerge from a shared field of energy and communicate information about meaningful differences. The capacity of group life for self-correction, the patterns which appear mindful, bring physicists if not mediators to the definition of consciousness. At the least, the internal capacity for adapting to new information and generating mechanisms of balance suggests group life is composed of levels of mind, each self-organizing and self-correcting.

Rhythm. Group life is a field of energy with internal rhythm. The activity of the patterns, the movements of dual aspects and the interactions of opposing tensions generate rhythm. Modern physics studies the universe as patterns of relationships where opposites are unified through rhythm.[131] The fundamental rhythm of the physical universe is the harmony of opposing tensions: the movements of quantum fields unify matter and energy.

In face-to-face group discussion, we mirror this harmony in the rhythm of separating and belonging.[132] In conversation, we stand alone and feel team spirit, we assert our unique individuality and voice the needs of group life. The rhythm of separating and belonging unifies individual and group needs, balances separation and togetherness. Whatever the content, the shared rhythm of interaction unifies the parts and the whole. The recurring movement between separation and belonging is a repeating melody in all living systems. Rhythms of harmony accompany all patterns of interaction. The rhythm of fields in nature is the unity of opposing forces.

In modern physics, patterns involve, connect or contain each other in a continuous dynamic process. In face-to-face discussion, psychological patterns also involve and connect with each other in a multi-dimensional and continual dynamic process. Larger patterns such as sub-grouping or scapegoating are composed of basic building blocks shaped as pairs, emerging from a shared field of energy, and connected to all other patterns. In group discussion, conflict contains balance and harmony.

Evolution. Over time, groups in dialogue evolve in the direction of increased complexity, increased coordination and increased awareness. In part, we experience this new meaning as the resolution of opposition and the growing connections of mutual support and maturity.

An "older" group is different from a "younger" group. The more mature group shares information more effectively, talks about internal tensions more easily and has greater respect for the knowledge found in different viewpoints. The more mature group is less likely to search for causes and sources of blame, it is more likely to observe and describe connections. Over time, groups hold together with stronger links and develop a culture with special language and shared myths. Group maturity can be measured as the increased sharing and coordination of information, roles, power, patterns and responsibilities.

A mature group balances the needs of individuals, the reality of differences and the necessity of unity. It takes some time for a face-to-face group to learn these skills of peacemaking. This philosophical view brings the last five principles of peacemaking:

25. Order emerges from interaction: The knowledge is in the system.
26. The rhythm of fields in nature is the harmony of opposing forces.
27. Group maturity can be measured as the increased sharing and coordination of information, roles, power, patterns and responsibilities.
28. Group life shows the characteristics of awareness and mindfulness.
29. Groups show equifinality—final results may be achieved with many different conditions and in many different ways.

The twenty-nine principles generate a theory of peacemaking: **People joined together in face-to-face dialogue tap patterns of balance and rhythms of harmony across multiple levels of reality.**

Peacemaking is alive and well. The technologies, dynamics and theories all point to common ground, internal mechanisms of balance and harmony and the existence of knowledge needed to solve major domestic and global problems. It is time to recognize our conflict resolutions skills and make a commitment to sustained dialogue.

Part IV

APPLICATION

Chapter 12:

DESIGNING PEACE CONFERENCES

CHAPTER 12

DESIGNING
PEACE CONFERENCES

"I am convinced the conference model made the difference."
Ambassador John W. MacDonald

Peace-seeking conferences bring people together to analyze conflict and solve problems. A well-designed conference is a tool for crisis intervention, introducing new ideas, managing conflict or planning long-term and complex projects.

Whatever the content, problem-solving conferences are typically divided into team meetings, sub-group negotiations and plenary (whole-conference) sessions. Such a conference takes on the qualities of a living system with internal patterns, rhythms and momentum. A careful design can focus this energy to deal with problems of purpose, policies, people, culture, technology, values or environment.

This chapter grounds technology, psychology and theory in the systems design of peace-seeking conferences.

CONFERENCE DESIGN

When ancient chieftains sent messengers to neighboring tribes calling for regional councils on war or peace, the idea of the modern conference was born. A working conference is a special meeting to exchange information or solve problems. In the 1980s, as program planners have become more sophisticated, conferences have become everyday tools to introduce new ideas, manage conflict and negotiate agreements.[133] In general, conference design has shifted away from the speaker-audience-cocktails format to a new emphasis on workshops and "relevant" agendas.

Problem-solving conferences can be useful in any organizational system—schools, hospitals, homes for the elderly, small or large businesses, state or federal agencies, community organizations or social institutions which exist for brief periods of time, such as traditional conference gatherings of psychologists, physicians, priests or politicians. Problem-solving conferences require a design which encourages interaction, works issues through and reports observations of conference dynamics as feedback for self-correction or action.

Conference planners have not always agreed that "dynamics" are useful information for conference participants. For example, in an excellent article called "Conference Arrangements," anthropologist Margaret Mead described a group "rebellion" led by Dr. Harry Stack Sullivan in the planning meetings for the 1948 Second World Congress on Mental Health.[134] Sullivan formed a planning commission whose objectives (support the new World Health Organization) conflicted with Congress goals (develop an international statement on mental health). Mead concluded that these conflicting objectives were never resolved and contributed to a period of disorganization for the World Congress and its parent organization, the World Federation for Mental Health.

Mead suggested that conference management be aware of conference dynamics, but concluded that "to bring the difficulties into the consciousness of the group . . . [would be] destructive and inefficient." (p. 57) Twenty-five years later, conference managers are bringing difficulties into consciousness in an open effort to teach participants how to manage conflict. For example, Herbert Kelman's workshops on international conflict resolution, described in Chapter 8, specifically use process observations to help the work of conference participants. Perhaps the general public is now more sophisticated about "psychology" and more comfortable talking about human behavior.

Conference Design. Many of the case studies in this book use variations of a general problem-solving, peace-seeking conference structure. There are eight basic components of the systems approach to conference design:

1. An **OPENING** statement by organizational leaders or outside consultants clarifies conference design, ground rules and expectations. A clear agenda gives added confidence in the structure and flow of conference events.
2. **INTRODUCTIONS** let people see who is present and how they operate, while feeling grounded in a sense of self.
3. **VISION** and **VALUES** include a purpose statement or a description of philosophy, style, expectations and shared vision.
4. **WARM-UP GAMES** are non-threatening exercises that teach lessons of group decision making, communication and group dynamics.
5. **PERSONALITY PROFILES, GROUP DYNAMICS** and **CULTURAL VALUES** can be discussed so that participants learn more about themselves, each other, group process, cultural values and different styles of communication.
6. **PROBLEM SOLVING** is accomplished through facilitated discussion and analysis of shared problems using problem-solving technologies. The focus is the analysis of the conflict situation and the generation of solutions and action plans through consensus.
7. **PROCESS REVIEW** and **FEEDBACK** is accomplished in small group and whole conference meetings leading to self-correction and evolution.
8. **CLOSING** rituals allow participants to debrief and report their learnings, feelings, observations or interpretations.

The eight elements listed here can be shortened, lengthened or modified as necessary. Here is a 3-day version which starts Tuesday after lunch and finishes Friday before lunch:

3-DAY AGENDA

TUESDAY
1:00 – 1:15	Opening
1:15 – 2:00	Introductions
2:00 – 3:15	Organizational Philosophy
3:15 – 3:30	Break
3:30 – 4:15	Warm-Up Game
4:15 – 4:45	Discuss Group Decision Making
4:45 – 5:00	Closing Activity

WEDNESDAY
8:30 – 9:00	Check In
9:00 – 10:30	Personality Tests
10:30 – 10:45	Break
10:45 – 12:00	Discuss Individual Differences
12:00 – 1:30	LUNCH
1:30 – 4:30	Brainstorm Problems, Choose Focus
4:30 – 5:00	Feedback and Process Review

```
THURSDAY
  8:30 –  9:00  Check In
  9:00 – 12:00  Small Problem-Solving Groups
 12:00 –  1:30  LUNCH
  1:30 –  4:30  More Problem Solving
  4:30 –  5:00  Feedback and Process Review
FRIDAY
  8:30 –  9:00  Check In
  9:00 – 10:00  Finalize Solutions and Action Plan
 10:00 – 11:00  Present Solutions to Large Group
 11:00 – 12:00  Process Review and Closing Ritual
```

This design has been adapted for use in hospitals, schools, manufacturing facilities, city and federal agencies, prisons and conference meetings of professional associations. Here's a one-day version, billed as a team-building workshop for thirty-two mid-level managers faced with problems in quality control.

```
                    1-DAY AGENDA
  8:00 –  8:15  Opening and Purpose Statement
  8:15 –  8:30  Introductions
  8:30 – 10:00  The Wilderness Game
 10:00 – 10:15  Break
 10:15 – 11:30  Personality Styles
 11:30 – 12:00  Process Review
                LUNCH
  1:15 –  4:00  Problem Solving
  4:00 –  4:30  Present Solutions to Large Group
  4:30 –  5:00  Process Review and Closing Ritual
```

Obviously, more time is needed for groups which are angrier, engaged in long, drawn-out conflict or deeply troubled by internal or external events. Nonetheless, anger can turn to analysis and solutions in even a one-day meeting with a clear agenda and focused purpose. The next case study shows the pivotal role of conference design in international settings.

The Global Scene. The Geneva and Iceland summit meetings showed the need for careful attention to the structure of peace-seeking negotiations. The impact of conference design and structure is pin-pointed in the next case study.

In 1984, the U.S. Department of State, Center for the Study of Foreign Affairs, published *International Negotiation: Art and Science*, a wonderful summary of a 1983 conference for Foreign Service officials, experienced negotiators and academics who have pioneered research in conflict resolution.[135] Discussing the design and dynamics of peace-seeking meetings such as U.N. conferences or international treaty negotiations, William Zartman, professor of political science at Johns Hopkins University, outlined three functions of complex negotiations: diagnosing all ingredients of the situation, finding a formula to serve as the basis for agreement (for example, the Egyptian-Israeli formula of security for territory) and then implementing details by applying the formula to the specifics of the situation. The three stages of **Diagnosis, Formula** and **Implementing Details** provide a framework to deal step-by-step with multiple, overlapping issues. Thomas Colosi of the American Arbitration Association then pointed out that participants in such discussions must learn to balance trusting people and trusting the process of negotiation. Harold Saunders, assistant secretary of state from 1978 to 1981, remarked that the negotiation itself occurs after the pre-negotiation phases of defining the problem, making the commitment to negotiate and arranging the negotiations. Ambassador John W. McDonald, then told the following story describing the critical role of conference design.

Case Study #34: The Role of Design

I would like to take Bill Zartman's formula and add a subheading to it and talk about the model of the conference itself. I am not talking necessarily about the size of the table. But I am talking about the design of the conference.

In 1979 I was involved in a conference to negotiate a treaty against the taking of hostages. This, of course, was a very delicate thing with Libya and Syria and the Soviet Union. Thirty-six countries were involved in the process. They met for three years, three weeks at a time, with no success whatsoever.

Before the last meeting, we looked at the model of what had happened before and why it had failed. We felt that it had failed because the previous sessions were public and on the record. In other words, every speaker was simply talking to his home audience, making the points that the Foreign Office had said he should be making. Nothing was happening. We were trying to develop a treaty which would fill a legal hole so that a hostage taker had to be either extradited for prosecution or prosecuted where he was arrested.

We tried something different in the third and probably final three-week session. After the opening morning, we proposed that this same group of thirty-six nations turn itself into an informal working group not open to the public. That meant no records of any kind, no secretary, no press and therefore, in practice, no speeches since no one was there to listen.

The delegates immediately got down to work and we negotiated and interacted informally, ten to twelve hours a day. The last day of the three-week session we reconvened in plenary session, open to the public, and adopted a draft treaty. I am convinced the conference model [conference design] made the difference. (p. 6)

• • • • •

Whatever one's opinion about the value of summit meetings, the influence of conference design is quite apparent. In 1986, Reagan and Gorbachev found themselves in Iceland with an unclear purpose amid grandiose public expectations and confronted with a media debating whether it was a "true summit." Carried away by the spirit of dialogue and the intensity of a conference setting, Reagan and Gorbachev negotiated agreements without sufficient time for thorough discussion and without input from allies who would be greatly affected by a total withdrawal of nuclear missiles. Perhaps magnified by global electronic transmissions, the Iceland summit seemed charged with archetypal energy where images of Wise One and Fool, Good versus Evil, Armegeddon and Golden Age of Peace had conscious and unconscious influence. No wonder the politicians went home exhausted.

The role of conference design must ultimately take into account the impact of culture on negotiation strategies. The study of cultural habits and peace-seeking strategies is a very recent development in the young science of peacemaking.

Culture and Peacemaking. In 1987, the U.S. Department of State, Center for the Study of Foreign Affairs published *National Negotiating Styles* which briefly describes the negotiating styles of China, France, Egypt, the Soviet Union, Japan and Mexico.[136] A few conclusions from that book show fascinating comparisons.

The Chinese culture stresses interpersonal relationships and inter-dependency rather than individuality. Thus, Chinese negotiators, who prefer to negotiate on their home territory, may use banquets and sight-seeing tours to cultivate a sense of "friendship." However, in the Chinese tradition, "friend-ship" implies obligations as well as personal relations and Chinese negotiators often encourage a sense of obligation in their counterparts. The Chinese approach to negotiation has been described as a linear process. In opening moves, they set ground rules with an emphasis on "principles" (e.g., "peaceful co-existence"); then, embark on a long period of assessment, probing to dis-cover the opponent's bottom line without revealing their own; then, perhaps years later, quickly conclude agreements; and, in the final phase of implementation, may reopen issues their opponents felt had been resolved. The Chinese are a very patient people and the American "can do" enthusiasm may be interpreted as impatience. It is not a good idea to negotiate with the Chinese if you have a deadline to meet.

The French diplomatic corps is one of the oldest in the world, with a strong and consistent intellectual and philosophical flavor to their thought and training. French diplomats are conservative, prefer concepts over facts and strive to maintain the autonomy of the individual negotiator. They often enter negotiations with a single, elaborate, carefully planned proposal and no fall-back positions. Since individuality and self-identity are so important, the French tend to dislike face-to-face negotiations which might call for compromise. When agreement appears impossible, they may break off discussions rather than persevere through laborious negotiations. Their intellectual style may create difficulties when faced with the pragmatics of participatory decision making, while their genious has led to the development of grand designs such as the Common Market.

Egyptian negotiators have a tremendous sense of history and national pride—they refer to their country as the cradle of civilization with a recorded history of 5,000 years. Following tradition, they want, expect and receive strong leadership, although presidential decisions may be blocked or delayed by a large, ingrained bureaucracy. Negotiation is influenced by the suq model and the Bedouin model. The suq is the marketplace, where preliminary discussions over coffee establish a personal relationship and bargaining begins with very high and very low prices, working toward the middle through haggling and maneuvering. Eventually, closure is the win-win result where both sides are satisfied with the outcome. In the Bedouin or tribal model, especially when blood has been shed and honor is at stake, saving face and not haggling is the key. In this model, a third-party intermediary, trusted by both sides, provides a face-saving solution.

The Soviet negotiating style flows from a history of isolation, invasion and violent conflict, influenced by a lack of natural frontiers. The consequences are a preoccupation with security and secrecy. Soviet decision making in foreign affairs is the province of a small group of men in the Politburo of the Communist Party and the views of the military are predominant if not controlling. Both decisions and details are generally decided by those at the top of the Soviet hierarchy. Thus, Soviet history, ideology and organizational structure lead to three perspectives: negotiation is seen as a means to advance power and influence; generalities and principles are preferred over details; and compromise in negotiations is perceived as weakness. The Soviet style is blunt and combative, with extreme, opening positions, reluctance to make concessions and denial of actual compromises. A favorite tactic is "salami-slicing"—making concessions slice by slice. While the Chinese work to develop a sense of obligation, the Soviets, who also prefer to negotiate on home territory, work to wear down their counterparts.

The Japanese dislike formal, negotiating sessions because they have long been taught to avoid social conflict. The Japanese culture emphasizes accommodation, personal obligation, understanding and satisfying the concerns of others. The Japanese negotiatiors will never say "no" to their counterparts in formal sessions, preferring a polite exchange and saving alternative proposals for informal sessions. Further complicating matters, Japanese diplomacy is very decentralized and government departments (while remaining dependent upon the policies of the majority political party) often negotiate with foreign governments. The Japanese consensus-building strategies mean their positions are often considered final proposals fair to all and not open to further bargaining. While Americans negotiate details, the Japanese negotiate a relationship. The communication patterns of the Japanese are highly dependent on the social context, rely on euphemism and vagueness, and require the negotiating partner to understand a complex web of relationships and interactions.

Mexican history is marked by Spanish rule, French occupation and American invasion and "penetration." The Mexican political system is quite hierarchical with great influence given to the presidency. Mexican negotiating teams present a united front, clearly dependent upon the senior negotiator who ultimately defers to the Mexican president. Mexican negotiatiors have a fondness for "lofty principles" such as "repository of moral values," although harsh economic reality has forced a true pragmatism.

According to the contributors in *National Negotiating Styles*, the lessons for American negotiators are clear: Don't assume the world communicates the way Americans do. Be prepared and do your homework. Be patient. Have clear objectives. Seek opportunities for informal sessions. Understand national sensitivities.

PROCESS, SHADOW AND PROJECTION

Somehow, the rational description of conference design and cultural styles obscures the intensity of conference process. The following case study demonstrates that problem-solving conferences draw forth the full range of archetypal behavior and images, where Hostility attracts Analysis, Good attracts Evil and Solutions attract our Shadows.

An event from a 1978 working conference for a national women's organization demonstrates the complexity of conference dynamics. The conference was designed in partnership with organization consultant, Georgia Strasburg. It was designed so the organization could clarify goals, priorities, philosophy and decision making during a period of rapid growth. The women's group had changed from informal local networks to a large, formal national organization.

Case Study #35: *Mirrors and Reflections*

The 2½-day conference was made up of a series of small problem-solving meetings, plenary sessions and task force events in which members discussed written questions about mission, objectives and priorities presented at the beginning of each session. The small problem-solving teams were the three naturally occurring organizational clusters: the Central Staff, the Board of Directors and two groups of Chapter Representatives (from across the United States). Each group had the services of a consultant.

During the conference, the small groups worked on basic issues and reported back to the large group their decisions about goals, values, structure and long-term plans. An "Open" time during the conference was scheduled so individuals could address issues which were emerging spontaneously.

By *Day 2* of the conference, the consulting team became aware that they felt "pulled" into the process of the small groups to which they were assigned. In a very general way, and sometimes in a very specific way, the consultants absorbed the dynamics of the group they were assigned. The consultants "mirrored" the dynamics of participants. That night, there was a dream about someone breaking into a house.

By *Day 3*, what the consultants said to **each other** was a mirror image of conference dynamics. Lynn (who consulted to the Staff) felt pressure to "take care of" tearful participants, just as Staff felt pressure to "take care of" the wandering Chapter Representatives from out-of-town. Georgia (consultant to the Board of Directors) was trying to control Lynn's "caretaking" behavior, just as the Board was trying to come up with ways to structure and control the Staff, who were networking beyond their budget.

Meanwhile, the two consultants to the Chapter Representatives were angry at Georgia (consultant to the Board) for not controlling Lynn (consultant to the Staff)who was now wandering the halls, talking to Chapter Representatives. About the time Chapter Representatives voiced disappointment about the Board's squabbles with the Staff, Lynn and Georgia were fighting out loud about conference design. The two other consultants complained of headaches and backaches while some Chapter Representatives roamed the halls, crying and ignored.

The tension of problem solving peaked and released as attention in the "Open" meeting turned to a spontaneously emerging issue: the lack of Board members from rural America. Chapter Representatives from farms, small towns and Indian reservations complained about the lack of representation on the Board of Directors. In an emotional, angry, then exhuberant session, the conference-as-as-whole decided on a formula to correct the Board imbalance.

In general, the conference helped the organization clarify internal roles and policies, balance power between Board and Staff, redefine the composition of the Board and encourage the emergence of Chapter Representative leadership. Events helped the consultants gain a healthy respect for the electric potential and archetypal intensity of conference dynamics. Georgia's observation was that the female issues and women's dynamics had split her and Lynn into the task-minded, time-bounded Bad Father (Georgia) and the mooshy, over-nurturant Good Mother (Lynn). Paradox and process being what they are, Georgia went off to have a baby and Lynn went off to write a book.

• • • • •

The power and range of conference dynamics are extraordinary. Group discussion generates a field of interconnnected patterns of universal dimension and archetypal impact. Visions of healing, wholeness and unity are stimulated along with their opposites—destruction, deceit and betrayal. Problem-solving participants and especially facilitators and consultants must learn the logic of this new universe.

Conference dynamics are primitive. The Shadow motivations have the energy of atoms: erupting, exploding and tearing apart. The facilitators and consultants are pulled into dark, eerie tunnels and stay sighted and grounded only through self-study and a focus on the system issues. Facilitators must process their own behavior (report observations of their personal reactions) as feedback for the consulting team or the conference itself. Facilitators must be willing to look in the mirror of conference process and observe personal biases, limitations and weaknesses. When the consulting team welcomes feedback and process review, entropy is exported and the system potential for balance emerges.

PEACEMAKING

Conflict is the opposition of forces. Peacemaking transforms conflict into the energy of creativity as opponents talk about shared problems and discover common ground and shared needs. Peacemaking brings together opposing forces for creative problem solving.

The problem-solving team is a complex organism. Group behavior and peacemaking dynamics have four levels: action, content, process and rhythm.

On the level of group action, peacemaking means making the decision to fight with words, not weapons and sabotage. On the level of content, peacemaking means bringing out the issues and waiting for consensus about action plans. Confronting issues is not tearing into each other, but taking events apart and looking for connections.

Whatever the content, peacemaking includes both individual and group process. At the level of individual dynamics, conflict and peacemaking mean questions about identity: What is this fight about? What side is my group on? Where do I fit in? Is there a right and wrong? Peacemaking requires participants to learn a problem-solving technology and then encounter rage and despair, deception and betrayal, unconscious images of Good and Evil, along the path of learning and healing. In peacemaking, people encounter their hatreds and their mortality. Success requires a willingness to assert personal heroism.

Joined in dialogue, the group as a whole is more than the sum of individuals. Group life is a galaxy of patterns with star players, clusters of relationships, archetypal connections and a surprising quality of balance and mindfulness.

Simultaneously, individuals joined together for dialogue generate a larger field of energy. In the space-time of group life, information is communicated across multiple levels of awareness, duality and unity are commonplace and group dynamics take shape as paired opposites. In face-to-face dialogue, Hostility draws out Analysis, Pain attracts Support and Perception attracts Action creating an intricate dance of balance.

These patterns of balance are influenced by rhythms which unify our physical and psychological reality. The fundamental rhythm of the universe is the harmony of opposing forces. The movements of space and time unify matter and energy, the movements of belonging and separating unify individual and group needs. In general, the fundamental rhythms of the universe unify the parts and the whole, unify opposing forces and generate creative, adaptive new structure.

Peacemaking is alive and well. Technically, conflict resolution includes the roles and procedures of creative problem solving. Mathematically, the statistics are available to track the nonlinear patterns of group consciousness. Psychologically, rational intention and intuitive wisdom turn unique individuals into synergistic teams. Theoretically, individuals joined together for dialogue have access to patterns of balance and rhythms of harmony across multiple levels of reality. Philosophically, these connections between physical and psychological reality are a stunning affirmation of nature's dignity and internal harmony.

EPILOGUE

For both musician and audience, the experience of SYMPHONY generates an awareness of the interconnectedness of nature. The notions of tone, pitch, rhythm, harmony, melody, balance and integration are part of this experience.

If you pluck a string on a violin, you hear a pitch, such as an "A" note. Pitch is the frequency of the vibration. Every pitch has an infinite variety of tones. Tone is what you add to the pitch, like someone says, "Watch your tone of voice."

Musicians often use words from other senses to describe tone, such as open or nasal, soft or hard, cold or warm and bright or dark. The tone is what musicians and listeners feel physically. In the words of musician Renie Wong Lindley:

> When I play second violin, I am in a perfect position to absorb the totality of a piece like Bach's B Minor Mass. Literally, second violin sits in the middle. I feel the music through the floor and through my feet and throughout my entire body. I feel the music like a shower of sound washing over and through me—that's tone. I also hear the inner harmonies and the inner subtleties.

For a musician, harmony is any combination of pitches. The notes may fit together in a pleasing way or they may fight each other and feel like disharmony.

Rhythm moves the music forward. Rhythm is pace or speed of the impulses generated. The rhythm may be short like a march or long like a waltz. According to Lindley, "Rhythm is the driving force. Unlike art, music moves through time because of rhythm. Rhythm plus harmony is melody—which distinguishes one piece of music from another."

Pitch, tone, rhythm, harmony and melody exist within the orchestra. The role of the conductor is balance and integration.

The conductor sets the balance in two ways. If the horns are playing too loud with respect to the violins, the conductor facilitates a correction. A conductor is also responsible for balance in terms of musical phrase—for drawing out what's important. People in the orchestra look to the conductor to get beat and visual image of the music. In Lindley's words, "The conductor

243

dances out the music. Some conductors are so expressive they never make a nonmusical gesture."

The music becomes whole as the conductor balances dynamics, structure and meaning. This is integration, which means bringing everything into a place of wholeness. Again from Lindley:

> The B Minor Mass is magnificent. I hear each single line make beautiful sense as a melody. At the same time, all the instruments line up vertically and make perfect sense in harmony. Each line has its own importance and also fits in with the total picture. As orchestra musicians, we each know how to submerge ourselves for the benefit of the whole.

> When the chorus is added to the orchestra, I hear the inner voices and the soft subtleties and I abandon myself to pleasure. I follow the conductor and the section leader and let go of my ego and find perfect freedom. The joy of music is this letting go and integrating with a total larger than myself. It's ironic that with all the rigid regimens of classical music that there is such joy and unlimited spirit.

In many ways, the facilitator who guides a problem-solving group through the intricacies of peacemaking is like a conductor guiding an orchestra through the intricacies of a musical score. The facilitator helps the group reach wholeness by raising differences into awareness and allowing interaction to generate harmony. Individual statements and combinations of patterns rise and fall within the efforts of the whole. Moments of integration and oneness are moments of inner peace, where participants feel both the strength of connectedness and the unlimited spirit of perfect self-expression.

The facilitator balances attention to content with respect for process and balances attention to history with an appreciation for the moment. Simultaneously, the facilitator maintains an eye on the common ground and shared energy which heals human systems split off into opposing forces. The facilitator guides a group to the point of conflict, through opposing tensions to a third position of balance, harmony and integration.

Both musician and facilitator are guided by the understanding that the internal rhythm of their total process is harmony and unity. In peacemaking as in a symphony, interaction may bring joy and unlimited spirit.

NOTES

INTRODUCTION

1. For conflict resolution technologies, see John Burton, "Conflict and Communication: The Use of Controlled Communication" in *International Relations,* London: Macmillan, 1969; Herbert Kelman, "The Problem Solving Workshop in Conflict Resolution," in Richard Merritt (Ed.), *Communication in International Politics*, Urbana, Illinois: University of Illinois Press, 1972, pp. 168-204; Michael Doyle and David Strauss, *How to Make Meetings Work*, Chicago: Playboy, 1976; Rensis Likert and Jane Gibson Likert, *New Ways of Managing Conflict*, New York: McGraw Hill, 1976; A. Delbecq and A. Van de ven, "A Group Process Model for Problem Identification and Program Planning," *Journal of Applied Behavioral Science*, 1971, 7, pp. 466-492; Lawrence Porter (Ed.), *Reading Book for Human Relations Training*, Arlington, Virginia: NTL, 1979; Roger Fisher and William Ury, *Getting to Yes*, New York: Penguin, 1983.

   See also the series from the U.S. Department of State, Foreign Service Institute, Center for the Study of Foreign Affairs, especially *International Negotiation: Art and Science*, John W. McDonald and Diane Bendahmane (Eds.), Washington, D.C.: U.S. Department of State, Center for the Study of Foreign Affairs, 1984; *Perspectives on Negotiation*, John W. McDonald and Diane Bendahmane (Eds.), Washington, D.C.: U.S. Department of State, Center for the Study of Foreign Affairs, 1986; *Multinational Peacekeeping in the Middle East*, Robert Houghton and Frank Trinka, Washington, D.C.: U.S. Department of State, Center for the Study of Foreign Affairs, 1987; *Conflict Resolution: Track Two Diplomacy*, John W. McDonald and Diane Bendahmane (Eds.), Washington, D.C.: U.S. Department of State, Center for the Study of Foreign Affairs, 1987; and *National Negotiating Styles*, Hans Binnendijk (Ed.), Washington, D.C.: U.S. Department of State, Center for the Study of Foreign Affairs, 1987.

   Portions of this book are revised versions of articles originally published as: Lynn Sandra Kahn, "The Dynamics of Scapegoating: The Expulsion of Evil," *Psychotherapy: Theory, Research, and Practice*, 17(3), May

1980, pp. 79-84, used with permission; Kahn, the following all appearing in *Proceedings*, Society for General Systems Research: "Group Process, Quantum Logic and Peacemaking," 1983, pp. 467-473; "The Concept of Duality in Philosophy, Physics, Psychology, and Peacemaking," 1984b; "Peace Development Systems: Cases and Concepts," 1986, pp. (L)88-91; "Case Studies in Peacemaking," 1987, pp. 548-553, all used with permission; Kahn, "The Science of Peacemaking," paper presented at the Society for General Systems Research, 31st Annual Conference, Budapest, 1987, used with permission; "Process and shadow moving through opposition to a third position of balance" is from conversations with Margaret Keyes, Muir Beach, California, 1983; Kahn, "Group Process and Sex Differences," in *Psychology of Women Quarterly*, Summer 1984a, pp. 261-281.

2.   Stephen Ludwig, "Japan Style Quality Circles Go from Fad to Trend," *Investor's Daily*, May 25, 1984; Robert Rehder, "What American and Japanese Managers are Learning from Each Other," *Business Horizons*, March/April 1981, pp. 63-70.

3.   For participatory management see Thomas Peters and Robert Waterman, *In Search of Excellence*, New York: Harper and Row, 1982; William Ouchi, *Theory Z*, Menlo Park, California: Addison-Wesley, 1981; Anthony Athos and William Pascale, *The Art of Japanese Management*, New York: Bantam, 1981; and Rosabeth Moss Kanter, *The Change Masters*, New York: Simon and Schuster, 1983.

4.   John Naisbitt, "Re-inventing the Corporation," *Financial Executives Magazine*, Vol.1, No.2, March 1985.

5.   For social and group psychology see Kurt Lewin, *Field Theory in Social Science*, New York: Harper and Row, 1950; Kenneth Benne, "The Processes of Re-Education: An Assessment of Kurt Lewin's Views," in W. Bennis, R. Chin, and K. Corey, *The Planning of Change* (3rd Edition), New York: Holt, Rinehart, and Winston, 1976, pp. 315-327.

6.   For group process see Wilfred Bion, "Experiences in Groups: I," *Human Relations*, 1948(a), 1, pp. 314-320; W. Bion, "Experiences in Groups: II," *Human Relations*, 1948(b), 1, pp. 487-496; W. Bion, *Experiences in Groups*, New York: Basic Books, 1961; A. K. Rice, *Learning for Leadership*, London: Tavistock, 1965; Graham Gibbard, John Hartman and Richard Mann (Eds.) *Analysis of Groups*, San Francisco: Jossey-Bass, 1974; Kahn, 1980, 1983, 1984a, 1984b.

7.   Herbert Kelman, "An Interactional Approach to Conflict Resolution and its Application to Israeli-Palestinian Relations," in *International*

Interactions 6(2), pp. 99-122; Herbert Kelman and Stephen Cohen, "Reduction of International Conflict: An Interactional Approach," in W. G. Austin and Stephen Worchel (Eds.), *The Social Psychology of Intergroup Relations*, Monterey, California: Brooks-Cole, 1979, pp. 288-303.

8. Leonard Doob (Ed.), *Resolving Conflicts in Africa: The Fermeda Workshop*, New Haven: Yale University Press, 1970; Leonard Doob and William Foltz, "The Belfast Workshop: An Application of Group Techniques to a Destructive Conflict," *Journal of Conflict Resolution*, 1973, 17, pp. 489-512.

9. Fisher and Ury, 1983.

10. For research methodology, see P. Stone, D. Dunphy, M. Smith and D. Ogilvie (Eds.), *The General Inquirer: A Computer Approach to Content Analysis*, Cambridge, Massachusetts: The M. I. T. Press, 1966; Elizabeth Aries, "Interaction Patterns and Themes of Male, Female, and Mixed Groups," *Small Group Behavior*, 7, 1976, pp. 7-18; Kahn, 1980, 1984a, 1984b.

11. Lynn Sandra Kahn, *Solving Problems and Managing Conflict*, San Francisco, California: LSK ASSOCIATES, 1984c.

12. For an introduction to Jungian psychology see Carl Jung, Marie-Louise von Franz, Joseph Henderson, Jolande Jacobi and Aniela Jaffe, *Man and His Symbols*, New York: Doubleday, 1964; C. Jung and Wolfgang Pauli, *Interpretation of Nature and the Psyche*, London: Rutledge and Kegan Paul, New York: Pantheon Books, Bollingen Series XLVIII, 1955; Carl Jung and Richard Wilhelm, *The Secret of the Golden Flower*, London: Rutledge and Kegan Paul, 1931; Violet de Laszlo (Ed.), *Psyche and Symbol: A Selection From the Writings of C.G. Jung*, New York: Doubleday, 1958.

13. For systems theory and quantum physics see Gregory Bateson, *Steps to An Ecology of Mind*, New York: Ballantine, 1972; Fritjof Capra, *The Tao of Physics*, Boulder, Colorado: Shambala, 1975; Daniel Katz and Robert Kahn, *The Social Psychology of Organizations*, New York: Wiley, 1976; Newton Margulies and Anthony Raia, *Conceptual Foundations of Organization Development*, New York: McGraw Hill, 1978; Charles Schoderbek, Peter Schoderbek and Asterios Kefalas, *Management Systems: Conceptual Considerations*, Dallas: Business Publications, 1980; Fritjof Capra, *The Turning Point*, New York: Simon and Schuster, 1982; Heinz Pagels, *The Cosmic Code*, New York: Simon and Schuster, 1982.

14. For early discussion of rhythm see Gibbard et al, 1974, especially pp. 247-277; Capra, 1982, p. 267.

Chapter 1: PROBLEM SOLVING AND PEACEMAKING

15. Kahn, 1984c; Ronald Kregoski and Beverly Scott, *Quality Circles*, Chicago: Dartnell, 1982.

16. For conference design, see Rice, 1965; Lynn Sandra Kahn and Georgia Strasburg, "Group Process and Organizational Change," unpublished manuscript, Washington, D. C., 1979; Jimmy Carter, *Keeping Faith*, New York: Bantam Books, 1982, used with permission.

17. Isabel Briggs Myers and Peter Myers, *Gifts Differing*, Palo Alto, California: Consulting Psychologist Press, 1980; David Keirsey and Marilyn Bates, *Please Understand Me*, Del Mar, California: Prometheus, 1978.

18. Donald T. Simpson, "Wilderness Survival: A Consensus-Seeking Task," in J. William Pfeiffer and John E. Jones (Eds.), *The 1976 Annual Handbook for Group Facilitators*, San Diego: University Associates, 1976, pp. 19-25, used with permission. (The answer is c.)

Chapter 2: TO THINE SELF BE TRUE

19. Carl Jung, *Psychological Types*, Bollingen Series, XX, Vol VII, 1931; and Jung et al, 1964.

20. Linda Groff, "Cultural Mindsets and Cross-Cultural Conflict Resolution," paper presented at Society for General Systems Research 30th Annual Conference, Philadelphia, May 1986.

21. Abraham Maslow, "A Theory of Human Motivation," *Psychological Review*, pp. 370-396, July 1943.

22. David McClelland, *Power: The Inner Experience*, New York: Irvington, 1975.

23. Kahn, 1983 and 1984b.

24. See also Chester Karrass, *Give and Take*, New York: Thomas Crowell, 1974; Chester Karrass, *The Negotiating Game*, New York: Thomas Crowell, 1970.

25. Kenneth Thomas and Ralph Kilman, *Thomas-Kilmann Conflict Mode Instrument*, Tuxedo, New York: Xicom, 1974.

26. For gender and roles see Louise Kaplan, *Oneness and Separateness: From Infant to Individual*, New York: Simon and Schuster, 1978; Nancy Chodorow, "Family Structure and Feminine Personality," in Michelle Zimbalist Rosaldi and Louise Lamphere (Eds.), *Women, Culture, and Society*, Stanford: Standford University Press, 1974; Dorothy Dinnerstein, *The Mermaid and The Minotaur*, New York: Harper and Row, 1976.

27. James O'Neil, "Male Sex Role Conflicts, Sexism, and Masculinity: Implications for Men, Women, and the Counseling Psychologist," paper presented at the American Psychological Association 88th Annual Conference, Montreal, September 1980.

28. Eleanor Maccoby and Carol Jacklin, *The Psychology of Sex Differences*, Stanford: Stanford University Press, 1974.

29. Aries, 1976.

30. Kahn, 1980, 1984a.

31. Sara Winter, "Interracial Dynamics in Self-Analytic Groups," in Gibbard et al, 1974, pp. 197-219; "Ethnic Issues in the Workplace," San Jose, California *Mercury News*, March 1982.

32. For organizational roles see Lewin, 1950; Terrance Deal and Allan Kennedy, *Corporate Culture*, Menlo Park, California: Addison-Wesley, 1982.

Chapter 3: GROUP ROLES

33. Jung, 1964; Katz and Kahn, 1976; Kahn, 1984a.

34. Sigmund Freud, *Group Psychology and the Analysis of the Ego*, in *The Standard Edition of the Complete Psychological Works of Sigmund Freud*, Vol. 18, London: Hogarth, 1955, originally published in 1921.

35. F. Redl, "Group Emotion and Leadership," *Psychiatry*, 1942, 5, pp. 573-596.

36. Robert Bales, *Interaction Process Analysis: A Method for the Study of Small Groups*, Reading, Masssachusetts: Addison-Wesley, 1950; Dexter Dunphy, "Social Change in Self-Analytic Groups," in Stone et al 1966, pp. 287-341.

37. Kahn, 1980, 1984a, 1984b; Dexter Dunphy "Phases, Roles, and Myths in Self-Analytic Groups," in Gibbard et al, 1974, pp. 300-314; Aries, 1976.

38. J. W. Ringwald, "An Investigation of Group Reaction to Central Figures," in Gibbard et al, 1974, pp. 220-246.

39. Jung, 1964.

Chapter 4: DEPENDENCY

40. Rosabeth Moss Kanter, *Men and Women of the Corporation*, New York: Basic Books, 1977.

41. Stanley Milgram, *Obedience to Authority*, New York: Harper Colophon, 1974.

42. Ernest Becker, *The Denial of Death*, New York: The Free Press, 1973; especially pp. 148-150, "Transference as Fear of Death."

43. James George Frazer, *The Golden Bough*, New York: Macmillan, 1922.

44. Kahn, 1986.

45. Simpson, 1976, used with permission. (The answer is "freeze.")

Chapter 5: REBELLION

46. John Fialka, "Botched benefits," *The Wall Street Journal*, October 5, 1981, p. 1.

47. Sigmund Freud, *Totem and Taboo*, in *The Standard Edition of the Completed Psychological Works of Sigmund Freud*, Vol, 13, London: Hogarth, 1955, pp. 1-161, originally published in 1913.

48. Gibbard et al, 1964.

49. Jung, 1964, p. 79 and especially pp. 110-128.

50. Donald Dudley and Graham Webster, *The Rebellion of Boudicca*, New York: Barnes and Noble, 1962, pp. 137-142 (courtesy of Anne Headley).

51. Fred Wright, "The Effects of Style and Sex of Consultants and Sex of Members in Self-Study Groups," *Small Group Behavior*, 1976, 7(4), pp. 433-457.

52. Carol Beauvais, "Dilemmas for Women in Authority," paper presented to the U. S. Commission on Civil Rights, Washington, D. C., September 1977.

53. Patricia Graham Wilson, "Towards a New Understanding of the Gender of Organizations," unpublished doctoral dissertation, Union Graduate School, 1979.

54. Kahn, 1984a.

55. Erich Neumann, *The Great Mother: An Analysis of the Archetype*, translated by Ralph Mannheim, New York: Bollingen Series, XLVII, 1955, p. 185.

56. Julia Sherman, "Power in the Sexes: Rape," paper presented at the American Psychological Association 86th Annual Conference, San Francisco, California, August 1977; Mary Daly, *Beyond God the Father*, Boston: Beacon Press, 1973, especially pp. 44-68.

57. Charlene Spretnak, *Lost Goddesses of Early Greece*, Berkeley: Moon Books, 1978.

58. Fred Wright and Laurence Gould, "Recent Research on Sex-Linked Aspects of Group Behavior: Implications for Group Psychotherapy," in Wolberg and M. Aronson (Eds.), *Group Therapy 1977: An Overview*, New York: Stratton Intercontinental Medical Book Corporation, 1977.

59. Vivian Hopkins Jackson, "Feminism, Racism, Group Process and Organizational Health: Part II," paper presented at the American Psychological Association 88th Annual Conference, Montreal, August 1980.

60. Phyllis Palmer, "White Women/Black Women: The Dualism of Female Identity and Experience," paper presented at the American Studies Association, September 1979.

61. Warren Bennis and Herbert Shepard, "A Theory of Group Development," *Human Relations*, 1956, 9, pp. 415- 437.

62. B. W. Tuckman, "Developmental Sequence in Small Groups," *Psychological Bulletin*, 1965, 63, pp. 384-399.

63. Philip Slater, *Microcosm: Structural, Psychological, and Religious Evolution in Groups*, New York: Wiley, 1966.

64. Bion, 1948a, 1948b.

65. William Shutz, *FIRO: A Three-Dimensional Theory of Interpersonal Behavior*, New York: Holt, 1958.

66. Gibbard et al, 1974, pp. 83-93.

67. Donald T. Brown, personal communication, 1983.

Chapter 6: SUB-GROUPS

68. F. Kenneth Berrien, *General and Social Systems*, New Brunswick, New Jersey: Rutgers University Press, 1968.

69. Likert and Likert, 1976.

70. Marie McGlone, "The Principles of Group Process Evidenced in the Development of the ERA Plank at the 1980 Republican Platform Committee Meeting," unpublished manuscript, George Washington University, May 1981.

71. Melody Brooks Balick, "The Group Dynamics of Decision Making: A Difference of Opinion Among Feminists at the 1980 Democratic National Convention," unpublished manuscript, George Washington University, May 1981.

72. Melanie Klein, *Contributions to Psycho-Analysis: 1921-1945*, London: Hogarth, 1948.

73. W. Elliot Jacques, "Social Systems as a Defense Against Persecutory and Depressive Anxiety," in Gibbard et al, 1974, p. 283.

74. Peter Vaill, "Strategic Planning," paper presented at the 1983 Organization Development Network Conference, Los Angeles, September 1983.

75. Inspired by Gibbard et al, 1974.

Chapter 7: SCAPEGOATING

76. Kahn, 1980.

77. Frazer, 1922, pp. 651-675.

78. Gordon Allport, *The Nature of Prejudice*, Reading, Massachusetts: Addison-Wesley, 1954; E. Vogel and N. Bell, "The Emotionally Disturbed Child as the Family Scapegoat," in W. Bennis, E. Schein, D. Berlew and F. Steels (Eds.), *Interpersonal Dynamics: Essays and Readings on Human Interaction*; Dunphy, 1974, pp. 300-314; Richard Mann, *Interpersonal Styles and Group Development*, New York: Wiley, 1967.

Chapter 8: PEACEMAKING

79. Kelman, 1972, 1979; Kelman and Cohen, 1979.

80. Burton, 1969.

81. Doob, 1970.

82. Doob and Foltz, 1983.

83. Kelman, 1972.

84. Kelman and Cohen, 1979, see especially p. 275.

85. Kelman, personal communication, Washington, D. C., 1981.

86. McDonald and Bendahmane, 1987, pp. 5-20.

87. McDonald and Bendahmane, 1984, pp. 1-9.

88. McDonald and Bendahmane, 1987, pp. 35-52.

89. Carter, 1982, especially pp. 269-429.

90. Robert Blake and Jane Mouton, "Overcoming Group Warfare," *Harvard Business Review*, December 1984, pp. 98-108.

91. A technique developed by Robert Reisett, Training Works, Chevy Chase, Maryland.

92. William Grier and Price Cobbs, *Black Rage*, New York: Basic Books, 1968.

93. Gayle Delaney, *Living Your Dreams*, San Francisco: Harper and Row, 1979; Sigmund Freud, *The Interpretation of Dreams*, London: Hogarth, 1955, Standard Edition, Vol. VI, originally published in 1900; Jung et al, 1964; Edward Whitmont, "Jungian Approach," on James Fosshafe and Clemens Loew (Eds.), *Dream Interpretation: A Comparative Study*, New York: Spectrum, 1978.

Chapter 9: SUPPORT

94. Wayne Merrill, "Group Phenomena Concepts," Washington, D.C.: Group Training Section, St. Elizabeths Hospital, 1980.

95. Kahn, 1980, 1984a.

96. Terry Stein, "Men's Groups," in Kenneth Solomon and Norman Levy (Eds.), *Men in Transition: Theory and Therapy*, New York: Plenum, 1982, pp. 275-307.

97. Nancy Chodorow, *The Reproduction of Mothering*, Berkeley: The University of California Press, 1978.

98. Gibbard et al, 1974; Dexter Dunphy, "Phases, Roles and Myths in Self-Analytic Groups," in Gibbard et al, 1974, pp. 300-314.

Chapter 10: HEALING

99. Capra, 1982.

100. Kenneth Cohen, "Taoist and Native American Healing," interview with KPFA, Berkeley, California, October 28, 1983.

101. Barry McWaters, *Conscious Evolution*, San Francisco: Evolutionary Press, 1982.

102. Maxwell Jones, *Beyond the Therapeutic Community*, New Haven: Yale University Press, 1968; Gordon Paul and Robert Lentz, *Psychosocial Treatment of Chronic Mental Patients: Milieu versus Social Learning Programs*, Boston: Harvard University Press, 1978; G. W. Fairweather, D. Sanders, D. Cressler and H. Maynard, *Community Life for the Mentally Ill: An Alternative to Institutional Care*, New York: Basic Books, 1961; *President's Commission on Mental Health*, Washington, D.C.: General Accounting Office, 1978; J. Borriello, L. S. Kahn, H. S. Leonard, Sara Stevenson and G. Zanni, "A Social Systems Approach to Integrating Saint Elizabeths Hospital Patients Into the Community: A Proposal," Washington, D. C. Group Training Section, St. Elizabeths Hospital, 1980.

103. Don Lathrop, "De-Institutionalization," unpublished manuscript, Los Angeles, 1978.

104. Richard Almond, *The Healing Community*, New York: Jason Aronson, 1974.

105. See also R. M. Kanter, *Commitment and Community*, New Haven: Yale University Press, 1968; Victor Turner, *The Ritual Process*, Chicago: Aldine, 1969.

106. Supported in part by a grant from the Maryland State Department of Mental Hygiene, 1977.

107. "Alternatives to Prison," NBC News Special, January 1983.

108. McWaters, 1982.

109. James Lovelock, *Gaia*, New York: Oxford University Press, 1979.

110. Fred B. Wood, "A Logical Division of the Development of Co-Evolution with the Biosphere into Philosophical, Scientific, Engineering, Educational, Decision and Action Components," *Proceedings*, Society for General Systems Research, 1987.

Chapter 11: THEORY

111. For General Systems Theory see also Ludwig von Bertalanffy, "An Outline of General Systems Theory," *British Journal of Philosophical Science*, 1950, 1, pp. 134-165; James Miller, "Toward a General Theory for the Behavioral Sciences," *American Psychologist*, 1955, 10, pp. 513-531; Boris Astrachan, "Towards a Social Systems Model of Therapeutic Groups," *Social Psychiatry*, 1970, 5, pp. 110-119; Fremont Kast and James Rosenzweig, "General Systems Theory: Applications for Organizations and Management," *Academy of Management Journal*, December 1972, pp. 447-465.

112. Wendell French and Cecil Bell, Jr., "A Brief History of Organization Development," in W. French, C. Bell and R. Zawaci, *Organization Development*, Dallas: Business Publications, Inc., 1978, pp. 15-19.

113. Lewin, 1950.

114. James G. Miller, *Living Systems*, New York: McGraw-Hill, 1978.

115. Jung, 1964.

116. Carter, 1982, pp. 371-379.

117. Dunphy, 1974.

118. Kahn, 1984b.

119. Jung, 1964; Ira Progoff, *Jung, Synchronicity, and Human Destiny*, New York: Delta, 1973.

120. Progoff, 1973.

121. Progoff, 1973, p. 171.

122. Kahn, 1983.

123. This section relies on Capra, 1976, 1982 and Pagels, 1982; see also Bateson, 1972 and 1979; Erich Jantsch, *The Self-Organizing Universe*, New York: Pergamon, 1980; Geoffrey Chew, "Bootstraps: A Scientific Idea?" *Science*, 161, May 1968, pp. 762-765.; Chew "Bootstrap Dynamics," lecture delivered at University of California, Berkeley, May 8, 1982.

124. Pagels, 1982.

125. Progoff, 1973.

126. Ilya Prigogine, *From Being to Becoming: Time and Complexity in the Physical Sciences*, San Francisco: Freeman, 1980.

127. Jantsch, 1980.

128. Bateson, 1972, 1979.

129. Capra, personal communication, 1982.

130. Bateson, 1972, p. 482 and 1979, p. 102.

131. Capra, 1982, p. 267.

132. Gibbard et al, 1974.

Chapter 12: CONFERENCE DESIGN

133. Warren Burke and Richard Beckhard (Eds.), *Conference Planning*, Washington, D.C.: NTL Institute, 1962; Rice, 1967.

134. Margaret Mead, "Conference Arrangements," in Burke and Beckhard, 1962, pp. 45-65 especially p. 57.

135. McDonald and Bendahmane, 1984.

136. Binnendijk, 1987.

137. Kahn, 1984c; Kahn and Strasburg, 1978.

INDEX

administrator, neutral 145–147
AU Research Groups xi, 39–40,
    50–52, 54–56, 67–72, 84–99,
    122–124, 181–182, 183–189,
    219–221
authority 33, 61, 65–72, 79,
    82–106, 107
    figures xii, 63, 67, 72, 77,
      99–101
    gender issues 67–70, 72, 87–89,
      94–101, 190
    race issues 101–102, 169–171
    rebellion xii, 79

balance of power xii, 29, 81, 84,
    102
Bateson, Gregory 225, 226
blame vii, xii, 117–120, 122, 125,
    221
boundaries vii, 114, 213
brainstorming 6, 7, 12, 37, 76, 77,
    148, 151–152

Camp David 36, 136–144, 145,
    146, 214–216
Capra, Fritjof 197, 223, 228
Carter, President Jimmy 36, 124,
    136–144, 145, 176, 214–216
celebrate 6, 7, 12, 13
communication viii, 109, 148, 153,
    154–155, 165, 168
    cross-cultural 40
Communitas 200

compromise 33, 215
conference, peace xiv, 3, 12,
    15–26, 29, 41, 211, 231–242
conflict
    analysis of viii, 116, 129–132
    defined 129
    international ix, 26–29, 36,
      129–133
    management xi, 212
    resolution viii, xi, 50, 116
    social 109–110
consensus viii, xi, 7, 16
consultant 9, 12–15, 16–26, 53, 57,
    67, 70, 73–74, 77, 84–99,
    148–164, 211
content
    defined 115–116
    of meetings 168
creative problem solving viii, xi,
    5–12, 78, 177, 211, 221
culture 11, 26, 28, 33, 38–41, 47,
    63, 106, 144, 219, 220,
    237-239
    organizational 41

decision making viii, xi, 7, 16, 81
dependency xii, 61–78, 102, 107
diplomacy, track two x–xi, 129,
    133–136
domestic violence 202–203
dreams 172–175
duality 116, 221

environment 11, 192, 212

facilitators vii, ix, xiii, 8, 12–15,
    75, 146
family 38–40, 202
feedback xiii, 21, 29, 50, 67, 73,
    131, 146, 176, 177, 212–213
Freud, Sigmund 82, 172

game, wilderness 21, 74
gender 33, 38–40, 47, 55
Geneva Summit 26–29, 36, 219,
    220
good vs. evil vii, xii, 107, 113–114,
    239
Gorbachev, General Secretary
    Mikhail 26–29, 36, 219, 220,
    237
Group
    development theories 102–104,
        190–192, 227
    dynamics xiii, 11, 12, 74, 83,
        164, 168, 214, 218
    dynamics and gender 39, 67–70,
        72, 87–89, 94–99
    identity 84–99, 104–107, 185
    life, defined 11, 217–219, 226
    process 50, 54, 58, 67, 176
    roles 41–58
    system 10–11, 57, 105, 115, 129
    theory xiii
    "whole group" model 147

harmony vii, xi, xii, 28, 58, 176,
    227–228, 241–242
Harvard Negotiation Project ix
Healing xi, 53, 104, 197–205
    defined 197
    global 204–205
heirarchy of needs, Maslow's 37

intimacy 182–190, 193

Jantsch, Erich 226, 227
Jung, Carl G. 33, 57, 83, 172, 176,
    213–214, 220, 221
Jungian psychology xiii

leadership 20, 72, 77–78, 219
Lewin, Kurt viii–ix, 175, 212
listening viii, 50, 182

management
    participating viii–ix, 204
    philosophy 16, 18–19, 63, 147,
        176
McDonald, John D. x, 133–136,
    236–237
mediation xi, 145–147
motivation 33, 37–38, 176
Myers-Briggs Type Indicator
    19–20, 31–35, 148, 214

nurturance 67–72, 183, 190, 193

paired opposite 130, 216–220, 226
participation viii, 61, 73, 78, 81,
    198
patterns 52, 54, 56, 77, 103, 117,
    176
peacemaker, defined vii
peacemaking
    defined vii, viii, 129, 176, 221
    interracial 169–172
    psychology vii, xi, xii, 41,
        63–138
    setting 12
    technology vii, ix, x, xi, xii, 3,
        41–62
    theory vii, xi, 209–228
peace-seeking dialogue vii, x, xiii, 3
personality
    profile 19–20, 34–35
    styles 33, 34–35, 37, 176

physics, quantum xiii, 116, 211, 221–225, 226–227
Prigogine, Ilya 227, 228
problem solving
10✳STEP℠ Model 5–12, 73, 75, 147, 149, 167
cases 13–31 41, 77, 147–164
Kelman workshops 129–132
process, defined 115–116

Reagan, President Ronald 26–27, 36, 219, 220, 237
rebellion xi, 74–106, 107
defined 81
recorder 8, 12, 19, 75
reorganization 16–26
representative 9, 75
revolution 81
role xii, 8–9, 41–58, 70
roles
5 basic meeting 8, 46
sharing 54, 56, 57

scapegoat xi, 17, 117–126
scapegoating, defined 119–120
self 33–41, 114–115, 176
self-help groups 203
Shadow 37, 57, 65, 114, 197
spirituality 191–192, 193
structure
of organizations 115–116
of meetings 168
support 48–49, 52, 54, 57, 155, 179–193
defined 177, 179
sub-groups 107–116, 117
system, larger 12, 121, 122, 124, 125
systems
analysis 7, 12
approach 116
defined 10, 212

living vii, 12, 108, 112, 197, 204, 213
model 12
science vii, xiii, 37, 209, 212–213
social 203–204, 213
view 10–11, 105, 211, 213

Tavistock Institute ix, xiii, 67
tension vii, xi, xii, 28–29, 79, 115, 120, 121, 146, 169, 200
racial 101–102, 169–172
therapeutic community 198–200
timekeeper 9, 12–15, 75
training 12, 13, 16–26, 37, 147, 148, 172
turning points 132, 135, 145–146, 171–172

U. S. Department of State 132
Center for the Study of Foreign Affairs x, 235, 237

values xii, 11, 18–20, 33, 176
vision vi, 18–19, 34, 131

Wedge, Bryant 133–136, 209
wordclusters xi, 39–40, 183, 216

About the Author

Lynn Sandra Kahn, Ph.D. is a psychologist and management consultant specializing in complex, organizational change. She received her Ph.D. in Clinical Psychology from The American University, Washington, D.C. in 1977. She lives in the San Francisco Bay area.